Agriculture and the Land

Edinburgh Critical Editions of Nineteenth-Century Texts

Published titles

Richard Jefferies, After London; or Wild England
Edited by Mark Frost

Marie Corelli, A Romance of Two Worlds: A Novel
Edited by Andrew Radford

Sensation Drama, 1860–1880: An Anthology
Edited by Joanna Hofer-Robinson and Beth Palmer

Agriculture and the Land: Richard Jefferies' Essays and Letters
Edited by Rebecca Welshman

Maxwell Gray, The Silence of Dean Maitland: A Novel
Edited by Julian Wolfreys

Jane Porter, Thaddeus of Warsaw: A Novel
Edited by Thomas McLean and Ruth Knezevich

Forthcoming titles

William Barnes, Dialect Poems in The Dorset County Chronicle
Edited by Thomas Burton and Emma Mason

Geraldine Jewsbury, Critical Essays and Reviews (1849–1870)
Edited by Anne-Marie Beller

Hartley Coleridge, The Complete Poems
Edited by Nicola Healey

George Gissing, The Private Papers of Henry Ryecroft
Edited by Thomas Ue

Philip James Bailey, Festus: A Novel
Edited by Mischa Willett

William Morris on Socialism: Uncollected Essays
Edited by Florence Boos

Hubert Crackanthorpe, Wreckage: Seven Studies
Edited by David Malcolm

Visit the Edinburgh Critical Editions of Nineteenth-Century Texts
website at: edinburghuniversitypress.com/series/ecenct

Agriculture and the Land

Richard Jefferies' Essays and Letters

Edited by Rebecca Welshman

EDINBURGH
University Press

Edinburgh University Press is one of the leading university presses in the UK. We publish academic books and journals in our selected subject areas across the humanities and social sciences, combining cutting-edge scholarship with high editorial and production values to produce academic works of lasting importance. For more information visit our website: edinburghuniversitypress.com

Edinburgh University Press Ltd
The Tun – Holyrood Road
12(2f) Jackson's Entry
Edinburgh EH8 8PJ

Typeset in 11/12.5 Baskerville and Times New Roman by
IDSUK (DataConnection) Ltd, and
printed and bound in Great Britain.

A CIP record for this book is available from the British Library

ISBN 978 1 4744 4088 2 (hardback)
ISBN 978 1 4744 4090 5 (webready PDF)
ISBN 978 1 4744 4091 2 (epub)

Contents

Abbreviations

AF	*Amaryllis at the Fair* 1887
AL	*After London* 1885
AP	*The Amateur Poacher* 1879
CH	*Chronicles of the Hedges* 1948
DM	*The Dewy Morn* 1884
FF	*Field and Farm* 1957
FH	*Field and Hedgerow* 1889
FW	*The Farmer's World* 2016
GFF	*Greene Ferne Farm* 1880
GH	*The Gamekeeper at Home* 1878
HHM	*Hodge and His Masters* 1880
HV	*The Hills and the Vale* 1909
JL	*Jefferies' Land: A History of Swindon and Environs* 1896
LF	*The Life of the Fields* 1884
LL	*Landscape and Labour* 1979
LSJ	*The Live Stock Journal and Fancier's Gazette*
NNL	*Nature Near London* 1883
OA	*The Open Air* 1885
PMG	*Pall Mall Gazette*
RD	*Red Deer* 1884
RGE	*Round About a Great Estate* 1880
RHH	*Restless Human Hearts* 1875
SFW	*Sport in the Fields and Woods* 2017
SMH	*The Story of my Heart* 1883
TF	*Toilers of the Fields* 1892
WE	*World's End* 1877
WLSC	*Wild Life in a Southern County* 1879
WM	*Wood Magic* 1881

Acknowledgements

Thank you to Malcolm Dixon for his assistance with preparing the texts.

The following texts are © British Library Board: Drought and Water, *Pall Mall Gazette*, 28 June 1870; Farmers at Bay, *Pall Mall Gazette*, 8 February 1871; The Old Sporting Man, *Pall Mall Gazette*, 1 February, 1872; The County Franchise, *Pall Mall Gazette*, 1 May 1872; The Rating of Personal Property, *Standard*, 23 May, 1872; The Poetry of Steam Ploughs, *Graphic*, 5 October 1872; The Farmer from his own Point of View, *Pall Mall Gazette*, 23 April, 1874; Patchwork Agriculture, *Examiner*, July 1875; The Cost of Agricultural Labour in 1875, *Standard*, 1 October 1875; Local Taxation, *Standard*, 29 December 1875; Joint-stock Agriculture, *Pall Mall Gazette*, 16 March 1877; The Landowners' Difficulties, *Pall Mall Gazette*, 29 March 1877; The Agricultural Labourer's Vote, *Pall Mall Gazette*, 24 May 1877; The Prospects of Farming, *Pall Mall Gazette* 1877, in two parts (19 July and 23 July); Milk Supply, *Pall Mall Gazette*, 26 December 1877; The Preservation of Game in England, *St. James' Gazette*, 25 October, 1881

A letter by Richard Jefferies to *The Times*, 15 October 1873, entitled 'The Future of Farming' is reproduced by permission of *The Times* Newspaper

Series Editor's Preface

The nineteenth century saw an unprecedented, prodigious production of literary texts. Many of these, often best-sellers or offering vital commentaries on cultural, political and philosophical issues of the period engendering debate, did not survive in print long into the twentieth century, regardless of putative quality, however measured. Edinburgh Critical Editions of Nineteenth-Century Texts seeks to bring back to the reading public and the scholarly eye works of undeniable importance during the time of their first publication and reception, which have, often unjustly, disappeared from print and readers' consciousness. Covering fiction, long and short, non-fiction prose and essays, and poetry, with comprehensive critical introductions and carefully chosen supporting appendices, germane to the text and the context of the volume, Edinburgh Critical Editions of Nineteenth-Century Texts provides definitive, annotated scholarly reprints.

Introduction

Richard Jefferies began his career in the 1860s as a local reporter in Wiltshire. By the time of his death in 1887 he had published nineteen books, many of these works including some of the finest essays in English literature in major publications such as the *English Illustrated Magazine, Chambers' Journal* and *Longman's Magazine*. His reflective natural history philosophy contributed to the popularisation of the natural world, particularly as he was writing for mainly an urban readership.[1] As a close observer of people and nature, in rural and urban areas, Jefferies was well aware of the inequalities of Victorian England. His beliefs, hopes and aspirations were crystallised in his spiritual autobiography, *The Story of My Heart* (1883).

Lesser known is Jefferies' large body of writings on agriculture, which comprise more than half of his total output as an author. His agricultural writing took the form of letters, essays and articles that expressed his hope for the future of agriculture as a science, offered practical advice to farmers, sketched rural characters, and commented on the political and social changes taking place. *Hodge and His Masters*, formed of articles contributed to the *Standard* between 1878 and 1879, was intended by Jefferies to 'remedy [. . .] the ills of the depression years of the 1870s',[2] which were a result of bad harvests, falling crop prices and an increase in foreign imports. Many of the works collected in this volume have significant affinities with *Hodge and His Masters*.

As a reporter, the young Richard Jefferies gained valuable experience of writing about the political and social conditions of rural south west England. In the early 1870s, when Jefferies began writing for national papers, it was widely recognised that England was in the grip of agricultural depression, and by the 1880s, the periodical press had declared that agriculture was in crisis.[3] Writing retrospectively, the

---

1. For many years Jefferies was known as 'the author of *The Gamekeeper at Home*', which was first published in serial form in the *Pall Mall Gazette* in 1878.
2. Richard Jefferies, *Hodge and His Masters* (London: Quartet, 1979), p. vi. The paper was known as the *Standard* but its full title was the *London Evening Standard*.
3. See, for example, 'The Crisis in British Agriculture', *Pall Mall Gazette*, 30 August 1881, and 'Agriculture in Crisis', *Standard*, 19 March 1881.

Reverend Monro Gibson likened the agricultural depression of the late nineteenth century to a cloud that hung over the country:

> 'Depression, depression, depression!' How sadly familiar the word has been for many years. It is not an unfamiliar word at any time, but lately it almost seems as if it had come, not to visit, but to stay. The depression in agriculture and commerce has been so long continued, that it is almost a weariness to speak of it.[4]

Jefferies was chronicling a vision of rural England that was vanishing. For a time, old methods, ideas and attitudes existed side by side with the new, before they were swept away by a changing infrastructure, new relations between the landowners, farmers and labourers, and the commercialisation of agriculture. In 'Patchwork Agriculture' he describes the simple wooden plough, essentially unchanged since prehistoric times, working alongside the noisy lumbering steam plough, and the contrast could not be greater. Jefferies writes, 'these are no fancy pictures; they are drawn from the reality; they exist at this hour within a radius of three miles. They are drawn to illustrate the extremely patchwork character of agriculture in our land.' He does not lament the introduction of mechanised farming. Rather he attempts to embrace it, even going so far, in 'The Spirit of Modern Agriculture', as to imagine a factory in the midst of a wheat field: 'the distillery and the refinery will even yet raise their tall chimneys upon the farm. Imagine a factory chimney in the midst of the yellow wheat and scarlet poppies!'

W. J. Keith has previously noted that Jefferies 'is quite capable of donning the mask' of different characters when writing for periodicals.[5] To some extent, this ability enabled Jefferies to write for a range of publications without a fixed political stance. In the preface to 'Thoughts on the Labour Question'[6] Jefferies declared that he represented no political party:

> In writing this book I am influenced by no political bias. I take no interest in politics, and belong to no party or political body. I am simply a student of nature and human life, and I paint only what I see; others must draw their own conclusions.

4. Monro Gibson, 'A New Year's Word of Cheer', *The Sunday At Home: A Family Magazine for Sabbath Reading* (1888), pp. 5–7.
5. W. J. Keith, *The Jefferies Canon: Notes on Essays Attributed to Richard Jefferies without Full Documentary Evidence* (Oxford: Petton Books, 1995), p. 19.
6. Dated to 1877 or 1878 by Graeme Woolaston ('Richard Jefferies: "Thoughts on the Labour Question"', *Notes and Queries*, March 1975, pp. 118–19; qtd in George Miller and Hugoe Matthews, *Richard Jefferies: A Bibliographical Study* (Aldershot: Scholar Press, 1993), pp. 51, 771.

This form of calm and rational objectivity allowed him vividly to bring to life pictures of the farmer, the labourer and the landowner.

The ownership of land, also known as the land question, was a central political concern of the late nineteenth century. As noted by Matthew Cragoe and Paul Readman, radicals 'saw in land reform a means to break the hold of the aristocracy over the destinies of the country'.[7] The agitation of the land question intensified in the 1840s and the 1870s.[8] In his writings from the 1870s Jefferies addressed many of the issues that came under the umbrella of the land question, which included access to allotments for labourers, taxation and the housing of labourers. In 1874 Jefferies proposed to Longmans publisher a 'great book in two volumes on the whole Land Question', with two parts – 'Tenant and Labourer' and 'Land and Landlord'. The manner of the proposed work was to be 'impartial and trenchant', yet with a 'slightly conservative tone, so as to counsel moderation'. On 8 June he sent 200 manuscript folios with a revised proposal that the first volume should be titled 'The Agricultural Life':

I. The Creed of the Agriculturalist
II. The Agriculturalist at Home
III. Agriculture as a Business
IV. Summary of the Farmer's Case
V. The Labourer's Daily Life
VI. The Labourer's Case
VII. The Gist of the Whole Matter[9]

Besant states that the project came to nothing. Matthews and Trietel note that the work 'would appear to have been conceived as a comprehensive analysis of the workings of contemporary agriculture'.[10] While some of the material can be traced in, for example, 'The Labourer's Daily Life' and 'The Farmer at Home', substantial material remains to be identified. As I suggest in my analysis in support of Jefferies' authorship of the new articles included in this volume, some of the material for the lost project was used by Jefferies in the *Pall Mall Gazette*.

Jefferies' articles are generally proactive, written in the spirit of reform. Yet they are also imbued with the author's characteristic ability

7. Matthew Cragoe and Paul Readman (eds), *The Land Question in Britain, 1750–1950* (Basingstoke: Palgrave Macmillan, 2010), p. 2.
8. Ibid., p. 3.
9. Walter Besant, *The Eulogy of Richard Jefferies* (London: Chatto and Windus, 1889), p. 119.
10. Hugoe Matthews and Phyllis Trietel, *The Forward Life of Richard Jefferies* (Oxford: Petton Books, 1994), p. 65.

to offer more than one side to a question. Jefferies' sympathies lay with the farmers, the labourers and the landowners. He recognised that the farmer was in a difficult position regarding increasing rents and pressure from agricultural labourers asking for higher wages. Yet he also observed the hardships of outdoor work endured by the labourers, and their genuine need for improvements – not only to their wages, but to their diets, their homes and their right to have the vote. In 'The Landowners' Difficulties' he declares, 'No one is more envied than the possessor of a great estate, and yet the residents in "the stately homes of England" have for some time past been labouring under a constantly increasing pressure.' These pressures took the form of labourers' demand for increased wages, demands from tenant farmers to reduce rents, and other local expectations.

Until 1874, when Jefferies' first child arrived, he had been living for the most part at his birthplace: the family home, Coate Farm, just outside of Swindon. It has been suggested that, before that, he included his address in his letters to *The Times* on the agricultural labourer, in order perhaps to give weight to his opinion.[11] It is interesting that he also does this in the letter dated 23 May 1872 to the *Standard* concerning the rating of personal property – a letter that is republished here for the first time. Writing letters clearly offered a way in to the national publications with which the young journalist wished to be associated. The letters about the labourer were followed by a letter on the future of farming, which is collected here for the first time. Matthews and Trietel note that, on the occasion of this letter, Jefferies was referred to as 'an eminent Agriculturalist'.[12] The letter formed the basis of the substantial article in *Fraser's Magazine* in December 1873 under the same title, which earned Jefferies further recognition as an agricultural expert. At the time, Swindon was primarily surrounded by agricultural parishes, yet it was also home to the Great Western Railway works and was connected directly to London by rail. Jefferies was there when the agricultural unions were being formed – Joseph Arch gave a speech at the Corn Exchange in Swindon in early January 1874 where the county franchise was discussed, and labourers were urged to join the Union to secure better wages.[13] Ten of the works collected in this volume were written while Jefferies was living in Swindon – before he left for Surbiton in 1874 and never returned to live in Wiltshire.

11. See Matthews and Trietel, p. 54.
12. Ibid.
13. See 'Mr. Joseph Arch at Swindon', *Bristol Mercury* (10 January 1874), p. 7.

While in Surbiton, Jefferies went on to contribute a year-long series of articles to the *Livestock Journal and Fancier's Gazette* (1877–8), based upon his observations of the Swindon area and addressing agricultural issues such as the import and export of meat, the processing of cheese, the role of mechanisation in farming, agricultural shows and fairs (which he attended), poaching, the harvest, and changing trends in livestock. However, despite him being recognised as an expert on agricultural subjects, very few publications belonging to the early years of Jefferies' career are known. The publication of *The Gamekeeper at Home* in 1878, which brought him nationwide critical acclaim, is considered to mark the turning point of his career – from journalist to author. As early as 1871, he claimed that he had been writing for the *Pall Mall Gazette* for several years,[14] and yet the earliest documented article by him in the paper is 'Joint-Stock Agriculture' (1877).[15] The earliest article in this collection – 'Drought and Water' (*Pall Mall Gazette*, 1870) – correlates with a section concerning drought in *Wild Life in a Southern County*, which was serialised eight years later in the same paper. This is just one article from that time and, taking Jefferies at his word, there could be many more.

This collection first of all brings together nineteen of Jefferies' contributions concerning agriculture and the land which have not been republished or have not been collected. While the focus is on these items, several already published works are also included – some of which have been previously collected alongside his nature writing. This arrangement provides context for the newly identified works, but also offers new context for the better-known works. The chronological order in which the items are presented aims to show the development of Jefferies' writing on agriculture and the land from the early 1870s to the mid-1880s: something that cannot be achieved so easily when considering pieces in isolation or out of chronological order. The selection also includes material from a range of periodicals – twelve in total – together with information about these publications and their significance. The collection includes essays, letters and short articles, which serve to illustrate the range of Jefferies' tone, subject matter and changing concerns over time. Subjects addressed include the extension of the vote to agricultural labourers, the welfare of labourers, the relation between employer and labourer, the use of steam power in the fields, the impact and regulation of local taxation, problems faced by landowners in light of

14. Richard Jefferies, letter to an unknown publisher (23 June 1871), quoted in Matthews and Trietel, p. 46. In the letter Jefferies writes, 'I have been over five years constantly connected with & writing for the Press – writing for papers, Pall Mall &c, besides a large amount of local work, local histories, correspondence &c.'
15. See Miller and Matthews, p. 41.

changing legislation, practical advice to farmers concerning the dairy industry and the supply of milk, and the demands placed on agriculture by changing market trends. While offering a rational perspective on the innovations and capital required to sustain British farming, Jefferies also reflects on progress and what it might mean for the future. As a whole, it is hoped that the collection offers a fresh picture of the changing conditions of British agriculture from the early 1870s to the mid-1880s.

All items are presented as complete full-length works as they originally appeared in the magazines or newspapers. Those items which have been previously collected in part, with omissions, are also reproduced in full for the first time. The twelve newly identified works presented in this collection anticipate the subject matters Jefferies addressed in the *Livestock Journal* from 1877 to 1878 and are reflected in style and theme by his other works of the period. They fill significant gaps in his publication record. As we might expect, they connect linguistically with his works from the 1870s, including *WLSC, HHM, GH, AP*, with *RGE* (1880), and with essays from the 1870s collected in *HV*. Evidence in support of Jefferies' authorship of the newly attributed items is given in the Appendices.

As Jefferies' writing matured in the early 1880s, his prose became increasingly imbued with the richness of his poetic vision. In 'The Beauty of the Fields' the threshing-machine and the reaper are enveloped by the sunlight in the cornfield to become part of the age-old natural environment:

> the sunlight (and once now and then the shadow of a tree) throws its mantle over, and, like the hand of an enchanter softly waving, surrounds it with a charm. So the cranks, and wheels, and knives, and mechanism do not exist – it was a machine in the workshop, but it is not a machine in the wheat-field. For the wheat-field you see is very, very old, and the air is of old time, and the shadow, the flowers, and the sunlight, and that which moves among them becomes of them.

The harshness and sterility of the machine are softened and smoothed away as it becomes part of a much older and larger dynamic: a form of ritual symbiosis between humans and the natural world that is embodied by the wheat itself. Yet in 'One of the New Voters' Jefferies questions how the spiritual value of nature can ever be fully integrated into human life when it seems divided from it by hardship – 'the wheat is beautiful, but human life is labour'. As expressed by Roger Ebbatson, Jefferies 'does not simply represent some "reality" of nineteenth-century rural life, he works to create meanings in ways that problematise the act of writing and produce texts of deep political and philosophical ambivalence, resonance and complication'.[16] The harsh reality of labouring life is depicted alongside the beauty of the fields in their summer vibrancy. Jefferies asks the reader to consider the true position of the reaper – to empathise, not out of pity, but through humane understanding. Again, in 'The State of Farming', Jefferies brings to the page the difficult truth about the impact of the agricultural depression: for farmers approaching middle age, who have worked all their lives, 'reason' cannot compensate for the loss that the heart feels – 'this today is the future they had looked forward to and strived for. They cannot put their future forward again.' Writing with characteristic astuteness and sensitivity, Jefferies observes that 'It is the people who feel it; the human beings, not the smiling fields.'

Jefferies was fully engaged with the spirit of the times, and nowhere does this show more than in 'The Spirit of Modern Agriculture'. This remarkable essay is broad in its scope and overarches an impressive range of topics that each required specialist knowledge. Agriculture embodied a new spirit of the age, where 'the sharp distinction drawn between the farmer and the manufacturer, and between the labourer and the mechanic, melts away daily and hourly as their interests become commingled'. With these dissolving social boundaries the divide between the city and the country became ever more permeable. 'Gone', Jefferies writes, is 'the farmer living isolated upon his fields, his horizon bounded by the double-mound hedge. . . . The modern agriculturist gives and takes with the manufacturer and the trader.' Agriculture was becoming a science, with a wide infrastructure – 'the locomotive rushes over the country in the service of the soil, the swift steamer skims the sea, and the busy brains of the speculator are for ever intent upon the agricultural supply and demand'.

Yet, not without a touch of melancholy, Jefferies observes how some of the older country characters perched uncomfortably on the cusp of these changes. In 'The Old Sporting Man' the squire is 'the last of his race' and his heir 'one of the new sporting school'. The squire, who fondly knows every corner of his fifteen hundred acres, laments the loss of the old ways and reluctantly finds himself on the threshold of a different world: 'Brocklehurst can never be what it was; no more than England.' Jefferies recognises that the new spirit of agriculture was irrevocably changing country society and the character of the land. The pieces collected here acknowledge what was being lost, and yet celebrate, with Jefferies' characteristic hope, the dawn of a new era.

Rebecca Welshman, June 2018

16. Roger Ebbatson, *An Imaginary England: Nation, Landscape and Literature 1840–1920* (Oxford: Routledge, 2017), pp. 3–4.

Notes on Periodicals

Examiner

The *Examiner* was a well-established national paper that, in the 1870s, discussed a range of subjects from a predominantly radical point of view. Jefferies' work was regularly reviewed in the paper, often quite favourably, but his contributions to the paper have so far remained unknown. Until the mid-1860s the paper had been known as a leading intellectual journal on politics, domestic economy and theatricals, and published the work of authors such as Byron, Keats and Hazlitt. After the paper changed hands to William McCullagh Torrens in 1867, who halved its cost, it lost its elite status as a journal and targeted a mass readership. In the 1870s the editor William Minto sought to revive the paper's reputation for radical intellectual commentaries, which coincided with the peak of Jefferies' contributions on the social and political conditions of agriculture.

Fortnightly Review

This monthly magazine (1865–1934), edited by John Morley, was described in the *Encyclopaedia Britannica* of 1973 as 'the leading journal of radical opinion',[1] and as 'one of the most influential English-language periodicals of the 19th century'. The idea for the periodical came from Anthony Trollope, and its purpose was 'to free the "higher journalists" of the time from "the views of an Editor or Political party"'.[2] Jefferies contributed 'The Power of the Farmers' (June 1874) and 'Nature and Books' (May 1887).

Fraser's Magazine

A monthly literary magazine published by Longmans, Green and Co. (1830–82), *Fraser's* published some of Jefferies' best works on agriculture and the land, including 'The Future of Farming' (1873), 'John Smith's

---

1. Miller and Matthews, p. 8.
2. Available at <http://fortnightlyreview.co.uk/about/> (last accessed 28 June 2018).

Shanty' (1874) and 'The Farmer at Home' (1874). In the early 1870s the paper was edited by James Anthony Froude, followed by William Allingham.

Graphic

The *Graphic* was a weekly illustrated paper (1869–1932), edited by Arthur Locker, that became the main rival to *The Illustrated London News*.[3] The paper serialised Thomas Hardy's *The Mayor of Casterbridge* (1886) and *Tess of the D'Urbervilles* (1891). An advertisement for the first edition of the paper described it as

> a journal combining literary excellence with artistic beauty [that] will deal with all the prominent topics of the day; especially those belonging to Literature, Arts and Sciences, Fashions, and Matters interesting to the Fashionable World, Sports and Pastimes, Music, the Opera, and the Drama.[4]

London Evening Standard

This was a daily paper that ran from 1827 to 1916. From 1878 to 1880, the *Standard* published a significant number of Jefferies' articles concerning agriculture and the land, the majority of which were collected as *Hodge and His Masters* (1880). In August 1880 a new series of articles began with a natural history theme, the majority of which formed *Nature Near London* (1883). Further contributions to the paper from 1883 to 1887 were collected in *The Life of the Fields* (1884), *The Open Air* (1885) and *Field and Hedgerow* (1889). Until 1878, the paper was edited by James Johnstone, and after that date by William H. Mudford.

Longman's Magazine

This magazine ran from 1882 to 1905 as a monthly literary number. Jefferies contributed 'Bits of Oak Bark' in March 1883. In a letter asking Jefferies for further articles, Longman wrote, 'I should very much like to have one of your out-of-door pictures – straight from nature for the spring.' Longman's request drew forth one of Jefferies' most eloquent pieces of writing – 'The Pageant of Summer' (June 1883) – prose infused with the light and movement of summer. In November 1883 Jefferies contributed 'The Wiltshire Labourer', also at Longman's request. Thomas

---

3. Miller and Matthews, p. 13.
4. *Dublin Evening Mail* (13 November 1869), p. 1.

Hardy's 'The Dorsetshire Labourer' was published in the magazine in July 1883. Several years after Jefferies' death in 1887, Mrs Jefferies sent Longman several manuscripts for publication in the magazine. Upon the publication of these later works Longman wrote,

> the following paragraphs will seem strangely familiar to readers of this Magazine to which Richard Jefferies was so constant a contributor. . . . They are but scraps, but they serve to recall 'the touch of a vanished hand, the sound of a voice that is still'.[5]

Several of the pieces were collected by Longman in *Toilers of the Field* (1892).

Magazine of Art

This illustrated monthly was printed by Cassell and Co., London, and ran from 1878 to 1904. The publication was devoted to the decorative arts and developed to become similar to the *Art Journal*.[6] Samuel Looker has attributed 'Horses in Relation to Art' (September 1878) to Jefferies. Jefferies' signed contributions to the magazine include 'The Beauty of the Fields' (1881), 'New Facts in Landscape' (1882) and 'Nature in the Louvre' (1887).

Manchester Guardian

This paper was edited by C. P. Scott, with whom Jefferies corresponded. It was a daily paper (1821–1959), known as the *Guardian*, and as Miller and Matthews point out, the only example of a local paper that became a national publication.[7] Jefferies contributed 'The Otter in Somerset' in August 1883, which was signed 'From a Correspondent'. This was followed by 'The Water Colley', also in August 1883, and signed 'From a Correspondent'. Scott was evidently pleased with 'One of the New Voters' (1885), writing to Jefferies, 'It is capitally done and I hope you will be able to follow it up speedily with others like it.'[8]

New Quarterly Magazine

This magazine ran from 1873 to 1880 and described itself as a 'High-Class Literary and Social Periodical'.[9] During the 1870s Jefferies

---

5. Miller and Matthews, p. 29.
6. Ibid., p. 30.
7. Ibid., p. 31.
8. Ibid.
9. Ibid., p. 35.

contributed papers on rural life and agriculture. Jefferies wrote to the editor, Oswald Crawfurd, in 1876 describing Coate and the reservoir of his childhood, and expressing a desire to write prose endowed with 'the magic of sunshine and green things and calm waters'. Crawfurd later recalled being 'immensely struck with the lucidity of these papers, the rare faculty of co-ordination possessed by the writer, and the strong, nervous, simple English which he had taught himself to use'. In Jefferies' writing, Crawfurd detected a 'fresh, rhythmic note in style, the stamp of an original artist'. Crawfurd also went as far as to say that Jefferies

> achieved more than Gilbert White ever attempted, for he not only observed, catalogued, and recorded the ways and doings of wild animals, but he saw all aspects of wild life through the eyes of a poet and interpreted them to us.[10]

Pall Mall Gazette

The *Pall Mall Gazette* was a daily evening newspaper and review (1865–1925) owned by George Smith, with a Conservative stance. The paper was edited by Frederick Greenwood until 1880, followed by John Morley to 1883 and William T. Stead to 1890. Greenwood was helpful and encouraging to Jefferies, and it was under his editorship that Jefferies produced *The Gamekeeper at Home*, *The Amateur Poacher* and other countryside books, which were first serialised in the paper. In 1880, when the paper changed hands and supported the Liberal Party, Greenwood resigned. The paper took its name from *The History of Pendennis*, by William Makepeace Thackeray, in which the *Pall Mall Gazette* 'is written by gentlemen for gentlemen'.[11]

St. James's Gazette

This daily paper was founded and edited by Frederick Greenwood in 1880 after he left the *Pall Mall Gazette*. Jefferies contributed articles and essays on farming, sport, nature notes and rural sketches. Several items which have previously been attributed to Jefferies, and published under his name, were in fact written by a naturalist from Westmoreland named John Watson. Further items listed in the Bibliographical Study by Miller

10. Rebecca Welshman, '"Concerning Coate": A Letter from Richard Jefferies to Oswald Crawfurd', *Richard Jefferies Society Journal*, 23 (2012), pp. 15–17.
11. 'A Chronology of the *Pall Mall Gazette*', *Sketch* (10 May 1893), p. 8.

and Matthews are also written by Watson: these include 'Conforming to Environment' (1886), 'In Summer Fields' (1886) and 'Notes-a-Field' (1885).[12]

The Times

Known as the leading national daily, *The Times* initially began as the *Daily Universal Register*.[13] From 1872 to 1873 Jefferies contributed four signed letters, followed by 'Farms out of Cultivation', which was signed 'From a Correspondent'. In 1881 Jefferies contributed two articles concerning Sussex, 'Some Uncultivated Country – Downs' and 'Some Uncultivated Country – Forest', both of which were unsigned and collected in *OA*. Jefferies' letters on the Wiltshire labourer were widely reprinted in papers all over the country and extensively commented on.

---

12. See Rebecca Welshman, 'Bibliographical Discoveries: Jefferies Imitators', *Richard Jefferies Society Journal*, 20 (2011), pp. 19–25.
13. Miller and Matthews, p. 62.

Richard Jefferies' Essays and Letters

DROUGHT AND WATER[1]

PALL MALL GAZETTE, 28 JUNE 1870

Their experience of the last three summers ought to send our farmers
to school in the sunny South. Hitherto the calamity they have had most
reason to dread has been a plague of rain and water, especially in spring;
they have been more used to see their hay crops rotting on the soaking
soil than eluding the scythe in dust and tinder. If they are wise, they may
turn their late experience to account, heavy as has been the price they
have paid for it. Even if their climate should change permanently for the
hotter and dryer, they have their remedy, or at least an alleviation, at their
elbow, and a small first outlay may assure a large future benefit. We English are not as other men with a short sharp rainy season breaking in on
a burning year. Taking one season with another, we may lay our account
for a heavy average rainfall. For long months, as we know to our cost,
fogs are chronic with us. Spite of all the grubbing and felling steadily
going forward, we have trees enough distilling copious moisture all over
the country. Above all, and except in our chalk ranges, we have springs
bubbling up in every hill and stream, bursting down every valley. In the
best part of each ordinary year all that moisture is running to waste, if that
can be called waste which we never miss. A season comes like this, and
the farmer thinks with idle regret of the rain he thought such a nuisance
when it was interrupting his field work in early spring. What little was
suffered to accumulate in the small duck pond by the farmyard or the
little hollows by the field corners has long given out, after the last bucket-
fuls had been economized as carefully as waterskins in the desert. There
is no sap in the shrivelled grass; the cattle and the very sheep have to be
driven twice a day to the distant stream. His horses, men, and waggons
are hauling the precious fluid, and the expenditure of labour on water carriage is something heart-breaking. The truth is, his farming is conduced
exclusively in deference to the popular idea and general character of our
English climate. He makes his book solely to hedge against the rain, and
never takes into account the chances of prolonged drought. If a man of
enterprise and capital, he spends his money on drains until rushes are

---

1. Newly identified and not since republished.

nearly as rare as the papyrus in his fields, and after a rainfall, the water goes hurrying off his farm, gurgling and choking itself in its anxiety to escape. Very properly, too; but he should recollect that every medal has its reverse, and when water is so abundant he should provide not against a rainy but a droughty day. What would be easier than a system of tanks and reservoirs, more or less extensive according to his soil, situation, and probably necessities – ponds, open or covered, or sheltered by timber against excessive evaporation, which should be regularly filled in case of the worst? He admits the principle in those hollows you see in every field where there is no running water; only instead of keeping the three or four weeks' supply he may very probably want, why should he not lay in for the three or four months' he may possibly have occasion for? The outlay would bear little more proportion to the possible expenditure in a single calamitous year than that he pays for the assurance of his premises against the chances of a fire.

What is perhaps even stranger is the utter absence of the very simplest arrangement for irrigation, when circumstances seem to force the idea upon farmers vociferating as savagely for rain as the prophets of Baal. You see everywhere elaborately solid works banking in the quiet-going stream, whereon the tradition lingers of some mediaeval flood. But rarely indeed do you see a sluice gate, except where the neighbouring land has been christened a water-meadow, and treated accordingly. Never does it seem to enter the conception of the farmer that by slight pressure, and at moderate cost, water may be made to ascend the few inches which shall bring the adjacent fields below its level; that in time of flood it will carry itself into ditches, where it may be shut off for his future use. The man who will pay enormously for Peruvian guano to enrich his crops, for patent oilcake to fatten his beasts, will not expend one shilling on English water to fertilise his fields, or rather to guard them against utter starvation. It is that element of uncertainty that is fatal to the economical and common place safeguard he might so often secure himself. If he knew he would have a visitation at stated intervals – lose £100, £1,000, as the case might be, in a single season – he would never hesitate. Counting on a run of damp seasons, in his penny wisdom, he shuts his eyes and backs his luck. Besides, at a moderate out-lay, he would often convert a curse into a blessing. In a blazing spring, with plenty of water, he might coin gold. The damp soil glows like a hot bed, forcing fabulous growth in a miraculously short time, yielding a second and a third crop. Look at the feats of husbandry performed on the Huerta Valencia for example. It would have been a stony desert but for its system of irrigation; with that system, the water regularly let over it steadily mani-cures it, and everything grows in tropical rapidity and luxuriance. In the tropics themselves, in South America and near the line, similar treatment produces results more surprising still. At Cairo, one sees cabbages and lettuces growing when the Nile water is thrown on the dust and sand of the old city. We do not look for results so satisfactory on Norfolk farms or the pastures of the Midland counties, but the idea is the same. When we do get something of a tropical season, why not have something of tropical crop? Seeing so little of the sun as he does, no wonder an Englishman has little conception of its power and uses; but his climate as it used to be ought to have taught him something of the properties of water, and his climate as it is will perhaps disabuse him of the idea that it is necessarily and invariably a nuisance.

FARMERS AT BAY[1]

PALL MALL GAZETTE, 8 FEBRUARY 1871

The "bucolic mind" has long been held a subject of legitimate merriment by every class of persons in this country which partakes in the enlightenment of cities. The picture of a fat man in a broad-skirted coat, leather gaiters, a low-crowned hat, and a thick stick, in a state of profound bewilderment over some very simple question of politics or economy, is the conventional type of the British farmer – how unlike the real in all these external characteristics we need hardly say. But as far as this exterior is intended for an outward sign of mental and moral characteristics it is not altogether wrong. It is not true to speak of the modern farmer as a man who passes his whole life in the predicament of perplexity. He understands his own business thoroughly, and as much of other people's business as other people understand of his. He has a great deal of mother-wit and a great deal of practical wisdom. But no doubt there is about all his intellectual processes a certain slowness and unreadiness, such as that with which the Norman Conqueror used to twit the Saxon. He is awkward in the evolution of ideas, chews the cud of a generalization a long while before he can digest it, and is liable consequently to be thrown into utter confusion by antagonists in every way inferior to himself except in mental nimbleness.

---

1. Newly identified and not since republished.

These defects are easily accounted for by the fact that for the station they occupy in life the ordinary tenant farmers of England are the worst educated class in the country. The gentleman has his liberal education which teaches him with more or less success both the art and the science of reasoning. The city tradesman, in the bustle and mental activity of a town life, picks up a rough-and-ready kind of dialectic which enables him to hold his own with considerable plausibility. But of these two kinds of training the unfortunate farmer has neither. In the educational race he has dropped quite into the rear. Schools originally meant for him have passed away from him; some into a lower, some into a higher grade. And as for establishing new ones of his own accord that was an idea without the range of his experience. Accordingly the education of his children fell into the hands of men who had no qualification for the task whatever, but who knew that the parents were, if possible, more ignorant than themselves; and that if they could supply the article at a cheap rate no questions would be asked. Many such men made a good deal of money, in return for which they turned their pupils on the world the helpless intellectual beings we now see them. That the next generation will be very different from the present we have reason to believe. The farmers as a class are becoming conscious of their own defects and anxious for the improvement of their children. Meantime the seniors are sorely beset when called on to defend themselves. Even when they have a good case they do not know how to make the most of it, and a consciousness of that perhaps keeps them silent. They will, however, when hard pressed occasionally turn to bay, and then, like Enceladus:

> *Once tame and wild,*
> *As ox unworried in the grazing meads*

they become really dangerous.

A venerable dignitary of the Church is just now experiencing the full force of this unpleasant truth. As our readers may be aware, a commission is just now sitting to inquire into the operation of the Truck Act; and evidence was required in regard to the prevalence of the truck system in agricultural labour. Among other witnesses summoned for this purpose was Archdeacon Stanton, of Wiltshire; and the evidence which he gave and the answers which it has provoked afford quite a remarkable instance both of the danger of making half-statements and of the inability of your rustic controversialist to hit a fallacy in the bull's eye, and separate what is true from what is false in propositions which are what the schools call "equivocal." The farmers of the neighbourhood have turned on the Archdeacon like a nest of hornets. The local paper, that is to say, the *Marlborough Times*, of which several numbers are before us, is crowded with their correspondence, and the whole neighbourhood is said to resound with their loud and angry hum. Now, we do not intend in this article to go very deeply into the question at issue between the two disputants. *Et vitulo tu dignis et hic.* The truth probably lies between them. But we do wish to take this opportunity of showing how it is that misunderstandings arise among men who have nearly equal faculties for arriving at the truth: and likewise of reminding people that some allowance must be made for farmers when they are driven to rush into print, their argumentative power being, generally speaking, quite unequal to their cause.

The three statements made by the Archdeacon which seem to have given the most umbrage are these: that wages in Wiltshire are 8*s.* or 9*s.* a week; that harvest money, Michaelmas money, and such like supplementary payments are not worth taking into account; and that farmers pay their men in public-houses. Now, in one sense all these statements may be quite true, while in another, and that the more obvious sense, they are quite false. Eight or nine shillings a week may be all that is given while the labourer is working by the day. But then he has his turn at piece-work, which swells the average by a third. The Michaelmas money or the pig, &c., may go for nothing, if by that is meant that it does not contribute to the weekly expenditure of the family. But it pays the rent. To call this going for nothing is like saying that if an inhabitant of Belgravia sets aside some portion of *his* income which he receives less frequently than others for the payment of *his* rent, *that* goes for nothing. When farmers employ half a dozen men on a job of draining or what not, they often give the foreman a cheque for the whole amount which he changes at the public-house, and doubtless that is to be regretted. But it is something quite different from what the general public would understand by being told that farmers habitually pay their men in public-houses. It is clear therefore that Archdeacon Stanton's statements, if true in the letter, are not true in the spirit, and we are firmly convinced that he would admit as much himself. But this only shows the evil of publishing scraps of evidence in the newspapers without any explanatory context, as well as of taking evidence, if it was so taken, on the bald "Yes or No" principle so much in favour with Old Bailey practitioners who wish to discredit a witness according to strict form of law. We do not for a moment blame the Archdeacon. But still less can we blame the farmers who in defence of their own characters are buzzing round his devoted head.

Owing, however, to the infirmities we have ascribed to them, their attack, though it can scarcely fail to give considerable pain to the object of it, has not cleared the ground of his mistakes. He and his advocates continue to repeat their statements, and the farmers continue to contradict them; and there the matter rests. What the first do not see is that what the public wants on this subject are practical results, not mere technical and barren definitions. And what the second do not see is that they will never establish their own case to the satisfaction of the world unless they subject their relations with the labourer to a searching analysis which shall place every fact connected with them in its true light and show its bearing upon other facts. A clerical advocate of the Archdeacon ingeniously observes that when you are asked what are a man's weekly wages, you are bound to state only the sum which is agreed upon, so to speak, as a retaining fee, without regard to anything he may earn in excess of it by work which is uncertain or irregular. If the answer disseminates a wrong impression that is the fault of the questioner, who should have elicited the truth by further inquisition. This gentleman has clearly mistaken his profession, and should have been a luminary in Westminster Hall. But several observations are suggested to us by the point he raises. In the first place, it was neither the intention nor the duty of the Archdeacon to baffle inquiry but to furnish information. And to represent him as standing on the defensive in this manner and taking advantage of the form in which the question was put to say as little as he could, regardless of the danger of totally misleading all who heard him, is truly humorous, and reminds us of the very old story of the Oxford man under examination who, when asked to say who Saul was, declined to answer, for fear, as he afterwards said, of being "led into the woody country of the kings." In the second place, neither the public nor the commissioners care twopence by what name the earnings of the labourers may be called; they want the amount. Nor is it anything to the purpose that the labourer does not "contract" to do piece-work, as long as he is perfectly certain to have the offer of it. While seed time and harvest, cold and heat, summer and winter continue to recur, his turn at piece-work is as certain as his weekly wages. That he does not contract is in his own favour, not the farmer's. But if we object to this kind of special pleading that it is utterly sterile and impractical, we object to the mode in which it is answered that it is chaotic and mentally indigestible. That is the fault of the farmer's education. He cannot deploy his forces; and for want of this power he often gives an apparent triumph to better trained minds who with a twentieth part of his knowledge are masters of intellectual strategy.

THE OLD SPORTING MAN[1]

PALL MALL GAZETTE, 1 FEBRUARY 1872

The old sporting man was young once on a time, although he has altered so little in the many years you have known him. Hard and hale, he still resembles what he was when fifty years ago he succeeded to the paternal acres. At two-and-seventy he retains the same square shoulders, the same broad, open chest. He has nothing to speak of in the way of a stoop, and calves that incline him to welcome knickerbockers, in spite of his prejudices against new-fangled fashions of dress. Still on the backs of his powerful hands you can see the muscles coiling themselves like whipcord, although they are lost somewhat in gathering flesh. The flesh has gained a little on him elsewhere, padding out his great flapped waistcoat, and giving his hunters and his cob a few stones more to carry. The extra substance in the ponderous fabric of bone compels him to look up weight-carriers at fancy figures. His eye is bright as it used to be, although his sight is scarcely so sharp as the old gentleman fancies for it is his vanity to believe he can find a hare or mark a covey with any boy about his place. Take Squire Badger all in all, were his father to rise from his fifty years' slumber under the yews of Brocklehurst churchyard, he would have little difficulty in recognizing the son he left to fill his boots. For if the squire has changed little in look, considering the fifty years that have flown over his hoary head, he has altered even less in dress. His wardrobe is much what it was when the sporting blood of '20 came home rusticated from the university. Cutaway coats in blue, green, and pepper-and-salt, white corduroy waistcoats, drab corduroy continuations, cream-coloured and blue birds'-eye scarves, tops, and boots that might be Hessians with the tassels of whips, from the four-in-hand to the hunting crop; of stuffed badgers, terriers, hawks, and silver-ringed pheasants; of foxes' heads and brushes and pads; of portraits of Bay Lucy, the famous trotting mare; of Rattle, the celebrated badger bitch; of Lord Harkaway, the Master of the Mid-Kent Hounds, flying the brook and five-feet post and rails – to say nothing of all these, the heavy white wraprascals, the many-caped white driving coats, and the low, hard, broad-brimmed white hats would tell you you were in the hall of a sportsman of the old school. Appearances out of doors are the same. The Brocklehurst property consists of the fifteen hundred acres that have been in the Badger family three hundred years and more. Its owners have always been as much the farmer as "the squire", and with the upland grazing downs have

---

1. Newly identified and not since republished.

kept the half of it in their own hands. Looking at it from three points of the compass, the Grange stands almost buried in its farm buildings. You see the clusters of its red brick angular chimneys rising over the spreading roofs of its outbuildings. Everything speaks of space and ease and plenty. The keeping up those roods of red-tile roof is as good as an annuity to the bricklayer, thanks to the flights of pigeons perpetually pecking at the mortar. The walls of the great barns bulge perilously, as with immemorial pressure of overflowing harvests. The great strawyards with their long rows of sheds are filled in winter time with droves of fattening bullocks, littered all the year round with sounders of fatted pigs, crowed over by long-spurred game-cocks, and pecked about by game fowls and game bantams. A pond and a patch of common at the one side are whitened with cackling geese. At the other an orchard of moss-grown apple and cherry trees shelters endless poultry coops and out-lying dog kennels. In the paddock behind, a blood colt or two and some superannuated brood mares are grazing round the old grey dovecot. Before the door, leaving the bare room for the carriage sweep, is the old-fashioned garden, with its clipped hedges. Nothing has gone to decay, and nearly as little has been done for ornament. The Badgers have strong tastes, but no sensibilities. They never discovered that they lived in one of the quaintest dwellings in Kent and one of the most picturesque nooks of England. But they were conscious and thankful that Providence had cast their lots in an excellent sporting country. They showed their gratitude by actions rather than words, although they might brag of their blessings among their boon companions, at the small hours. Brocklehurst furzes were always a sure find, and although it was hard to get the foxes away, and the country was cramped according to modern notions, the old hounds and men were slow. They liked a run none the worse because they took it leisurely. Brocklehurst Bottom, with the matted copse wood hanging over the trout stream, was known far and wide as an otter haunt. There used to be badgers, too, in the thick fur scrub, although latterly these namesakes of the Brocklehurst family had to be imported for drawing purposes. Of course, with his small property and his antiquated ideas, the squire never dreamed of battues. Although there were generally a couple of fox litters in his woods, yet, thanks to the abundance of rabbits, they left him a sprinkling of pheasants. The hares he spared for his harriers or greyhounds; but partridges there were in plenty, and snipes in the undrained meadow-land by the Brockle, and ducks occasionally in the sedgy ponds in the gloomy wood of the Springshaws, while those Springshaw rills were sure for woodcock in the winter.

The Badger family has been more considered than it is, and the present squire has sad suspicions he is an anachronism. Times are not what they were. England is going to the dogs. He knows himself to be right and all his neighbours in the wrong. Yet social opinion is strangely tolerant to him. It regards him as a type of the English gentleman-yeoman of the old school and leaves him to time to deal with. It admits his redeeming qualities in atonement of much that scandalizes it. For the life the squire looks back upon with jovial melancholy and an honest conscience was anything but edifying according to modern ideas, and the rector and the churchwardens think "old Badger" sets the parish a most discreditable example now. Yet he holds himself a staunch pillar of the parish church. He would as soon think of missing a meet as morning service and the worst is that his virtues recommend his vices for imitation. He is the kindest master in the whole neighbourhood, and the labourer who has done easy work for him through a lifetime need have no fear of the union. Yet in Mr. Badger's opinion, drinking is an amusement like another, provided you drink discreetly after working hours. For himself, as his people know, and for all the tremendous strength of his head, the squire seldom goes to bed "not to say exactly sober." He points triumphantly to his evergreen health in proof of his asseveration that he was never the worse for liquor in his life. With what propriety can local magistrates proceed against the parish roughs for dog-fighting, when the squire of Brocklehurst fights dogs still and draws badgers, and improvises on occasion a cockpit in his parlour? The roughs quote him as an excuse for brutalizing themselves. They cannot be expected to draw nice distinctions or appreciate the strange contrasts of a character which seems perfectly harmonious to the owner. He was reared from the nursery in the faith that the end of animal existence is the sport of man. In petticoats still, his father chuckled while he stoned a cat out of an apple tree to be torn piecemeal by the terriers. As the reward of boyish good conduct, he was permitted to see his pet cocks peck each other to death, and he would clap his small hands with delight while his friend the great mastiff of the yard rolled over and over with his fangs locked in a death-worry. So in a match against time he would trot a favourite horse to the gates of death, through the most cruel sufferings. But if the animal crippled its constitution in the effort he would pension it for life in his paddocks, and as soon think of selling Brocklehurst as parting with it. It must be remembered, in common fairness, that he spared himself no more than the brute creation. He might urge his favourite dog to a worry, or send him into an earth to be horribly mangled by a badger; but then there was nothing he enjoyed so throughly himself as a "turn-up" with a man supposed to be a trifle better than himself. He never knew when to throw up the sponge, and would come up round after round, to receive a renewal of the most tremendous punishment. He might trot his mare almost to the death, nor spare the whipcord, although he knew her blood and game; but when he backed himself, in no particular condition as he was, to do his thousand miles, fair toe and heel, in a thousand hours, his physical sufferings were greater and far more prolonged than hers. He did limp in a winner on his swollen feet; but for the last few days relays of friends had to prevent his collapsing in sleep as he walked, notwithstanding the excruciating pain.

Old Badger is something more than a local celebrity. Although always well forward in the hunting-field, his weight prevented his achieving great triumphs in the silk, but on the box he was celebrated far and wide. He was as well known on the Kentish coast-roads as any of the regular professionals – better, indeed, for he used to work all the coaches promiscuously. He was always making himself objects for journeys to fairs or races or coursing meetings. He was hand-in-glove with all the coachmen, who regarded him as a gentleman of means content to do their profession some grace. The most self-satisfied were willing to confess that there was something to be learned from the squire in the matter of style. A single glance at this amateur would silence the objections of the most timid passanger. With his splendid physique and superb air of confidence, ignorance itself saw he must be the right man for the place. He neither sat bolt upright like a veteran corporal of pensioners, nor lolled over his work like a punt-fisher over his float. With his lithe, powerful frame bending itself to his horses, the wildest team of half-broke, over-fed thoroughbreds might have tried in vain to tear themselves out of those iron hands that could be light on occasion as feathers. Strength, skill, and swagger always make a demigod with the million. Travellers used to accost him with distant reverence during the rapid changes. Buxom landladies beamed on him from bar-parlours. Boots and ostlers lay grovelling under his heavy boots. For some seasons he horsed the Canterbury Eclipse himself for the three stages that lay past his doors. That cost him more money than he liked, so he very sensibly gave it up, for it had never been the way of the Badgers to let their sporting tastes gallop away with their acres. For that reason, although a frequent attendant on race meetings, he never "went upon the turf." He attended for sport and not for business, and as he could throw his soul into a race, he did not think it worth while sending money after it. Not that he did not make his races pay, or back the good things he was put up to by any of his friends down the road. And these friends had learned to be exceedingly careful of the tips they gave him. The squire was rough in his ways as with his words. He generally lost his temper when he lost his bets, for losses stung his pride as well as his pocket. Then when he next encountered the false prophet, it was very apt to be a word and a blow, and a sheer toss-up which of them came first. Last of his race, the squire is the first of it who had lived in celibacy at Brocklehurst. He has always been hospitable in his own way, and, as may be surmised from his habits, was never over-particular in his company. But he only cares to associate with inferiors whom he can respect for their attainments. In the decay of old English sport he has no liking for the sport-talking boors of his neighbourhood, and the neighbouring gentry have little liking for him. So he often sits solitary, with the memories of the jolly old times for his sole boon companions. Ah! In those jolly old times Brocklehurst was a very different place. He has a horse or two still that he need be ashamed to show to no one. But his stables are a solitude compared to what they were in the times when he horsed the Eclipse. He mechanically sallies forth by himself in the old way, his old white bull-terrier at his heel. The yelp of welcome from the mastiff chained at the corner gives the alarm; it is echoed by a couple or so rough otter-hounds on one side, by a small kennelful of harriers on the other, by the setters penned away by the woodshed, and the terriers, rough and smooth, condemned to separate confinement in the orchard. His face brightens only to cloud again. Brocklehurst can never be what it was; no more than England. Not that it greatly signifies. He is the last of the Badgers in the direct line, and must soon be run to earth in the churchyard. But his heir? His next of kin is one of the new sporting school, and the new sporting school is one of his antipathies.

THE COUNTY FRANCHISE[1]

PALL MALL GAZETTE, 1 MAY 1872

The various proposals which have from time to time been made for equalizing the town and county franchise are the natural product of the pecuniary qualification introduced in 1832. And in 1859, when the Conservative Government proposed to carry out this object by extending the £10 franchise to the counties, one of the arguments adduced in favour of their plan was that unless something of the kind were done, we should sink by degrees through a process resembling "a Dutch auction" to universal household suffrage. We are now promised, it appears, and that at no remote period, the fulfilment of the prophecy. An organized agitation for that purpose is not unlikely to be established. A young and ambitious member of Parliament has taken up the question. Mr. Gladstone has spoken of it in doubtful language. Opposition to the change would come with a very ill grace from the Conservatives had they cause to be afraid of it. And the conclusion seems to be that if taken up in earnest by any considerable section of the Liberal party, the movement is likely to succeed.

1. Newly identified and not since republished.

In theory, of course, there is no more to be said for the £12 county franchise than there was for the £10 borough franchise. Such limitations are purely arbitrary, resting on no principle, and only safe as long as they are not attacked. They may happen to work so well as not to be seriously assailed for many years. But the moment a sufficient number of people are found to say that their practical utility is no warrant for their logical absurdity, their fate is sealed. The practical argument was exhausted by Mr. Lowe in 1866, with a warmth of eloquence, a vigour of argument, and an abundance of illustration which are not likely to be surpassed. And what was the result? It seems, therefore, that unless something more can be said for this kind of limitation in the counties than Mr. Lowe could find to say for it in the towns, it must share the same fate. There is, indeed, one thing to be said in its favour which could not be said equally of the elder system. The new settlement is only five years old, while its predecessor was five-and-thirty. To disturb again so soon an arrangement which was complete with so much difficulty and under circumstances so little likely to recur may be thought the part rather of a pedant than a patriot. There is no doubt that a tendency to vexatious and meddlesome legislation is one of the vices of the age: and let this argument therefore be taken for what it is worth. But the central consideration, of course, is how would household suffrage operate in the counties; how far would it affect the present distribution of power; how far would it violate those implied compacts on which our present electoral system is confessedly based?

At first sight it might appear that the enfranchisement of the agricultural labourer would throw great additional power into the hands of the farmers. Whatever the effect of the ballot, supposing it to exist, in large towns, we doubt whether any artificial contrivance could ensure secrecy in a country village. We may assume practically that farmers would always be able to ascertain with more or less certainty how their labourers had voted. Their relations with them are so much more personal than between employers and employed in towns; the social circle is so much narrower in the country, and every one knows so much more about his neighbours' concerns, that we take it for granted the ballot would be a dead letter. Then, of course, the farmer can bring to bear upon his labourer a kind of pressure, both moral and material, about impossible for the manufacturer. All his men know him. They see him and speak to him every day of their lives. Their fathers worked for his father. To offend or thwart one with whom you have these close personal relations is something very different from thwarting a man who is little more than an abstraction to you. The sum of it, in short, is this: the man who employs twelve workmen, all of whom he knows well, can influence them and manipulate them much more effectually than he who employs twelve hundred who are practically strangers to him. The small army would be much more manageable than the large one. But, secondly, the farmer can exert a potent material coercion over the labourer. He can turn him out of his cottage, keep him out of work, and almost make his village too hot to hold him. For, independently of professional interests, there is a homogeneity of politics among farmers which would enable them to present a more impenetrable front then the manufacturers. For these various reasons it might seem as if household suffrage in the country would almost throw our county representation into the hands of the farmers. But there are certain conflicting considerations which tend greatly to modify this conclusion.

In the first place, we must remember that the dependence of the farmer on the labourer is just as great as that of the labourer on the farmer. If a manufacturer cannot execute a given order for want of hands, he loses the profit on that particular transaction, and there's an end of it. But if a farmer cannot get his land ploughed, his corn sown, and his crops carried at the right season of the year and when the weather gives him his chance, the consequences are tenfold more serious. He knows pretty well the whole stock of labour on which he has to depend. He cannot import it from a distance; and will perhaps be less able to do so hereafter than he is now. Thus it is clear that farmers would have to think twice before dismissing any number of workmen because of an obnoxious vote; and that if they dismissed them one day they might have to take them on again the next. But, secondly, we must remember what some people do not know, and what many are apt to forget, that the population who would be enfranchised by household suffrage in the counties is far from exclusively agricultural. There are counties of England in which every village has a large percentage of artisans, stocking-makers, lawmakers, or what not. There are towns in England without representatives in Parliament, and with little agricultural connections, whose vote even now materially affects the county. What would it do if every householder could vote? There is the mining population in the north, and, in short, there is a very large miscellaneous element outside the area of the borough population which is not agricultural, and would if enfranchised go far to counteract the possible effects of giving greater power to the farmers. Still we have further to consider in common fairness how far it is equitable to pour this alien element into the county constituencies. Though it may be undesirable to see town and county constituencies and town and county representatives divided from each other by a hard and sharp line, it would be still more undesirable to upset the political balance which is still, however imperfectly, maintained among us.

THE RATING OF PERSONAL PROPERTY[1]

STANDARD, 23 MAY 1872

SIR, – The opponents of the scheme for rating personal property allege the difficulty of localising it; and there is an indefinite but none the less powerful opposition arising from the want of precedent. If it had been the custom to do so for centuries, as it has been the custom to rate the land, no objection would be raised. The following items, however, extracted from a poor-rate made in the year 1687, show that our forefathers found no difficulty in localising personal property, and that it actually was their practice to rate such property for the relief of the poor:–

"A tax made for the poor in the parish of Swindon of Ano 1687, and ye same to be collected as often as ye necessity of ye poore require:–
Thomas Goddard Esq. Item for tithe   0s. 8d.
Mr. Thomas Vilett, for tithe   1s. 8d."

Both these gentlemen were laymen. The Vilett family (now Rolleston) were the lay rectors of the parish. These paid a rate upon the tithe they received. Now it certainly does appear that an income from tithe is precisely the same as an income from funded property. And here we find the income from tithe rated to the relief of the poor furnishing the requisite precedent. There was no difficulty in localising income from tithe. Why should there be a difficulty in localising income from any other kind of property? Mr. Lowe appears to rely chiefly upon the income tax for his Indian rubber budgets; he finds no difficulty in localising that, at least in so far as collection goes. The vast works of the Great Western Railway here have recently been rated at a much higher figure than formerly, and in so doing the increased amount of traffic was taken into consideration. That traffic passes between London and Bristol, yet the income from it was localised to pay rates to the Highworth and Swindon Union. There is no difficulty in discovering to what parish an inmate of the workhouse belongs or where he has gained a settlement; what difficulty can there be, then, in discovering in what parish the rate derived from personal property should be applied? In point of fact it actually is done at the present moment. If a man from illness, for instance, becomes an inmate of the workhouse, and, as is often the case, he is found to possess a little funded property, or 20l. or 30l. in a bank, he is informed that he must repay the cost of his maintenance. If a man's father, from age, falls upon the workhouse, and the son is found to possess property in a bank or elsewhere, or to possess an

---

1. Newly identified and not since republished.

ascertained income from any source, he is informed that he must contribute from that property or income to the support of his parent. And if he neglects to do so the magistrates issue an order upon him to pay 1s. 6d. or 2s. per week according to the circumstances. What is this 1s. 6d. or 2s. a week but a rate upon personal property? In these cases there is no difficulty in localising it. – I am, Sir, faithfully yours, Richard Jefferies. Coate Farm, Swindon, April 18.

THE POETRY OF STEAM-PLOUGHS[1]

GRAPHIC, 5 OCTOBER 1872

Ex fume dare lucem – Horace.

That now common sight of a well-farmed district – the steam-plough – is seldom associated with the romantic and picturesque. All who do not regard it with the glance of an agriculturist look upon its foul volumes of smoke as an ugly blot upon the beauty of the country, and recoil from its monotonous rattle with aversion. If they are so unlucky as to meet it on the Queen's high-way, slowly advancing, with much noise and seemingly uncertain devious steps, like Samson led captive in his blindness, they execrate it as a nuisance to timid horses and bad drivers. But the steam-plough, like its brother the railway locomotive, has now passed through the cloud of mistrust and abuse which envelopes the birth of every innova-tion. It is even possible (as we hope to show) to discern a poetic side to its struggling, panting existence. And, at all events, it is better that the dweller in the country should attempt to evolve its aesthetic aspects, and learn to regard its advent amongst the stubbles with equanimity, than chafe at the incongruity which it presents to his ideas of natural beauty, and grumble while it remains in the neighbourhood. It is a nuisance, we freely grant, when encountered as a man is driving a young horse, and the attendant who is bound by law to precede it some hundred paces, give notice of its approach, and assist any horseman in difficulties, is lagging behind to chat with his mate, or absent in the road-side public house when most wanted. But let a dispassionate pedestrian stand aside while the huge groaning giant, dragging his load of coal and water, and a plough which would have amazed Ceres or Triptolemus, works its way past him, and he need be at

1. Newly identified and not since republished.

no loss to see some poetic elements in the creature. The attendant who precedes (supposing him to be in his proper place), supplies a charming piece of colour to the grey distance, as he waves his red flag of warning. It is not unpleasing to behold the terror of partridges and hares, as they flee from the monster's approach. And when the ungainly fabric, puffing out clouds of smoke, and snorting jets of steam from its enormous interior, draws near with slow yet imposing motion, its immensely broad iron wheels crunching the gravel into dust, with a loud murmurous rattle, such as might proceed from some fabulous creature of the nether world, it is impossible to escape a sensation of awe. The advance of the monstrous bulk of Juggernauth himself could not be more terrific. No Gorgon or Chimaera dire could utter more hideous sounds. Yet the creature is completely under the control of human will, as those two sooty stokers evince, who calmly smoke their pipes while they regulate the monster's steps from their seats behind. It has a very complicated arrangement of taps and tubes; yet the internal arrangements of an elephant are probably far from simple until you have learnt to look at them with the eye of an anatomist; and, indeed, this creature as it slowly feels its way over a dubious brick bridge, spanning a country brook, is not unlike the elephant, who cautiously explores with foot and trunk the plank bridge which crosses a jungle torrent, before he will trust his vast weight upon it. A fanciful mind might almost recognise instinct in this ungainly iron monster, while the store of coal and water which it bears proclaims loudly enough, that it has an appetite, like any sentient creature. Make way, make way, my masters! else as some resistless natural force it will speedily grind you to powder!

Few as the elements of the picturesque contained in a steam-plough seem to an ordinary observer, even he must recognise them when he thinks a minute on the influences which the vast machine represents. All the material progress of the country, nay of the world, during the last sixty years is contained in it. The plough is but the latest development of ingenuity which the monster, steam, has been compelled to work, as the Orientals typified by Aladdin and his Genie. When the locomotive approaches a spectator, resistless, black, and awful, he finds himself mentally comparing it with the modern ironclad; like it in its outward misshapen ugliness and the mighty forces which lurk within; but beneficent instead of deadly, lightening the old curse of labour, abridging man's toil during the bitter, dark days of winter, when exposure to the elements in our climate tries the strongest constitution. A blessing is in it; let us be slow to condemn its unsightliness. At once the earliest instrument of civilisation and the latest, the history of mankind's progress from the savage is contained in the grimy boiler which works the plough. All the future of agriculture as a science pulls from the disproportionately narrow funnel. It is a perpetual monument of human enterprise amongst the arable fields on which the earliest Autocthon[1] himself but one degree removed from his kindred clods, worked of old. It is a standing miracle of discovery, a marvel which men disregard only because other applications of steam are so familiar to them. What "fairy-tale of science" can be more wonderful than the one which tells how the bright-eyed lad stopped the spout of his grandmother's kettle, and when the steam forced up the lid, awoke to the idea that there, rather than in Solomon's sealed vessel, lay the imprisoned giant which would one day fill the world with its smoke? These and the like reflections beset us, as the plough drags along its ponderous weight to the field which it is to tear up.

Unpoetic as it is, too, it has not been forgotten by the poets, though at first sight it would seem as hopeless to bring it into verse as did the introduction of some such word as "gunpowder" appear to us when toiling as schoolboys over Latin "longs and shorts." Mrs. Browning, in the first edition of "Lady Geraldine's Courtship," says of her charming heroine:–

> She has halls, and she has castles, and the resonant steam eagles
> Follow far on the directing of her floating dove-like hand.

Indistinct as is this imagery (like the golden woodlands seen through the smoke of a steam-plough), it might be assigned to either a railway or a ploughing locomotive; but that the authoress intended her magniloquent "steam-eagles" for steam-ploughs, may probably be gathered from what took the place of the above quotation in subsequent editions –

> And the palpitating engines snort in steam across her acres,
> As they mark upon the blasted heaven the measure of the land.

Naturally enough in his "Northern Farmer," old style, the Laureate delights in the juxtaposition of the modern implement with the time-honoured plough, and happily touches that hostility to all innovation which marks the ignorant farmer –

> Summun 'ull come ater mea mayhap wi' 'is kittle o' steam
> Huzzin' an' mazin' the blessed fealds wi' the Divil's oan team.

But the steam-plough has had too short a lease of life so far to have become familiar to our poets. Doubtless the day will come when it will figure in a Pastoral. Meanwhile it must be left to prose to point out its poetic aspects. *Caret vate sacro.*

---

1. Actual spelling in text.

Most persons would allow it the praise of picturesqueness could they see it at work on a breezy day in the Wolds of Lincolnshire. The two locomotives are planted opposite to each other at the ends of one of the fine arable fields of that well-farmed county, containing, it may be, a hundred acres. Dimly, as you stand by one of them, is the other descried through its drifting sooty clouds, and the rattle of its huge drum, as it winds up the wire rope which drags the plough is scarcely heard – it is so far off. Sunny gleams every now and then sweep over the red clay furrows, much to the delight of the gulls and plovers on the look out for worms. The farmer rides about in stately majesty (like the Homeric king on the shield of Achilles); all farmers in this well-to-do county ride to do their farming, while the labourers stand about watching "her," and remarking that "*she* does her work well." Suddenly the traction is reversed, the engine near us puts on the steam, the drum revolves, the wire-rope tightens, and the monstrous plough turning up its four or five furrows at once under the guidance of the man who sits on it with a rudder-like wheel in his hand, resolutely makes its way across to where we stand. Slowly at first, but soon quicker, with much shaking and groaning of the engine, does it draw near. The wheel by which it is directed is but a small item in its general resemblance to a ship, ploughing up the waves before it, and tossing them from its prow. Onward rushes the plough, and the thick, fat, oozy clay is turned up with the utmost precision, and falls to right and left in long piled-up furrows. Resistless and almost superhuman in its might does the machine seem; and the difficult work on which three horses would scarcely make any impression, is accomplished with an appearance of ease which much adds to the beauty of the sight. The hedges are yet dark and dusky after the winter's buffeting, the few ash trees which alone are suffered to grow in them at sparse distances are black in bough, and, still blacker in bud. The skies are grey and leaden; occasionally a heavy shower falls; the chill east wind cuts you to the bone. Instinctively you feel that the grimy, smoke-polluted locomotives with their huge plough are quite in harmony with the landscape. Who could even think of shallops, balloons, feathery birches, melodious girls and madrigals, in connection with such a rough climate? It is a stern country, much heavy work has to be done, and the steam plough is here an invaluable assistant.

Take another sketch from the same county, but in one of the well-wooded valleys that cut through its chalky up-lands. The little village (its name certain to end in -by, thanks to the Northmen of old) nestles round its square, plain church tower, and many a substantial farmstead, filled with mighty stacks of hay and clover, wards off from the natives the west wind, here so much dreaded. Far away in a long line crowning the hill, a procession of sugarloaf-shaped wheat-ricks appears to prance into the next county. No small freeholders starve here on their pitiful three-acres. Everything is done on a gigantic scale. There are at least 1,400 acres in the farm on which we tread, while its owner hunts in pink, with relays of horses, and keeps plenty of "Chateau Margaux" and "Veuve Clicquot" in his cellars. In fact, though he holds of Lord Broadfield, he is too big a man to be called a tenant-farmer. No wonder that he requires so large a plough. We involuntarily find ourselves, as we look at him, thinking of George Eliot's Lowick farmers – "as curious as any buffaloes or bisons – monsters – farmers without landlords – one can't tell how to class them." Meanwhile he sits on horseback, quietly musing, as the huge plough draws near. Is he captivated with the fair rural scene? Does he meditate on some aspect of the steam-plough radiant with light and sweetness? Do not expect him "whose talk is of bullocks," to transcend his kind. Now he turns to ride off, having first shouted to his factotum: "Bill! see thou to yon engine's water, and then supper'up the *tups*!" (Anglice "sheep.")

If an observant eye can thus find poetry in a spring or autumnal landscape with a steam-plough in the foreground, we must fain confess that the poetry resides rather in its concomitants than in the useful implement itself. It is easy to see that this theory is right when the machine leaves the fields and takes to its lumbering journeys along the high-roads. It is generally surrounded by a crowd of children looking with great eyes at the portent, as little Alice did at the marvels of Wonderland. Like all beneficent forces, it yet contains a mighty terror latent in its womb; the boiler might explode and carry devastation around. But at present the awe-struck faces of the children, in all the beauty of their young life, typify the wondrous future development which we may well believe is inherent in the steam-engine. Much as our age has innovated upon its predecessors, its discoveries are probably as nothing to the wonders which physical science has in store for our children. But characteristically enough, the village lads soon grow familiar with the steam-plough after all their original amazement; and here, too, a practical mind sees the result upon man of the mightiest physical discoveries. Familiarity speedily breeds, if not contempt, at least indifference.

THE WILTSHIRE LABOURER[1]

THE TIMES, 14 NOVEMBER 1872

LETTER I. (To the Editor)

Sir, – The Wiltshire agricultural labourer is not so highly paid as those of Northumberland, nor so low as those of Dorset; but in the amount of his wages, as in intelligence and general position, he may fairly be taken as an average specimen of his class throughout a large portion of the kingdom.

As a man, he is usually strongly built, broad-shouldered, and massive in frame, but his appearance is spoilt by the clumsiness of his walk and the want of grace in his movements. Though quite as large in muscle, it is very doubtful if he possesses the strength of the seamen who may be seen lounging about the ports. There is a want of firmness, a certain disjointed style, about his limbs, and the muscles themselves have not the hardness and tension of the sailor's. The labourer's muscle is that of a cart-horse, his motions lumbering and slow. His style of walk is caused by following the plough in early childhood, when the weak limbs find it a hard labour to pull the heavy nailed boots from the thick clay soil. Ever afterwards he walks as if it were an exertion to lift his legs. His food may, perhaps, have something to do with the deadened slowness which seems to pervade everything he does – there seems a lack of vitality about him. It consists chiefly of bread and cheese, with bacon twice or thrice a week, varied with onions, and if he be a milker (on some farms) with a good "tuck-out" at his employer's expense on Sundays. On ordinary days he dines at the fashionable hour of six or seven in the evening – that is, about that time his cottage scents the road with a powerful odour of boiled cabbage, of which he eats an immense quantity. Vegetables are his luxuries, and a large garden, therefore, is the greatest blessing he can have. He eats huge onions raw; he has no idea of flavouring his food with them, nor of making those savoury and inviting messes or vegetable soups at which the French peasantry are so clever. In Picardy I have often dined in a peasant's cottage, and thoroughly enjoyed the excellent soup he puts upon the table for his ordinary meal. To dine in an English labourer's cottage would be impossible. His bread is generally good, certainly; but his bacon is the cheapest he can buy at small second-class shops – oily, soft, wretched stuff; his vegetables are cooked in detestable style, and eaten saturated with the pot liquor. Pot liquor is a favourite soup. I have known cottagers actually apply at farmers' kitchens not only

---

1. Letters collected in *TF*.

for the pot liquor in which meat has been soddened, but for the water in which potatoes have been boiled – potato liquor – and sup it up with avidity. And this not in times of dearth or scarcity, but rather as a relish. They never buy anything but bacon; never butchers' meat. Philanthropic ladies, to my knowledge, have demonstrated over and over again even to their limited capacities that certain parts of butchers' meat can be bought just as cheap, and will make more savoury and nutritive food; and even now, with the present high price of meat, a certain proportion would be advantageous. In vain; the labourers obstinately adhere to the pig, and the pig only. When, however, an opportunity does occur the amount of food they will eat is something astonishing. Once a year, at the village club dinner, they gormandise to repletion. In one instance I knew of a man eating a plate of roast beef (and the slices are cut enormously thick at these dinners), a plate of boiled beef, then another of boiled mutton, and then a fourth of roast mutton, and a fifth of ham. He said he could not do much to the bread and cheese; but didn't he go into the pudding! I have even heard of men stuffing to the fullest extent of their powers, and then retiring from the table to take an emetic of mustard and return to a second gorging. There is scarcely any limit to their power of absorbing beer. I have known reapers and mowers make it their boast that they could lie on their backs and never take the wooden bottle (in the shape of a small barrel) from their lips till they had drunk a gallon, and from the feats I have seen I verily believe it a fact. The beer they get is usually poor and thin, though sometimes in harvest the farmers bring out a taste of strong liquor, but not till the work is nearly over; for from this very practice of drinking enormous quantities of small beer the labourer cannot drink more than a very limited amount of good liquor without getting tipsy. This is why he so speedily gets inebriated at the alehouse. While mowing and reaping many of them lay in a small cask.

They are much better clothed now than formerly. Corduroy trousers and slops are the usual style. Smock-frocks are going out of use, except for milkers and faggers. Almost every labourer has his Sunday suit, very often really good clothes, sometimes glossy black, with the regulation "chimneypot." His unfortunate walk betrays him, dress how he will. Since labour has become so expensive it has become a common remark among the farmers that the labourer will go to church in broadcloth and the masters in smock-frocks. The labourer never wears gloves – that has to come with the march of the times; but he is particularly choice over his necktie. The women must dress in the fashion. A very respectable draper in an agricultural district was complaining to me the other day that the poorest class of women would have everything in the fashionable style, let it change as often as it would. In former times, if he laid in a stock of goods suited to tradesmen, and farmers' wives and daughters, if the fashion changed, or they got out of date, he could dispose of them easily to the servants. Now no such thing. The quality did not matter so much, but the style must be the style of the day – no sale for remnants. The poorest girl, who had not got two yards of flannel on her back, must have the same style of dress as the squire's daughter – Dolly Vardens, chignons, and parasols for ladies who can work all day reaping in the broiling sun of August! Gloves, kid, for hands that milk the cows!

The cottages now are infinitely better than they were. There is scarcely room for further improvement in the cottages now erected upon estates. They have three bedrooms, and every appliance and comfort compatible with their necessarily small size. It is only the cottages erected by the labourers themselves on waste plots of ground which are open to objection. Those he builds himself are, indeed, as a rule, miserable huts, disgraceful to a Christian country. I have an instance before me at this moment where a man built a cottage with two rooms and no staircase or upper apart-ments, and in those two rooms eight persons lived and slept – himself and wife, grown-up daughters, and children. There was not a scrap of garden attached, not enough to grow half-a-dozen onions. The refuse and sewage was flung into the road, or filtered down a ditch into the brook which sup-plied that part of the village with water. In another case at one time there was a cottage in which twelve persons lived. This had upper apartments, but so low was the ceiling that a tall man could stand on the floor, with his head right through the opening for the staircase, and see along the upper floor under the beds! These squatters are the curse of the community. It is among them that fever and kindred infectious diseases break out; it is among them that wretched couples are seen bent double with rheumatism and affections of the joints caused by damp. They have often been known to remain so long, generation after generation, in these wretched hovels, that at last the lord of the manor, having neglected to claim quit-rent, they can defy him, and claim them as their own property, and there they stick, eyesores and blots, the fungi of the land. The cottages erected by farmers or by landlords are now, one and all, fit and proper habitations for human beings; and I verily believe it would be impossible throughout the length and breadth of Wiltshire to find a single bad cottage on any large estate, so well and so thoroughly have the landed proprietors done their work. On all farms gardens are attached to the cottages, in many instances very large, and always sufficient to produce enough vegetables for the resident. In villages the allotment system has been greatly extended of late years, and has been found most beneficial, both to owners and tenants. As a rule the allotments are let at a rate which may be taken as £4 per annum – a sum which pays the landlord very well, and enables the labourer to remunerate himself. In one village which came under my observation the clergyman of the parish has turned a portion of his glebe land into allotments – a most excellent and noble example, which cannot be too widely followed or too much extolled. He is thus enabled to benefit almost every one of his poor parishioners, and yet without destroying that sense of independence which is the great characteristic of a true Englishman. He has issued a book of rules and conditions under which these allotments are held, and he thus places a strong check upon drunkenness and dissolute habits, indulgence in which is a sure way to lose the portions of ground. There is scarcely an end to the benefits of the allotment system. In villages there cannot be extensive gardens, and the allotments supply their place. The extra produce above that which supplies the table and pays the rent is easily disposed of in the next town, and places many additional comforts in the labourer's reach. The refuse goes to help support and fatten the labourer's pig, which brings him in profit enough to pay the rent of his cottage, and the pig, in turn, manures the allotment. Some towns have large common lands, held under certain conditions; such are Malmesbury, with 500 acres, and Tetbury (the common land of which extends two miles), both these being arable, &c. These are not exactly in the use of labourers, but they are in the hands of a class to which the labourer often rises. Many labourers have fruit-trees in their gardens, which, in some seasons, prove very profitable. In the present year, to my knowledge, a labourer sold £4 worth of apples; and another made £3, 10s. off the produce of one pear-tree, pears being scarce.

To come at last to the difficult question of wages. In Wiltshire there has been no extended strike, and very few meetings upon the subject, for the simple reason that the agitators can gain no hold upon a county where, as a mass, the labourers are well paid. The common day-labourer receives 10s., 11s., and 12s. a week, according to the state of supply and demand for labour in various districts; and, if he milks, 1s. more, making 13s. a week, now common wages. These figures are rather below the mark; I could give instances of much higher pay. To give a good idea of the wages paid I will take the case of a hill farmer (arable, Marlborough Downs), who paid this last summer during harvest 18s. per week per man. His reapers often earned 10s. a day – enough to pay their year's rent in a week. These men lived in cottages on the farm, with three bedrooms each, and some larger, with every modern appliance, each having a garden of a quarter of an acre attached and close at hand, for which cottage and garden they paid 1s. per week rent. The whole of these cottages were insured by the farmer himself, their furniture, &c., in one lump, and the insurance policy cost him, as nearly as possible, 1s. 3d. per cottage per year. For this he deducted 1s. per year each from their wages. None of the men would have insured unless he had insisted upon doing it for them. These men had from six to eight quarts of beer per man (over and above their 18s. a week) during harvest every day. In spring and autumn their wages are much increased by piece-work, hoeing, &c. In winter the farmer draws their coal for them in his waggons, a distance of eight miles from the nearest wharf, enabling them to get it at cost price. This is no slight advantage, for, at the present high price of coal, it is sold, delivered in the villages, at 2s. per cwt. Many who cannot afford it in the week buy a quarter of a cwt. on Saturday night, to cook their Sunday's dinner with, for 6d. This is at the rate of £2 per ton. Another gentleman, a large steam cultivator in the Vale, whose name is often before the public, informs me that his books show that he paid £100 in one year in cash to one cottage for labour, showing the advantage the labourer possesses over the mechanic, since his wife and child can add to his income. Many farmers pay £50 and £60 a year for beer drunk by their labourers – a serious addition to their wages. The railway companies and others who employ mechanics, do not allow them any beer. The allowance of a good cottage and a quarter of an acre of garden for 1s. per week is not singular. Many who were at the Autumn Manoeuvres of the present year may remember having a handsome row of houses, rather than cottages, pointed out to them as inhabited by labourers at 1s. per week. In the immediate neighbourhood of large manufacturing towns 1s. 6d. a week is sometimes paid; but then these cottages would in such positions readily let to mechanics for 3s., 4s., and even 5s. per week. There was a great outcry when the Duke of Marlborough issued an order that the cottages on his estate should in future only be let to such men as worked upon the farms where those cottages were situated. In reality this was the very greatest blessing the Duke could have conferred upon the agricultural labourer; for it ensured him a good cottage at a nearly nominal rent and close to his work; whereas in many instances previously the cottages on the farms had been let at a high rate to the mechanics, and the labourer had to walk miles before he got to his labour. Cottages are not erected by landowners or by farmers as paying speculations. It is well known that the condition of things prevents the agricultural labourer from being able to pay a sufficient rent to be a fair percentage upon the sum expended. In one instance a landlord has built some cottages for his tenant, the tenant paying a certain amount of interest on the sum invested by the landlord. Now, although this is a matter of arrangement, and not of speculation – that is, although the interest paid by the tenant is a low percentage upon the money laid out, yet the rent paid by the labourers inhabiting these cottages to the tenant does not reimburse him what he pays his landlord as interest – not by a considerable margin. But then he has the advantage of his labourers close to his work, always ready at hand.

Over and above the actual cash wages of the labourer, which are now very good, must be reckoned his cottage and garden, and often a small orchard, at a nominal rent, his beer at his master's expense, piecework, gleaning after harvest, &c., which alter his real position very materially. In Gloucestershire, on the Cotswolds, the best-paid labourers are the shepherds, for in that great sheep-country much trust is reposed in them. At the annual auctions of shearlings which are held upon the large farms a purse is made for the shepherd of the flock, into which every one who attends is expected to drop a shilling, often producing £5. The shepherds on the Wiltshire downs are also well paid, especially in lambing time, when the greatest watchfulness and care are required. It has been stated that the labourer has no chance of rising from his position. This is sheer cant. He has very good opportunities of rising, and often does rise, to my knowledge. At this present moment I could mention a person who has risen from a position scarcely equal to that of a labourer, not only to have a farm himself, but to place his sons in farms. Another has just entered on a farm; and several more are on the highroad to that desirable consummation. If a labourer possesses any amount of intelligence he becomes head-carter or headfogger, as the case may be; and from that to be assistant or under-bailiff, and finally bailiff. As a bailiff he has every opportunity to learn the working of a farm, and is often placed in entire charge of a farm at a distance from his employer's residence. In time he establishes a reputation as a practical man, and being in receipt of good wages, with very little expenditure, saves some money. He has now little difficulty in obtaining the promise of a farm, and with this can readily take up money. With average care he is a made man. Others rise from petty trading, petty dealing in pigs and calves, till they save sufficient to rent a small farm, and make that the basis of larger dealing operations. I question very much whether a clerk in a firm would not find it much more difficult, as requiring larger capital, to raise himself to a level with his employer than an agricultural labourer does to the level of a farmer.

Many labourers now wander far and wide as navvies, &c., and perhaps when these return home, as most of them do, to agricultural labour, they are the most useful and intelligent of their class, from a readiness they possess to turn their hand to anything. I know one at this moment who makes a large addition to his ordinary wages by brewing for the small inns, and very good liquor he brews, too. They pick up a large amount of practical knowledge.

The agricultural women are certainly not handsome; I know no peasantry so entirely uninviting. Occasionally there is a girl whose nut-brown complexion and sloe-black eyes are pretty, but their features are very rarely good, and they get plain quickly, so soon as the first flush of youth is past.

Many have really good hair in abundance, glossy and rich, perhaps from its exposure to the fresh air. But on Sundays they plaster it with strong-smelling pomade and hair-oil, which scents the air for yards most unpleasantly. As a rule, it may safely be laid down that the agricultural women are moral, far more so than those of the town. Rough and rude jokes and language are, indeed, too common; but that is all. No evil comes of it. The fairs are the chief cause of immorality. Many an honest, hard-working servant-girl owes her ruin to these fatal mops and fairs, when liquor to which she is unaccustomed overcomes her. Yet it seems cruel to take from them the one day or two of the year on which they can enjoy themselves fairly in their own fashion. The spread of friendly societies, patronised by the gentry and clergy, with their annual festivities, is a remedy which is gradually supplying them with safer, and yet congenial, amusement. In what may be termed lesser morals I cannot accord either them or the men the same praise. They are too ungrateful for the many great benefits which are bountifully supplied them – the brandy, the soup, and fresh meat readily extended without stint from the farmer's home in sickness to the cottage are too quickly forgotten. They who were most benefited are often the first to most loudly complain and to backbite. Never once in all my observation have I heard a labouring man or woman make a grateful remark; and yet I can confidently say that there is no class of persons in England who receive so many attentions and benefits from their superiors as the agricultural labourers. Stories are rife of their even refusing to work at disastrous fires because beer was not immediately forthcoming. I trust this is not true; but it is too much in character. No term is too strong in condemnation for those persons who endeavour to arouse an agitation among a class of people so short-sighted and so ready to turn against their own benefactors and their own interest. I am credibly informed that one of these agitators, immediately after the Bishop of Gloucester's unfortunate but harmlessly intended speech at the Gloucester Agricultural Society's dinner – one of these agitators mounted a platform at a village meeting and in plain language incited and advised the labourers to duck the farmers! The agricultural women either go out to field-work or become indoor servants. In harvest they hay-make – chiefly light work, as raking – and reap, which is much harder labour; but then, while reaping they work their own time, as it is done by the piece. Significantly enough, they make longer hours while reaping. They are notoriously late to arrive, and eager to return home, on the hay-field. The children help both in haymaking and reaping. In spring and autumn they hoe and do other piece-work. On pasture farms they beat clots or pick up stones out of the way of the mowers' scythes. Occasionally, but rarely now, they milk. In winter they wear gaiters, which give the ankles a most ungainly appearance. Those who go out to service get very low wages at first from their extreme awkwardness, but generally quickly rise. As dairymaids they get very good wages indeed. Dairymaids are scarce and valuable. A dairymaid who can be trusted to take charge of a dairy will sometimes get £20 besides her board (liberal) and sundry perquisites. These often save money, marry bailiffs, and help their husbands to start a farm.

In the education provided for children Wiltshire compares favourably with other counties. Long before the passing of the recent Act in reference to education the clergy had established schools in almost every parish, and their exertions have enabled the greater number of places to come up to the standard required by the Act, without the assistance of a School Board. The great difficulty is the distance children have to walk to school, from the sparseness of population and the number of outlying hamlets. This difficulty is felt equally by the farmers, who, in the majority of cases, find themselves situated far from a good school. In only one place has anything like a cry for education arisen, and that is on the extreme northern edge of the county. The Vice-Chairman of the Swindon Chamber of Agriculture recently stated that only one-half of the entire population of Inglesham could read and write. It subsequently appeared that the parish of Inglesham was very sparsely populated, and that a variety of circumstances had prevented vigorous efforts being made. The children, however, could attend schools in adjoining parishes, not farther than two miles, a distance which they frequently walk in other parts of the country.

Those who are so ready to cast every blame upon the farmer, and to represent him as eating up the earnings of his men and enriching himself with their ill-paid labour, should remember that farming, as a rule, is carried on with a large amount of borrowed capital. In these days, when £6 an acre has been expended in growing roots for sheep, when the slightest derangement of calculation in the price of wool, meat, or corn, or the loss of a crop, seriously interferes with a fair return for capital invested, the farmer has to sail extremely close to the wind, and only a little more would find his canvas shaking. It was only recently that the cashier of the principal bank of an agricultural county, after an unprosperous year, declared that such another season would make almost every farmer insolvent. Under these circumstances it is really to be wondered at that they have done as much as they have for the labourer in the last few years, finding him with better cottages, better wages, better education, and affording him better opportunities of rising in the social scale. – I am, Sir, faithfully yours,

Richard Jefferies.

Coate Farm, Swindon, Nov. 12, 1872.

WILTSHIRE FARMERS AND LABOURERS

THE TIMES, 27 NOVEMBER 1872

LETTER TO THE EDITOR

Sir, – I did not intend to make any reply to the numerous attacks made upon my letter published in the Times of the 14th inst., but the statements made by "The Son of a Wiltshire Labourer" are such as I feel bound to resent on the part of the farmers of this county.

He says he wishes the landed proprietors would take as much care to provide cottages for their labourers as I represent them as doing. I repeat what I said, that the cottages on large estates are now, one and all, fit habitations for human beings. The Duke of Marlborough is a large proprietor of cottages in this neighbourhood, and his plan has been, whenever a cottage did not appear sufficiently commodious, to throw two into one. The owner of the largest estate near Swindon has been engaged for many years past in removing the old thatched mud hovels, and replacing them with substantial, roomy, and slate-roofed buildings. Farmers are invariably anxious to have good cottages. There is a reluctance to destroy the existing ones, both from the inconvenience and the uncertainty sometimes of others being erected. Often, too, the poor have the strongest attachment to the cabin in which they were born and bred, and would strongly resent its destruction, though obviously for their good. Farmers never build bad cottages now. When a tenement falls in, either from decay or the death of the tenant, the cottage which is erected on its site is invariably a good one. A row of splendid cottages has recently been erected at Wanborough. They are very large, with extensive gardens attached. Some even begin to complain that the cottages now erected are in a sense "too good" for the purpose. The system of three bedrooms is undoubtedly the best from a sanitary point of view, but it is a question whether the widespread belief in that system, and that system alone, has not actually retarded the erection of reasonably good buildings. It is that third bedroom which just prevents the investment of building a cottage from paying a remunerative percentage on the capital expended. Two bedrooms are easily made – the third puzzles the builder where to put it with due regard to economy. Nor is a third bedroom always required. Out of ten families perhaps only two require a third bedroom; in this way there is a large waste in erecting a row. It has been suggested that a row should consist of so many cottages with two bedrooms only for families who do not want more, and at each end a building with three bedrooms for larger families. In one instance two cottages were ordered to be erected on an estate, the estimate for which was £640; these when completed might have let for £10 per annum, or 1¾ per cent, on the capital invested! The plans for these cottages had so many dormer windows, porches, intricacies of design in variegated tiles, &c., that the contractor gave it up as a bad job. I mention this to show that the tendency to build good cottages has gone even beyond what was really required, and ornamentation is added to utility.

Then it is further stated that the labourer cannot build cottages. I could name a lane at this moment the cottages in which were one and all built by labourers; and there are half-a-dozen in this village which were erected by regular farm labourers. The majority of these are, as I said before, wretched hovels, but there are two or three which demonstrate that the labourer, if he is a thrifty man, earns quite sufficient to enable him to erect a reasonably good building. The worst hovel I ever saw (it was mentioned in my letter of the 14th) was built by a man who is notorious for his drinking habits. Some forty years ago, when wages were much lower than they are now, two labourers, to my knowledge, took possession of a strip of waste land by the roadside, and built themselves cottages. One of these was a very fair building; the other would certainly be condemned now-a-days. The lord of the manor claimed these; and the difficulty was thus adjusted:– The build-ers were to receive the value of their tenements from the lord of the manor, and were to remain permanent tenants for life on payment of a small per-centage, interest upon the purchase-money, as quit-rent. On their deaths the cottages were to become the property of the lord of the manor. One man received £40 for his cottage, the other £20, which sums forty years ago represented relatively a far higher value than now, and demonstrate con-clusively that the labourer, if he is a steady, hard-working man, can build a cottage. Another cottage I know of, built by a farm labourer, is really a very creditable building – good walls, floors, staircase, sashes, doors; it stands high, and appears very comfortable, and even pleasant, in summer, for they are a thrifty family, and can even display flower-pots in the window. Other cottages have been built or largely added to in my memory by labourers. On these occasions they readily obtain help from the farmers. One lends his team and waggons to draw the stones; another supplies wood for noth-ing; but of late I must admit there has been some reluctance to assist in this way (unless for repairs) because it was so often found that the buildings thus erected were not fit habitations. The Boards of Guardians often find a difficulty from the limited ownership of some of the labourers, who apply for relief, of their cottages. Perhaps they have not paid quit-rent for a year or two; but still they cannot sell, and yet it seems unjust to the ratepayers to assist a man who has a tenement which he at least calls his own, and from which he cannot be ejected. I know a labourer at this moment living in a cottage originally built by his father, and added to by himself by the assistance of the neighbouring farmers. This man has been greatly assisted by one farmer in particular, who advanced him money by which he purchased a horse and cart, and was enabled to do a quantity of hauling, flint-carting for the waywardens, and occasionally to earn money by assisting to carry a farmer's harvest. He rents a large piece of arable land, and ought to be comparatively well off.

'The Son of a Wiltshire Labourer' complains that the farmers or proprietors do not make sufficient efforts to supply the cottages with water. The lord of the manor and the tenant of the largest farms in this immediate neighbourhood have but just sunk a well for their cottages; previously they had got their supply from a pump in an adjacent farmyard thrown open by the proprietor to all the village.

It is the labourer himself who will not rise. In a village with which I am acquainted great efforts have been made by a farmer and a gentleman living near to provide proper school instruction for the children. One labourer was asked why he did not send his children to school. He replied, "Because he could not afford it." "But," said the farmer, "it is only threepence altogether." "Oh, no; he could not afford it." The farmer explained to him that the object was to avoid a School Board, which, in other places, had the power to fine for not sending children to school. "No, he could not afford it." The farmer's books show that this labourer, his wife, and two children received 28s. 6d. per week, his cottage rent free, and a very large garden at a low rent. Yet he could not afford the 3d. a week which would enable his children ultimately to take a better position in the world! The same farmer, who is a liberal and large-minded man, has endeavoured, without success, to introduce the practice of paying in cash instead of beer, and also the system of payment for overtime. The men say no, they would rather not. "In wet weather," they say, "we do no work, but you pay us; and if we work a little later in harvest, it only makes it fair." They would not take money instead of beer. In another case which came under my personal observation in the middle of last summer, a farmer announced his intention of paying in cash instead of allowing beer. In the very press of the haymaking, with acres upon acres of grass spoiling, his men, one and all, struck work because he would not give them beer, and went over to a neighbour's field adjacent and worked for him for nothing but their share in the beer. If labourers work longer hours in harvest (corn), it is because it is piece-work, and they thereby make more money. I contend that the payment in kind, the beer, the gleanings, the piece-work, the low and nominal cottage rent, the allotment ground and produce, and the pig (not restricted to one pig in a year), may fairly be taken as an addition to their wages. I am informed that in one parish the cottage rents vary from 10d. to 1s. 2d. per week; nearly all have gardens, and all may have allotments up to a quarter of an acre each at 3d.

per lug, or 40s. per acre. I am also informed of a labourer renting a cottage and garden at 1s. per week, the fruit-trees in whose garden produced this year three sacks of damsons, which he sold at 1s. 6d. per gallon, or £6, 18s. I know of a case in which a labourer– an earnest, intelligent, hard-working man – makes £2 a week on an average all the year round. But then he works only at piece-work, going from farm to farm, and this is, of course, an exceptional case. The old men, worn out with age and infirmity, are kept on year after year by many farmers out of charity, rather than let them go to the workhouse, though totally useless and a dead loss, especially as occupying valuable cottage-room. There is a society, the annual meetings of which are held at Chippenham, and which is supported by the clergy, gentry, and farmers generally of North Wilts, for the object of promoting steady habits among the labourers and rewarding cases of long and deserving services. There is also a friendly society on the best and most reliable basis, supported by the gentry, and introduced as far as possible into villages. The labourers on the Great Western Railway works at Swindon earn from 15s. a week upwards, according as they approach to skilled workmen. Attracted by these wages, most of the young men of the neighbourhood try the factory, but, usually, after a short period return to farm-work, the result of their experience being that they are better off as agricultural labourers. Lodgings in the town close to the factory are very expensive, and food in proportion; consequently they have to walk long distances to their labour – some from Wanborough, five miles; Wroughton, three and a half miles; Purton, four miles; and even Wootton Bassett, six miles, which twice a day is a day's work in itself. Add to this the temptations to spend money in towns, and the severe labour, and the man finds himself better off with his quiet cottage and garden on a farm at 12s. a week, and 1s. for milking, with beer, and a meal on Sundays. The skilled mechanics, who earn 36s. to £2 per week, rent houses in the town at 6s. to 8s.; and in one case I knew of 12s. per week paid by a lodger for two rooms. These prices cannot be paid out of the mechanic's wage; consequently he sub-lets, or takes lodgers, and sometimes these sub-let, and the result is an overcrowding worse than that of the agricultural cottages, around which there is at least fresh air and plenty of light (nearly as important), which are denied in a town. The factory labourer and the mechanic are liable to instant dismissal. The agricultural labourers (half of them at least) are hired by the year or half-year, and cannot be summarily sent along unless for misconduct. Wages have recently been increased by the farmers of Wiltshire voluntarily and without pressure from threatened strikes. It is often those who receive the highest wages who are the first to come to the parish for relief. It is not uncommon for mechanics and others to go for relief where it is discovered that they are in receipt of sick pay from the yard club, and sometimes from two friendly societies, making 18s. a week. A manufacturing gentleman informed me that the very men whom he had been paying £8 a week to were the first to apply for relief when distress came and the mills stopped. It is not low wages, then, which causes improvident habits. The only result of deporting agricultural labourers to different counties is to equalise the wages paid all over England. This union assisted emigration affords the improvident labourer a good opportunity of transporting himself to a distant county, and leaving deeply in debt with the tradesmen with whom he has long dealt. I am informed that this is commonly the case with emigrating labourers. A significant fact is noted in the leader of the Labour News of the 16th of November; the return of certain emigrants from America is announced as "indicative that higher quotations are not always representative of greater positive advantages." The agricultural labourer found that out when he returned from the factory at 15s. per week to farm labour at 12s. I am positive that the morality of the country compares favourably with that of the town. I was particularly struck with this fact on a visit to the Black Country. One of the worst parishes for immorality in Wiltshire is one where glovemaking is carried on; singularly enough, manufactures and immorality seem to go together. "The Son of a Labourer" says that all the advantages the labourer does possess are owing to the exertions of the clergy; pray who support the clergy but the farmers?

I think that the facts I have mentioned sufficiently demonstrate that the farmers and the landlords of Wiltshire have done their duty, and more than their mere duty, towards the labourers; and only a little investigation will show that at present it is out of their power to do more. Take the case of a farmer entering a dairy-farm of, say, 250 acres, and calculate his immediate outgoings – say fifty cows at £20, £1,000; two horses at £25, £50; waggons, carts, implements, £100; labour, three men at 12s. per week, £94; harvest labour, £20; dairymaid £10; tithe, taxes, rates, &c., £100; rent, £2 per acre, £500. Total, £1874. In other words (exclusive of the capital invested in stock), the outgoings amount to £724 per annum; against which put – fifty cows' milk, &c., at £10 per head, £500; fifty calves, £100; fifty tons of hay at £3, 10s., £175. Total income, £775; balance in hand, £51. Then comes the village school subscription; sometimes a church rate (legally voluntary, but morally binding), &c.

So that, in hard figures (all these are below the mark, if anything), there is positively nothing left for the farmer but a house and garden free. How, then, is money made? By good judgment in crops, in stock, by lucky accidents. On a dairy-farm the returns begin immediately; on an arable one there is half a year at least to wait. The care, the judgment, required to be exercised is something astonishing, and a farmer is said to be all his life learning his trade. If sheep are dear and pay well, the farmer plants roots; then, perhaps, after a heavy expenditure for manure, for labour, and seed, there comes the fly, or a drought, and his capital is sunk. On the other hand, if the season be good, roots are cheap and over-plentiful, and where is his profit then? He works like a labourer himself in all weathers and at all times; he has the responsibility and the loss, yet he is expected to find the labourer, not only good cottages, allotments, schooling, good wages, but Heaven knows what besides. Supposing the £1874 (on the dairy-farm) be borrowed capital for which he must pay at least 4 per cent. – and few, indeed, are there who get money at that price – it is obvious how hard he must personally work, how hard, too, he must live, to make both ends meet. And it speaks well for his energy and thrift that I heard a bank director not long since remark that he had noticed, after all, with every drawback, the tenant farmers had made as a rule more money in proportion than their landlords. A harder-working class of men does not exist than the Wiltshire farmers.

Only a few days ago I saw in your valuable paper a list, nearly a column long, of the millionaires who had died in the last ten years. It would be interesting to know how much they had spent for the benefit of the agricultural labourer. Yet no one attacks them. They pay no poor-rates, no local taxation, or nothing in proportion. The farmer pays the poor-rate which supports the labourer in disease, accident, and old age; the highway rates on which the millionaire's carriage rolls; and very soon the turnpike trusts will fall in, and the farmers *i.e.*, the land will have to support the imperial roads also. With all these heavy burdens on his back, having to compete against the world, he has yet no right to compensation for his invested capital if he is ordered to quit. Without some equalisation of local taxation – as I have shown, the local taxes often make another rent almost – without a recognised tenant-right, not revolutionary, but for unexhausted improvements, better security, so that he can freely invest capital, the farmer cannot – I reiterate it, he cannot – do more than he has done for the labourer. He would then employ more skilled labour, and wages would be better. And, after all that he does for them, he dares not find fault, or he may find his ricks blazing away – thanks to the teaching of the agitators that the farmers are tyrants, and, by inference, that to injure them is meritorious. There is a poster in Swindon now offering £20 reward for the discovery of the person who maliciously set fire to a rick of hay in Lord Bolingbroke's park at Lydiard.

If any farmers are hard upon their men, it is those who have themselves been labourers and have risen to be employers of labour. These very often thoroughly understand the art of getting the value of a man's wage out of him. I deliberately affirm that the true farmers, one and all, are in favour of that maxim of a well-known and respected agriculturist of our county – 'A fair day's wage for a fair day's work.'

I fear the farmers of Wiltshire would be only too happy to ride thorough-breds to the hunt, and see their daughters driving phaetons, as they are accused of doing; but I also fear that very, very few enjoy that privilege. Most farmers, it is true, do keep some kind of vehicle; it is necessary when their great distance from a town is considered, and the keep of a horse or two comes to nothing on a large farm. It is customary for them to drive their wives or daughters once a week on market-days into the nearest town. If here and there an energetic man succeeds in making money, and is able to send his son to a university, all honour to him. I hope the farmers will send their sons to universities; the spread of education in their class will be of as much advantage to the community as among the labouring population, for it will lead to the more general application of science to the land and a higher amount of production. If the labourer attempted to rise he would be praised; why not the farmer?

It is simply an unjustifiable libel on the entire class to accuse them of wilful extravagance. I deliberately affirm that the majority of farmers in Wiltshire are exactly the reverse; that, while they practise a generous hospitality to a friend or a stranger, they are decidedly saving and frugal rather than extravagant, and they are compelled to be so by the condition of their finances. To prove that their efforts are for the good of the community I need only allude to the work of the late Mr. Stratton, so crowned with success in improving the breed of cattle – a work in the sister county of Gloucester so ably carried on at this present moment by Mr. Edward Bowly, and by Mr. Lane and Mr. Garne in the noted Cotswold sheep. The breeds produced by these gentlemen have in a manner impregnated the whole world, imported as they have been to America and Australia. It was once ably said that the readings of the English Bible Sunday after Sunday in our churches had preserved our language pure for centuries; and, in the same way, I do verily believe that the English (not the Wiltshire only, but the English) farmer as an institution, with his upright, untainted ideas of honour, honesty, and morality, has preserved the tone of society from that corruption which has so miserably degraded France – so much so that Dumas recently scientifically predicted that France was *en route à prostitution générale*. Just in the same way his splendid constitution as a man recruits the exhausted, pale, nervous race who dwell in cities, and prevents the Englishman from physically degenerating. – I am, Sir, faithfully yours,

Richard Jefferies

Coate Farm, Swindon, November 25, 1872.

THE FUTURE OF FARMING[1]

THE TIMES, 15 OCTOBER 1873

LETTER TO THE EDITOR

Sir, Sixty years ago the farmers were the ruling class. The towns then had not acquired their present preponderance, and the electors in the country districts, whether for county or borough, were entirely in the landed interest. Perhaps nothing so contributed to their loss of power as the practical introduction of steam and the consequent enormous development of trade. But after half a century indications are not wanting of the inevitable compensation which sooner or later follows human changes. The development of trade and manufacture caused a corresponding increase of population, until at the present moment the demand for bread so largely exceeds the home supply that the imports of foreign corn are enormous in bulk. At first this reduced the political and commercial status of the farmer still lower; his produce was driven out of the market by vast consignments from abroad. But with the demand for corn came a still larger – a disproportionately larger – demand for meat. Corn could be imported, meat could not (at least not in appreciable quantities or quality), and the immediate result, as soon as this was felt, was a rise in the prosperity and importance of the farmer. His attention was at once turned to the production of meat. The cattle, it is true, were not actually fed on the corn which should be human food, but in effect they were, since the vegetables and products upon which they were fatted were either manufactured from or took up the room of such food, thus still further reducing the real – though not, perhaps, the apparent – supply of English corn. Gradually, in fact, England is becoming a meat-producing country as opposed to cereal crops, and the land is turned into vast fatting stalls for the city markets. So closely does the actual supply of meat correspond with the demand that a very slight derangement of ordinary conditions is sufficient to cause an appreciable disturbance, and even a permanent increase in prices. Such a derangement was the visitation of various contagious diseases. The numerical loss from these inflictions was comparatively small, where arrayed against the tale of the vast flocks in the kingdom, yet it exercised a very decided effect, and prices took a rise which has never since been lowered. Without taking an

1. Uncollected. Previously republished in the *Richard Jefferies Society Journal* (1993), no. 2. This letter led to the extended article under the same title in *Fraser's Magazine* in December 1873.

alarmist view of the question, it has become sufficiently clear to all that, if the population should continue to increase in its present ratio, the margin between an inadequate supply and the chances of a partial famine would be very small indeed. The consciousness of this state of things has been already making itself felt in attempts to increase the production of meat. Obviously, to do this requires an increase in the number of cattle kept. To a Londoner, who has seen the crowded dairies of Islington or Bayswater, this may appear easy enough. If a hundred cows can be kept in a building which occupies no more space than an ordinary garden, surely the farmers, with their hundreds and thousands of acres, can support a proportionable number. The number they now keep is ridiculously small in comparison. But these dairies are chiefly fed from the refuse of distilleries, and the result is milk, indeed – London milk – but the beast becomes skin and bone. There is no meat here, unless, indeed, the cattle are fed on artificial food; but, first, how is sufficient artificial food to be obtained to feed these contemplated additional millions of stock; and, secondly, how is it to be paid for? Where is the artificial food to be derived from? It must be grown somewhere, but if it is grown in exceptional quantities it must be by the use of exceptional and expensive manures. Where are these manures to be got from in such incalculable quantities? Another attempt has been made – by increasing not the number, but the meat-bearing power of stock – to so modify their shape and so increase their assimilating powers that one animal might carry the meat of three. This has been attempted, and with considerable success, both with sheep and cattle; but the result is practically the same. These beasts require more artificial food, and hence more artificial manure. They cost more to produce. The problem, therefore, simply increases in difficulty, it is not solved. In meditating over it the agriculturist places the blame partly upon certain antiquated restrictions as to his dealings with the land under his occupation. He is restricted to a particular rotation of crops, which was reasonable enough in the olden time, when the debris of one crop made the manure of the next, but utterly untenable in these days of artificial manure. But the principal difficulty is the fact that he may lay out a large amount of capital, sink it, and receive no return for unexhausted improvements. This grievance implies that if he could only employ a larger amount of capital he could greatly increase the produce. To some extent this is undoubtedly true, but only to some extent. In the first place, there are already many individual cases in which compensation is guaranteed, and what is the result? These favoured persons do probably produce slightly in excess of their competitors, but it is only by an extension of the same conditions. They employ no more powerful manure; they invent no more efficient artificial food; and until this is done, enabling a vastly larger number of cattle to be kept, no appreciable alteration will ensue. The same question occurs: Supposing compensation for unexhausted improvements was the rule, and supposing unlimited capital was ready to invest, where then would the artificial food and the artificial manure in such enormous quantities be obtainable? The present sources would simply materially raise their price; not that such a movement should be opposed, but it is a delusion to think that by that means alone any serious alteration is possible. Since, however, England is to be a meat-growing country it is clear the Colonies must be retained in close connexion with the Mother Country as sources of corn supply. It may yet come to pass that those vast uninhabited regions may produce some vegetable in quantities sufficient to feed the stock of the future, or some mineral manure with power to treble the number and amount of our home crops of cattle-food. The real question is this, – Where are the necessary supplies of artificial manure and artificial food to be obtained? The questions of lease or yearly tenancy, of local taxation, compensation, &c., are all mere minor matter, before the great national demand for meat. It is obvious that if they can become the agents for the production of sufficient meat, a great future lies before the English farmers. They will occupy their old position as the most powerful class in the country. Coal and iron, all must yield to meat; and the denser the population the more secondary will become these hitherto all-powerful materials. But, on the other hand, with increased prosperity and increased political weight, there will come corresponding responsibilities; and the force of public opinion is now so great that any abuse of these advantages will be certain to bring retributive ruin. Should the population still increase, and no further addition be made to our present means of providing meat, the concentration of interest upon the farmer, as the very middleman between food and famine, will become almost painfully intense.

Faithfully yours,

Richard Jefferies

Coate Farm, Swindon

THE FARMER FROM HIS OWN POINT OF VIEW[1]

PALL MALL GAZETTE, 23 APRIL 1874

It is not our intention in this article to contribute anything to the advice bestowed upon the British farmer in his dispute with the agricultural labourer. In some quarters, at least, he has been judged rather harshly, or, at all events, rather prematurely. He probably knows his own business as well as men knew it who are not farmers, and if his labourers are not so well off as he represents them to be, they are, we suspect, much better off than they are represented to be by other people. It is not on these grounds that we propose to criticise him at present. Nor, in fact, in what we are about to say shall we bring any accusation against him to which other trades and professions are not in some degree obnoxious also. But the farmer has for many years past occupied rather an exceptional position among the English industrial classes, and the mental peculiarities which it has produced in him, as they have been remarkably conspicuous in the present controversy, will perhaps repay investigation.

There is no doubt that for a great many years the "working men," by which were meant exclusively men engaged in those departments of trade and manufacture which are carried on by manual labour, were so beflattered and belauded, partly by silly sentimentalists and partly by interested schemers, that the moderation with which they have borne it seems almost to justify the flattery. But it was rather their personal virtues than their public importance that was so warmly dilated on by the class of orators we are just now thinking of, and so engrained in the British mind is belief in capital that the merchant prince and his fraternity never failed to get their due share of deference and homage. In agriculture the case has been somewhat different; and the conditions under which it is pursued, as well as the constitution of rural society in general, have brought the farmer into a kind of prominence which even the working man never obtained. In commerce the employer represents capital and the employed represents labour. There is a hard and fast line between the two. But the farmer in some respects represents both. And this circumstance of course contributes to widen the area which he occupies in the province of agriculture. This, however, is the smallest and least influential item in our account of the causes which have made the farmer what he is. In many parts of England where the estates are very large, and the landlord

---

1. Newly identified and not since republished.

is only occasionally visible, the farmers might go weeks, months, even years, without seeing any one superior to themselves except the clergyman, whom they could mostly "buy up," and who, at all events, would have little to do with agriculture. In most country villages the half-dozen principal farmers constitute a little oligarchy, who in parochial and ecclesiastical matters yield a modified obedience to the vicar as the "families" did to George III, but come in contact with nothing else to diminish their sense of self-importance. Now no merchant or manufacturer is ever placed in a position exactly analogous to this; and if he was he would probably have a much better education to help him counteract its influence. But there is a third cause at work still more potent than the last in producing the particular result which is now before our minds, and that is the political importance of the farmer. All county elections are supposed to be conducted more or less with an eye to the agricultural interest. Other considerations no doubt come in; but the agricultural interest plays on these occasions a far more undivided and preponderating part than the commercial interest ever does in large cities, and the farmer is the pivot on which it all turns. The farmer is the man to whom candidates address themselves. The farmer is the hero of agricultural dinners. The farmer at all times and seasons when politics appear upon the stage finds himself the principal personage. The late Reform Bill may have made some difference in his position; but it has not had time to make itself felt yet, or to work any perceptible alteration in the character acquired by the tenant farmer during the eventful period which stretches back to 1832. Of course in a county election the squires and freeholders are a very influential body. But the squires are comparatively few; and the freeholders who are neither squires nor farmers are, or were, comparatively few too. Nor can they be knitted together by the same compact and formidable band. It is to the farmers accordingly that political aspirants and their friends chiefly pay their court, and for whom they promise either to uphold existing advantages or to obtain the concession of new ones.

It is easy to calculate beforehand what kind of effect would be produced by these causes on minds exposed to the operation of them, and we find in fact that it is produced. Accustomed only to hear of himself when the agricultural interest was discussed; hearing nothing till recently of the labourers' partnership in the business, and comparatively little of the landlords', the farmers have gradually come to think that they themselves are the agricultural interest; that when this interest is spoken of only themselves can be intended; and that what is good or bad for this is simply and exclusively what is good or bad for themselves. The naiveté with which they represent any advocacy of the labourers' claims as a desertion of the agricultural interest would be amusing if it were not the source of the most serious obstacle to a settlement. They seem to forget altogether that the agricultural interest consists of three parts – the owner, the occupier, and the tiller of the soil of the country. They speak sometimes as if they thought that the first and the third were merely appendages of the second. It is needless to assert that the landlord's stake in agriculture is at least equal to the farmer's; for on its prosperity depends not only his livelihood but the maintenance of an ancient family and a great position. Of the labourer it is sufficient to say that all he has is at stake. But the farmer evidently considers himself not only the most important of the three, but the one whose voice in all things which sheet the common interest should be paramount, and who should be entitled to regulate all internal matters of business entirely from his own point of view. We do not mean to say that there are not many exceptions to the rule, or that one anywhere finds the above doctrine laid down in so many words. But we find something very like it in letters which we have read from farmers in the columns of the *Standard*, and it is an irresistible inference from the argument by which they always meet the demand of the labourers. The tacit assumption which inheres in every statement they advance is that the sum which the labourer deserves must be measured by what the farmer can afford. But is that the case? What the labourer deserves is a fair day's wage for a fair day's work. That the farmer cannot afford to give it may be an excellent reason why the labourer does not get it, but it is no reason at all why he should not ask for it. But this the farmer, apparently at least, cannot see. He looks straight before him, like a horse between blinkers, and sees nothing on either side. When he says that he cannot afford to give more he implies that the labourer has no right to want more. Now we say that this contracted vision on the farmer's part is the most serious obstacle which exists to a settlement of the question. It necessarily prevents the farmer looking at it with the labourer's eyes or from conceiving the possibility that while he does all he can the labourer can never have anything to complain of. We need not say that it entirely precludes him from asking himself whether the sense which he attaches to the word "afford" has anything to do with the difficulty, and whether expenses which he honestly considers to be necessary are consistent with a satisfactory division of the profits of agriculture between the three partners.

It is a curious circumstance that while the farmer thus acts in the spirit of *l'état c'est moi*, as if *he* were the agricultural interest in his own person, he is in reality the member of that interest who is the least essential to its existence. We do not mean to deny that he is indispensable to the English system, or that we should be sorry to see that system superseded by any other to which he was not indispensable. But in the nature of things the middle man is only a convenience. Somebody must own the land, and somebody must cultivate it. These are primary necessities. But the contractor between the two, as the farmer really is, is a later invention. It does not signify what system of land tenure you adopt. You must have ownership in some shape or another, and you must have either tillage or pasturage. Proprietors, then, on the one hand, and ploughmen, shepherds, or herdsmen on the other are inseparable from the existence of land in any civilized community. But the tenant farmer, as we know him in the present day, is a modern development of agriculture, and decidedly not essential to it in the sense in which the other two are. Of course we do not mean that these remarks have much practical significance: we merely call attention to the contrast between the farmer's estimate of himself and his real importance to agriculture, considered upon first principles, as to an interesting phenomenon. Finally, we are led by these reflections to a few remarks on the reduction of rents which the farmer will claim in compensation if obliged to raise the rate of wages. The landlord will plead in vain that he, too, cannot "afford" it; and that the rent which the farmer ought to pay must be measured by the sum on which the proprietor can live. The farmer, we may depend upon it, will refuse to recognize his own argument when it comes in this unpleasant shape. But we may venture to suggest what it is by no means improbable that the landowner on his part will do if driven to reduce his rents. He will say to himself that, if it must be so, he will have the advantages of poverty as well as its drawbacks; and, with a reduction in his own style of living, he will restore the old race of small farmers who gave him no trouble about anything. Such a change as that would very soon settle the game difficulty, which arises not so much from the destructiveness of game as from the coveted privilege of shooting it. This and several other rather troublesome questions would be set at rest for half a century by exchanging the present race of farmers for a smaller, poorer, less ambitious, and more dependent class of occupiers. Any very material reduction in rents would not improbably lead to such a change; and if it did the country gentlemen might find, in the long run, that they had got the best of the bargain.

THE POWER OF THE FARMERS[1]

FORTNIGHTLY REVIEW, 1 JUNE 1874

There can be very little doubt that whichever side ultimately gains the victory, the struggle between the farmer and the labourer will in many things result in evil. Without laying much stress on the oft-talked-of sympathy and good feeling between master and man, now broken up for ever, there still remained bonds which it is a mistake to have severed. The character of Englishmen is averse to much sympathy: it is a form of sentiment against which a straight-forward and independent man revolts. The ideas and feelings which in the town are refined and softened, in the country come out in their blunt abruptness; and there is perhaps no section of the population which sets so low a value upon sympathy as the agricultural. The very rudeness of the life, the strife with the weather, the battle with the soil, tends to produce a sturdy and somewhat surly manliness, which cannot understand the meanings conveyed under the fine phrases of mutual forbearance, and so on, which have been so largely used in this controversy. But there certainly was an appreciable amount of esprit de corps, extending throughout the ranks of farmer and labourer up to a recent period. There was a common dislike of the town, its ways and men – a growling kind of pride in the country, and masters and men growled in concert. They found fault with the same things; they grumbled together; they could always agree in abusing the weather; they talked freely and without distrust; and there was not that sharpness of definition between the two classes that exists in manufacturing districts. The farmer did not set himself up as superior to the labourer in a coarse and insulting manner. He conversed familiarly with his men; walked with them a mile upon the road, without feeling in the least degree that he was lowering his dignity as an employer, or showing condescension to them; asked after their wives and families, and how the potato-patch or allotment was looking; and generally showed an interest in their concerns. After the agitation first commenced, this species of intercourse was a long time in dying out. The indignation of the farmers was poured entirely upon the agents who were spreading disaffection. No one found any fault with the labourers themselves. If they thought they were really worth more per week than they were receiving, they had a right to ask for an increase of pay; but when,

---

1. Uncollected. Previously published in the *Richard Jefferies Society Journal*, 19 (2010), pp. 4–11. The article was followed in the magazine for July by 'The Power of the Labourers' by J. O. Cox.

after an increase of pay was granted, as the farmers maintain, to a reasonable amount, and the agitation still continued, there arose a gradual coolness, and the two classes slowly arrayed themselves into opposing forces. It was now that the employers began to blame the employed, and to set themselves firmly against any further movement.

The lock-out in Suffolk was only what every one had seen must in the end take place, if the aspect of affairs continued unchanged. Throughout the country the agriculturists had come to a distinct although unexpressed determination that the matter could not go on without a firm resistance being offered. In the markets, at the market-ordinaries, wherever the agricultural world met, the tone that universally prevailed was that some decided step must be taken. When it was at last taken, and the news spread of the lock-out, the tone of conversation in these places of assembly grew at once firmer more defiant. The agriculturists are slow to combine, slower still to give utterance and shape to their resolves; but they possess a depth of feeling and a strength which is hardly acknowledged. The latent energy of resistance which exists among the agriculturists of the whole country is incalculably great. The Suffolk movement will be endorsed, if not followed in kind, in almost every county. The suppressed bitterness of two or three years of what they, rightly or wrongly, consider unjust treatment, will bear fruit in harsh and rigid measures which it would have been to the interest of all to avoid.

The farmers have an immense power in their hands – a power little understood and much underrated. It extends into the smallest affairs, especially, of course, in rural districts. Take the Boards of Guardians for instance: they are almost exclusively formed of farmers and landed gentry. We may regret the fact, but there is no doubt about it, that many such guardians will carry, perhaps have already carried, their resentment into the Board-room. In these days of open meetings and free newspapers, absolute tyranny is out of the question as much as absolute injustice, but there is still sufficient liberty of action to enable a man, and more particularly a body of men, to make their ruling ideas felt by those under them. Hitherto the agricultural poor certainly cannot complain of their treatment at the hands of the unions. They have been far more liberally dealt with than the poor inhabitants of towns. They have received, too, an amount of humanity over and above the strict administration of the poor law. Allowance has been made, often rather illegally, for circumstances. Now as the local rates come chiefly from the land, the guardians must be more than men if they did not feel, under provocation, a degree of inclination to administer strict law, and nothing more nor less, to the applicants. This same system of reprisal has already been carried into effect in districts hundreds of miles remote from the Suffolk lock-out.

In most villages there are adherents of the Labourers' Union. Generally the first members are the disagreeable inhabitants – the two or three perpetual grumblers and ne'er-do-wells. They join the Union and become marked men. Perhaps they make themselves peculiarly obnoxious in parish matters, or did so at the late election. They very soon find that employment cannot be found in the parish, no one will give them a job; certain perquisites are cut off; harsh refusals to grant time-honoured privileges follow; finally they find it necessary to migrate, having first of all held themselves up as martyrs in a public cause. It may be said that all this is an argument in favour of the agitation, but then it must be remembered that the farmers did not begin the conflict: they made no opposition till what they believed an unbearable pitch of overbearing insolence was reached.

So much for the power of the farmers in small things. The agitators argue that the farmers cannot possibly persist in the lock-out, because their work must be done or they will be ruined. Whether this particular lock-out continues or not, it is certain that this belief is a most mistaken one. The farmers are quite able to repeat or to continue the lock-out, as may suit them best. The reason is obvious: the landlords are at their back. If the tenant finds that he cannot cultivate his fields, and therefore cannot raise the money to pay his rent, the landlord seeing the condition of affairs, and feeling that his interest is identical, has only to remit the rent or part of it, and the struggle may go on indefinitely. The Union agitators are consequently quite in the wrong if they imagine they can coerce the agriculturists; provided that the latter are determined to fight. The funds of the Union are as nothing to the wealth at the back of the farmers; and in these days, the cause with the longest purse invariably wins. The twopence per week of the Unionist is of very little account when placed in the balance with the thousands of pounds accessible to the other side. Every hundred men locked out or on strike, while they in some measure embarrass the farmers, at the same time weaken the Union funds, and just at the very moment when the Union appears strongest, and can show an immense number of men doing nothing, it is really worst off, because of the incessant drain of money.

The labourers never for a moment dreamt that the farmers could do without them for so long as they have. They thought that a fortnight, or three weeks at least, would reduce their employers to their own terms. At the first glance there is indeed no trade or occupation in the country which seems to depend so much upon the labouring man as farming. The tenant of a large farm appears perfectly helpless without them. If the strikes or lock-outs had happened some years ago, the labourers would have doubtless been right in their calculations. But it is a notorious fact that while the art of agriculture has been carried to a length never imagined possible formerly, and while the produce has been doubled, the number of men employed has steadily decreased. Without going into statistics, though such aids to inquiry are forthcoming if necessary, it may be fairly reckoned that each farmer on an average employs less men by one-fifth, taking all the year round, than he did ten years since. If the harvest and busy season alone be considered, the decrease is far larger, and may amount to one third. Machinery has of course a good deal to do with this. The hay is mown by machines, made by machines, elevated on the ricks by machines, and the fields cleaned with rakes drawn by horses. The arable farmer ploughs by machinery, sows by machinery, reaps and threshes by iron and steel instead of thews and sinews. In the aggregate the difference is something serious. The very price of labour has taught the tenant to do his utmost to reduce the expenditure in that direction. Farmers who used to employ six men to mow, now only put on a couple.

There is less too of the system of keeping men all the year in order to secure their services at a busy season. Something must be put down to the growing scarcity of labourers themselves, which also tends to teach the tenants to get on with less help. Very few farmers now have sufficient labourers employed on their farms to get through the threshing. They have to borrow men from their neighbours.

The Labourers' Union, therefore, has not taken the farmers so much at a disadvantage as they at first supposed. There were a vast number of old men, past hard work but still capable of small services, who would have been glad of a job, but who found it impossible to get one. Now they come in and assist. Then, there are the regular men – the herd-men, carters, shepherds, with cottages and gardens. Many of these are too well paid to risk the loss of their wages. In this way the farmers may manage to get over the harvest without much loss. Another feature of the agriculture of late years has been the number of men and women who come out from the towns to work in the fields, particularly at harvest. In the neighbourhood of large towns, and especially where there are factories, they come out by hundreds. Many of them like a spell of work in the open air, and the women are glad of a chance of adding to their slender incomes. The immense numbers of women and girls who have absolutely nothing to do in great towns, eagerly grasp at a few weeks employment and fair pay in the harvest fields. In addition there are the loads upon loads of Irish whom the steamers bring over, with their brogue and their sickles, to reap the English corn. A stream of them pours into Bristol and other western ports about June. Harvesting, in fact, becomes every year more and more similar to the Kentish hop-picking season. Instead of being done by the regular residents on the spot, it is got through by what may be called casual labour. The farmers have a certain amount of resources in this floating population.

But then it may be said, with all these aids, still the produce cannot be so large as it would be if the labourers were at work, and there must be loss. For the first year it is doubtful if the loss would be appreciable; there would be some, but not much – not enough to lower the receipts of an individual farmer by a serious figure. But the next year, if the lock-out and strike and agitation should continue, would of course show some considerable decrease. And upon whom would this fall chiefly? If the landlord and the tenant are agreed, and the former remits his rent, or subscribes heavily, it is clear that the farmer will not suffer. The first to suffer will be the labourers. If the produce is smaller and prices rise, while wages, or rather Union pay, continues at the present 9s. per week, it is obvious that the labourer must partially starve. It matters very little whether the lock-out in Suffolk fails or succeeds. The same thing is nearly sure to occur again and again else-where, and each time over a wider area of country. Conceive for an instant, what is not at all beyond the regions of probability, the lock-out and strike extended to the greater part of England. The farmers say "We can wait; we are not dependent upon a certain weekly income of a few shillings!" What would be the consequence? The men must either starve or emigrate. That this is the fact is already practically acknowledged by the Union, which does all in its power to induce the labourers to go to America, or else-where abroad. It recognises its own incapacity to keep thousands of men in idleness for any length of time.

Again, the pressure of the population, and the demand for food, proves that anything like a general lock-out or strike would be attended with seri-ous consequences; and these consequences must principally fall upon the lower classes, who have no resources, no banker's balance, to fall back upon. There is no trade or manufacture the proprietors of which can afford to wait so long as the agriculturist. Farming is naturally a waiting business. Its professors possess that greatest of all powers, the capability of patience. They have no need to hurry. The tone and feeling of the agricultural world at present is in such a condition that a few energetic men in a county could easily form an association for resisting the demands of the Union. The only organization which now exists in agricultural districts is the very weak and feeble one of the farmers' clubs or chambers, from which politics are excluded, and the discussion is confined to the narrow limits of cultivation and subjects associated with it. The very exclusion of politics acts as a sedative, and keeps these chambers in a lukewarm state. There is no enthu-siasm, no life about them. But once let an organization be set on foot hav-ing for its object the suppression of Union agitation, and the farmers will throw themselves into it with energy and determination. They feel deeply on the matter. Rightly or wrongly, they believed that they have been inso-lently ill-treated, and held up as monsters of iniquity. This personal feeling would at once give such organizations a cohesive power never before experienced in a society of agriculturalists. They will not spare either money, time, or exertion to render their efforts successful. The farming world was probably never so united and unanimous before. It is even possible that the agitation may result in permanent good to them, since it will teach them the strength that lies in unity. Already in parts very distant from that where the lock-out occurred, the idea of sending money in aid of the movement has been mooted and warmly supported. Some think that it would be better to forward men to a locked-out district, who would be willing to work on the terms offered by the employer. The only objection to this is that it might result in a collision between the Union men and the imported labourers. The Union men would certainly have no right to complain. It has long been the policy of the Union to denude a district of men as much as possible in order to force up the rate of wages there. If it is fair to take men away, it is equally fair to the other side to bring bodies of labourers from a distance. As to a collision, the police must take charge of that; and it must be remembered that either party commencing a disturbance will at once place itself in the wrong in the eyes of the impartial observers. There can be very little doubt if the movement continues, and is extended to other counties, that the system of sending labourers from one part to another will be put into execution by the farmers. It will be far more efficacious than money. As to the possibility, that is beyond question. There are men enough to be found ready to work for reasonable wages in those districts to which the Union has not thoroughly extended itself, and such districts are well known.

There is such a thing possible, too, as importing Irish labour. A well organized gang of men thoroughly conversant with their work and under proper leaders, could be sent into a disaffected district, and pass on from farm to farm, doing the work as they go. This would answer better than sending a mob of men to spread themselves about and get work as they could. It would be preferable to forward them in companies, officered as it were, with a given extent of country to work over. This concentration of labour would finish the operation in half the time, and would enable the imported men to present a bold front to the labourers on strike, who would scarcely care to attack a strong gang.

But would such imported men work for less wages than the rest were out on strike for? The farmers would not stop at a few shillings a week extra to such men. They say that they do not object to the rise of wages; what they object to is the Union. Give up your Union card, and we will not refuse an extra shilling. It is, therefore, quite possible that a body of men from a distance may be found working in the midst of a strike or lock-out, for wages as high as those the locked-out men require, simply because they are non-Unionists.

The Union tactics are very bad. They follow a course which must, if persevered in, ultimately bring them to ruin. They deport as many men as possible from a district in which the farmers are obdurate. They employ every agency to induce the men to emigrate. Nothing is left undone to thin the agricultural population. There are two pleas for this course. The first is, that the greater the scarcity of labour, the higher price will it command. The second is one of necessity. They cannot keep so numerous a body on the Union funds; but they should reflect that the larger the number of men who emigrate, by so much do the twopences a week diminish, and that the force of any association consists in the numbers of its members. They should let the men on strike or locked-out go on the parish for relief. That would touch the farmers nearest. They all pay local rates, and many very heavily. A sudden increase of paupers would be a sore point indeed. It is true that the theory of the poor-law is that relief cannot be given to an able-bodied man; but in practice, if an able-bodied man presents himself at the workhouse, and shows that he is utterly destitute and without a penny, the guardians must offer him the house. As a rule they will not relieve him in the house, and his wife and children out, or vice versa. Imagine, then, the effect of some thousands of labourers, and their wives and families, applying at the workhouse for relief. The poor-rates must immediately rise to a heavy figure. The Union, however, does all in its power to lighten the rates by deporting the men who served to swell them. The Union agitators actually boast in the papers, that since the formation of the Union and the rise in wages, and flow of emigration, the expenditure at the workhouses has decreased one-third, and the poor-rates in equal proportion. Of course they have. The Union has taken away the cause of poor-rates – has deported it elsewhere; but this does not injure or embarrass the farmers – it actually relieves them. The tactics of the Union, therefore, are extremely ill calculated, and their plans for coercing the agriculturists very badly laid. If the Union has succeeded in raising the wages of labourers, and in making England such a paradise for them, how is it that the men emigrate in shoals, and do not stay at home to enjoy the high wages and other advantages the Union has obtained for them?

Any one who will carefully consider the arguments adduced, will at once see that the power of the farmers is no imaginary theory; it is a real hard fact which cannot be got over. Every one must deeply regret that the exercise of such a power should ever be necessary; but it must also be admitted that the farmers have been slow to avail themselves of it. Granted that it was quite fair, quite open to the labourers to form an organization for their benefit as a class, then it must also be conceded that the farmers have an equal right to associate together to defend their interest. It must never be forgotten that the farmers did not begin. They did not form their

association first, and by injudicious treatment, and insolent language, force
the labourers into a union in their own defence. The labourers commenced
the agitation, and the farmers did not retaliate for a long period of time. It is
at least two years since the Union made itself notorious; it is only after two
years that the farmers show any signs of combination and resistance. They
did not refuse an increase of wages. They did not give way to their tempers,
however much they may have been provoked. They remained quiet, waiting for the agitation to subside.

What substantial point is there that the most passionate unionist can
say that farmers denied their men up to this spring? They have shown an
amount of patience and forbearance which no other business men in the
kingdom would have shown. Neither the colliery-owners, nor the ironmasters, nor the cotton-mill men – none of the great trades would have waited
so long. The extreme agitators are to blame for forcing matters to such a
crisis. They would be wise if they counselled moderation: but at what stage
of the whole affair have they ever counselled that? Who began the affray?
No one can say it was the farmers. The labourers at this period of the movement cannot complain if their own measures are returned upon them. The
worst feature of the case is that the labourers seem completely in the hands
of the agitators; to do as they are bid, and go as sheep to the slaughter.
Ill-educated, ignorant, and prejudiced, they take every statement made to
them by their so-called friends as literally true. They have no power of
criticism – no penetration to distinguish the facts from the fictions. They
take it all on trust: just as they start from Liverpool on the ocean-going
steamers with the most dim and visionary ideas of the land they are about
to visit. Whether it be honourable of educated and well-informed men such
as certain leaders of the agitation are, to take advantage of their simplicity,
the world can decide for itself.

What may occur in time is, of course not to be foreseen; but it must be
admitted on all hands that, hitherto the conduct of the labourers has been
wonderfully good. Whether congregated in immense numbers, listening to
the inflammatory harangues of the Union orators, or slowly spelling out
in solitude the broad hints of the Union paper of rick burning and "beacon
fires," they have ever remained quiet, peaceable, and orderly. It is doubtful
if any other section of the population under the same circumstances would
so long have continued well behaved. They are a rude lot, primitive in
their ideas, prejudiced in the extreme, blunt and coarse in their expressions:
but they are not "roughs." That expressive word must be confined to the
produce of the back streets of great cities. The agricultural labourer, rude
as he may be, is no "rough". There is nothing of the rowdy about him. He
has not been induced to commit any excesses which present the faintest
resemblance to a civil war.

The question remains, is there no hope of real good from arbitration? Arbitration certainly seems the natural outcome from such a state of things. The doubt is whether the Unionists, as represented by the agents, will ever cordially accept any decision which does not endorse all their demands. In that case, of course, the attempt must fail. Putting the agents aside, if that were possible, then without hesitation it may be affirmed that the labourers would soon come to terms of their own accord. If it were possible to get at the men apart from their organization, it may be asserted that arbitration would be successful. The farmers, as men of education, and many of them men of position, would not hold out in the face of public opinion provided that no ultra demands were made upon them. But, on the whole, there is little reliance to be put on arbitration. It may decide a lockout here and a strike there, but it does not, and cannot, settle the question. There will still remain a feeling on both sides ready to break out. It may even be asked whether or no the best way, after all, is to let the affair come to an issue and decide itself. With that, however, the subject of the present article has little to do. The aim of the moment was to show that the farmers are possessed of immense, if unrecognised, power. In the face of such facts, which on consideration no one can doubt, it may reasonably enough be questioned whether those are the true friends of the labourer who urge him to persist in courses which embitter the two classes more and more. At the same time, conscious of this power, the farmers need not continue their measures, till they force a victory. They can afford to accept fair terms without loss of dignity or prestige.

PATCHWORK AGRICULTURE[1]

EXAMINER, JULY 1875

The history of farming is a history of compromises between the desire of improvement upon the one hand and the restraining influence of immediate profits and ineradicable traditions upon the other. The result is the present patchwork appearance of the face of the country. In one field may be

1. Signed 'Richard Jefferies'. Newly identified and not since republished. 'Patchwork Agriculture' is the only signed item by Jefferies in the paper. This connection with the *Examiner* so early in his career indicates that he was publishing more widely on political subjects than previously thought.

seen (as the writer saw only in the beginning of last spring) a rude agricultural implement whose very share is wood tipped with iron, drawn slowly over the surface by a pair of oxen, just scratching an inch or two deep. An old man of sixty winters guides the machine, and a boy of fourteen walks beside the oxen, now speaking to one, and now to the other. It is surprising how quickly these slow-witted animals catch the prolonged "woa-a" which orders them to stop; and stop they do, in an instant, only too glad to escape for awhile the heavy pull of the dead weight behind them. The ploughman is aged, for it is difficult now to find young men at once willing and experienced enough to undertake this task, and the boy earns almost as much per week as he does. By how much does this patriarchal implement differ from the wooden ploughs depicted upon the monuments of Egypt which were in use upon the teeming soil of that land thirty centuries since? How closely it resembles the true primitive and prehistoric original of the plough which was a forked branch torn from a tree – one fork shorter than the other, and this pressed into the earth by the strength of one man, while another dragged it along. This is our boasted civilisation and improvement indeed!

The very next field, parted from this one only by a closely-cropped hedge and shallow ditch, is attached to a sewage farm, where every latest agricultural invention and discovery is in use. Here the poisonous and fever-tainted stream from the slums of two thousand houses fertilises the soil, and is in turn rendered innocuous and inoffensive. Only a little further two gigantic steam traction-engines are tearing up the soil with a vast expenditure of energy. The field under cultivation is a one hundred-acre piece, situated on the slope of a hill – a rather rapid slope too; yet these engines are ploughing it up and down despite the tremendous resistance offered to the upward journey of the plough, which seems to drag along as if it would pull the very hill out by the roots. The white steam curls in puffs over the summit of the down; the fly-wheel hums as it spins round; the wire rope stretches taut as the windward shrouds in a gale. But the firm earth must yield: iron and steam are its conquerors. Wandering yet a little further, we approach a low-built cottage, long and narrow, thatched, with a double mound and ditch on one side, and a small garden and orchard – in which orchard the pigs are running free – upon the other. This, forsooth, is the homestead of a dairy farm, eighty-five acres, of which forty are "bull-poles",[1] "rowety"-grass, and useless furrows filled with dried up aquatic vegetation alike unwelcome to horse and cow, ten are broad hedges and ditches, and thirty-five fairly good pasture land, but shallow, and clay beneath, liable in a dry summer to burn up brown, and starve the yearlings. The cottage has two habitable rooms, a small dairy,

---

1. A provincial term for a useless grass growing in marshy, undrained places.

two sleeping apartments, made to do duty as three (the fogger uses one). They, the master and the fogger, rise at five in winter, at half-past four in summer, and then barely make up the rent at fifty-five shillings per acre, and no allowance for outhouses or small improvements from the land-lord's agents. Barely a mile distant stands a large modern-looking dwell-ing, with no architectural beauty, but suggestive of much comfort. Here are no pigs loose in the orchard, spoiling all pleasure, with their dirty habits, that man may take in a sultry day in that most delicious of retreats, under a Blenheim Orange, with pipe and book. Here are extensive ranges of brick buildings for the stall-feeding system; a steam-engine to drive chaff and turnip-cutter, pump water, and do a score of things which save manual labour and its terribly increased cost. Fertile low-lying meadows, judiciously irrigated by the adjacent brook, but not soddened with water where the land has drunk its fill. A few acres of arable land for sanfoil, turnips, and so forth. A splendid herd of shorthorns, realising high prices, producing good meat, giving the owners a name and a position. Well-paid skilled labourers in good cottages – no talk of emigration.

These are no fancy pictures; they are drawn from the reality; they exist at this hour within a radius of three miles. They are drawn to illustrate the extremely patchwork character of agriculture in our land. They are not exceptional cases. Similar examples may be seen by any one who will take the trouble to look for them. We hear much of the waste lands of the realm, of the woods and hills, deer forests, parks, morasses, heaths, double-mound hedges, and so on. Undoubtedly there is a great deal of truth in the argu-ments adduced about this waste. But is there not an equal amount of truth, and more practical and immediate benefit to be found in a more systematic extension of improved cultivation of the fields already in use. What is the use of one gentleman farmer here and there going to vast expense in the purchase of steam traction-engines, ploughing and scarifying gear, erecting ranges of buildings, improving the yield of corn, improving the size and quality of stock, if, on the other side of his boundary fence, slow oxen drag the ponderous old implements along, wretched rough-coated cattle starve on "bull-poles", and all is stagnation. There must be a uniform system of cultivation before a material – a national – good is reached. The very par-tial use of such improved gear and tackle tends to keep up this high and somewhat prohibitory price of which many farmers complain. Whenever the demand for an article is large, its price naturally falls; first, because of the greater number of factories employed in its production; secondly, because the manufacture of a thousand of the same pattern can be more cheaply achieved in proportion than that of one hundred. Even the use of artificial manure, greatly as it has extended of late years, is still very much restricted. True that most arable farmers use it, but so many sow such small quantities and use so sparingly of it. It may be safely taken as an axiom of our modern existence that whatever tends to increase the population is a national good. Now how thinly are those districts populated where the land is imperfectly cultivated; how thin the population, even where in spots at least comparatively high cultivation is resorted to. There must then be some radical defect in the present system, for the agricultural population seems practically at a standstill. Of what use is it if a man grows excellent asparagus in one corner of his garden if all the rest is overgrown with weeds and yields about a third of its potential cabbage and potatoes. Such is the aspect of the country. In an odd corner or two we have gentlemen cultivating agricultural asparagus, and the broad expanse devoted to the *vis inertia* of prejudice and lack of capital.

THE COST OF AGRICULTURAL LABOUR IN 1875[1]

STANDARD, 1 OCTOBER 1875

The agricultural atmosphere during the present year has been apparently free from disturbance. There have been no determined strokes such as have marked preceding seasons. Yet it would not be too much to say that the practical and material effects of the great change in the condition of the labouring classes have come home to the agriculturalist and all who are interested in the land as they have never done before. There has been less talk; there has been no vortex of agitation around which a mass of literature could group itself. With the exception of a few isolated meetings of labourers there has been no attempt at organisation, yet never before have the rural working classes succeeded so thoroughly in making their power felt. What was previously almost confined to the neighbourhood of two or three centres has now spread itself far and wide. From all parts of the country, from the most outlying districts as well as those which are affected by their proximity to large towns, there comes the same complaint. The price of unskilled labour is so high that, added to other burdens, it absorbs that percentage upon capital invested which is called profit. The labourer is not so much independent in a sturdy, manly sense, as beyond all restraint either of respect, self-interest, or legal contract. At

1. Signed 'From a correspondent'. Attributed by Walter Besant and not since republished.

the same time that he acquires higher wages he appears to have freed himself from all obligations whatsoever. When, with extreme difficulty, enough hands are secured to perform the work the product is not sufficiently valuable to compensate. The incidence of the labour question has been so severely felt principally because of the unfavourable character of the season. The early part of the year was fairly equal to the average, but the summer was chiefly remarkable for the continuous fall of rain. It is well known that the largest proportion of the cultivated area of England consists of grass or pasture land. The hay crop is, therefore, one of great value. Apart from considerations of food for the people – looked at in a pecuniary light only – it is probably of far higher value than the wheat crop. It also possesses this advantage. It is a crop which at least maintains a remunerative price, if it does not absolutely advance. Speculations in wheat are notoriously risky – the rise of one day may be followed by a fall on the next; and it requires a clever man, indeed, to place the balance of the account upon the right side. But it has long been known that hay is a profitable investment: and it is a common remark that one may always buy a hay-rick safely. Taking a series of years the seasons in which hay has been dear are more frequent than those in which it has been cheap. Changes in the agricultural world are slow to come about, but there is now a decided preference for grass land as more profitable than arable. The object of these remarks is to point out that whatever affects the pasture farmer is as important as that which affects the wheat-grower, for of late the latter has almost entirely, and very unjustly, absorbed attention. Now a summer of continuous wet weather is a serious matter to the occupiers of grass land. A certain amount of rain in the earlier part may be welcome to the riverside farmer who relies for a double crop upon irrigation, but when haycocks, swathes, implements and all are carried away by inundations, as they were this season, his year becomes practically a blank. To the pasture farmer whose meadows are not liable to inundations the continuous or intermittent rain means an equally continuous and useless expenditure upon labour. Meadows which might have been mown, made, and carried in a fortnight, and the whole farm cleared by the end of June, were still encumbered with mouldering, rotten, half-made hay two months after the scythe had been first applied. As at any moment during that time the sky might have cleared it was necessary to retain the whole of the harvest staff, so as to seize an interval of sunshine. Instead of paying a month's wages for a month's work, two months' wages had to be paid for enforced idleness. It will now be clear how the increased cost of labour, and the change that has taken place in the tone of the working classes, was brought home to the pasture farmer with greater force during the past season than it has ever been previously. He could recall to memory similar wet weather as having happened in former years, but his accounts showed that then he had only paid little more than half the present expenditure. With stalwart labourers at 15s., lads at 10s. a week, women at 1s. 3d. per day, and mowing from 5s. 6d. to 7s. per acre. If it were possible to calculate the whole amount of the extra sums thus paid by the grass farmers throughout the country during the past summer the total would be something enormous. Looking at the grass farmers as a body in the aggregate this total represents as much per cent. subtracted from their returns. Taking individual cases – as those where the agriculturalist works with borrowed capital – this extra expenditure means no little hardship, and even reparable loss. Since the larger proportion of cultivated land is grass it follows that the high price of labour in a bad season is a matter for very serious consideration. Vegetation upon arable land appeared at the commencement of the year to be in a forward and favourable state. Even the heavy rains of summer – excepting a few places – did not in appearance materially affect the growing crop. To the eye there was not much the matter. The first indication of an unfavourable state of things was afforded by the sales of standing corn towards the approach of harvest. Shrewd men of business had now handled the ears and inspected the interior of the fields, and the prices obtained exhibited a remarkable depreciation as compared with the previous year. When at last the sickle was set to work, and almost at the same moment the threshing machine, it was at once known that the yield was far below the average. The fine appearance of the crop, the tall straw and large ears, had deceived correspondents of the newspapers in all parts of the country. When threshed out the ears were found to contain only a few corns each – all the rest was chaff. Even upon really good land, where the wheat looked extremely handsome, the actual product was in some places as low as six sacks per acre, and upon light uplands not more than five sacks. These are outside cases, but they forcibly illustrate the general fact of the low yield. As a natural consequence, the arable farmer, like the occupier of grass lands, has felt the burden of high-priced labour more this season than he has ever done before. As high as 25s. has been paid per acre, and 20s. has been a common price. With wheat at the present value, or even at considerably above that value, such a low yield, coupled with heavy labour expenditure, means a dead loss to the arable farmers of an immense sum in the aggregate. To add to the evil it is now asserted that the root crops, from which much had been hoped, are more or less a failure. A little reflection upon these facts will show that the grass farmer, having lost in pocket by the continuous rain and cost of labour, will put a high value upon the product of his land, in order in some measure to recoup himself. Hay – the food of horses and cattle – must be dearer; grazing land, or "feed" as it is called, will be more valuable; and the butcher will be asked to pay more for the bullock. In the same way the arable farmer, who cannot force up the price of wheat owing to foreign competition, can, and doubtless will, do a good deal towards raising the price of mutton. The extraordinary spread of the foot and mouth disease, which is now exciting so much alarm, comes in as another factor in the calculation. Though his cattle be depreciated in value, and the market be virtually closed against him, the owner of infected stock must still continue to pay the same high price for labour. Here too, again, the change in the position of the working class falls with increased weight upon the shoulders of the agriculturalist. Here, too, again, the difficulties of the agriculturalist recoil upon the public, who as a consequence must pay an increasing price for meat. If from this series of facts any conclusion may be drawn with tolerable safety, it is that at the Christmas markets meat will reach a price beyond anything that has hitherto been given for it. It is well known that a very large number of agriculturalists are using borrowed capital. In addition to the rent they have to pay the interest upon the loan. In ordinary times, with moderate luck, farming in this way is possible – that is to say, a man may live and support a family, though he could not possibly advance. But the slightest disturbance of the equilibrium causes a strain which he cannot bear. When, therefore, an unfavourable season is accompanied with increased outlay upon labour, farming becomes a mere hand to mouth existence. Hence it is frequent now to hear of men talking of giving up agriculture, as it is impossible to pay two rents, meaning rent and interest. Much stress has been laid of late upon the necessity of attracting additional capital to the land, and with that avowed object legislation has been effected. But when an agriculturalist who occupies a large area and uses his own money finds that an unfavourable season – upon the occurrence of which at intervals he must count – reduces, by means of the cost of labour, his profit or per centage to nil, is he likely to invest more cash in the soil? The difficulty consists not only in the cost of labour, but the unreliable character of it when obtained.

In the height of a sunshiny interval between the rain the mower gets intoxicated, and sleeps the precious time away. His employer ventures to remonstrate, and at once up he starts, takes his tackle, and returns no more; and well for the employer if he escapes a torrent of abuse. Or the whole gang strike work because they are not supplied with beer, which was not in their agreement. The number of labourers who, after working during the winter at a fair price, desert their masters at the approach of harvest, increases rapidly. Doubtless, the new process for recovering compensation for a broken contract will be resorted to even more freely than the old method of summoning; but the effect will probably be that still fewer men will be found to enter into written agreements of any kind. There is already a wide-spread belief (and practice) among agricultural labourers that, although they engage for a week, they can leave any evening without notice. If they find the law stricter they will follow the example of the workmen in some trades, demand payment by the hour, and leave at the expiration of either quarter of the day. The wandering, restless spirit which seems to have come over the labourers of late is even more detrimental to the agriculturalist than the increase of wages, because he never can rely upon his work being done at the moment when it should be. Whether men of large capital will go into a business in which the occurrence of bad weather may reduce their profit to nothing, and in which they must coax and persuade men to do their work as well as pay them highly, appears to be extremely doubtful. It, therefore, is evident that the labour question is now more than ever a great practical difficulty.

LOCAL TAXATION[1]

STANDARD, 29 DECEMBER 1875

SIR., – As the question of local taxation appears to be forcing its way to the front, and we are informed that it is to be mentioned in the Queen's Speech, perhaps those gentlemen who are now preparing their arguments for the house may be glad of a few facts and figures upon which to base their flights of rhetoric. The question is not one of sentiment, but of hard £ s d, therefore it is only by actual results that the existing system can be judged, and the best method of arriving at a general conclusion will be by the comparison of statistics collected from each district.

The district here alluded to is that officially described as the Highworth and Swindon Union; but which, as Swindon, is incomparably the most important place within it, may be very properly called the Swindon district.

The union is composed of 17 parishes represented by 21 guardians. Out of these parishes twelve are in every sense of the term strictly rural. One is in a sense urban in so far as a small town or village supported by agriculture can be called urban; three, though mainly rural, are partially populated by

---

1. A letter, signed 'Richard Jefferies' and addressed to the Editor, which appeared under the heading 'Local Taxation'. Not since republished.

workmen walking several miles to their labour in the town of Swindon. Obviously, the greater proportion of the parishes are agricultural, and have nothing whatever in common with a town. Their interests are thoroughly separate. Nevertheless these parishes are grouped with Swindon for the purposes of poor rate, Swindon being, as every one knows, in every sense a town. The total population of the 16 other parishes amounted in 1871 to 14,158, and the population of Swindon to 11,720. But since that date the Great Western Railway have erected vast additional works at Swindon, and the population has very largely increased, and cannot now be calculated at less than 15,000; so that Swindon is equal in population alone to all the rest of the union. The rateable value of Swindon is 58,132*L*., out of which Swindon contributed 2141*L*., or more than a third, and in addition there was a balance in favour of Swindon at the same time of 957*L*., making a total of 3098*L*. The point of these figures is this, that in the same half year the cost of maintaining the paupers of the whole union, indoor and outdoor – the expenditure upon simple maintenance – was only 2993*L*., 8s. 11/4d., so that the single parish of Swindon actually contributed over 100*L*. more than was necessary to maintain all the poor of the union, including its own poor. This is a striking fact for the consideration of gentlemen now preparing to legislate upon local taxation and anxious to arrive at a fair and equal distribution of the burden. During this half year Swindon was credited with 8912 days of indoor relief, and the other parishes of the union with 15,224 days. At the same time Swindon had only 136 outdoor paupers, and the other rural parishes no less than 544. These figures may suggest the impolicy as well as the injustice of grouping rural parishes with urban districts for the purposes of local taxation. This is not the place to introduce local disputes, but so distinguished are the urban residents with their position, and with the assessments made by gentlemen whose interest is rural, that an association has been formed whose object is to promote appeals against the rates – a course of procedure likely to cost more than a complete revaluation of the union.

With the figures of the taxation imposed for highway purposes in the same, or nearly the same, district we are not yet quite so familiar, although no doubt they will soon have to be made public. The official Sphinx has, however, so far opened its lips as to vouchsafe the statement that the total expenditure for the year ending December, 1874 (the accounts not yet being complete for 1875), was 1403*L*., out of which 1117*L*. went in road repairs, etc, and 288*L*. in expenses such as salaries – that is to say, that as near as may be one-fifth part of the expenditure was upon working the highway board system. But next year, as the turnpike trusts fall in and the last gates are abolished, there will be an additional expense of 1000*L*.

Dismissing for the time the district, let us turn to the central town of Swindon, and see what the local taxation in the town itself amounts to.

Swindon is divorced into two local board districts, new town and old town. The accounts of the old town district are partially accessible, those of the new town are not. Therefore the figures given here relate only to the old town district, which taken by itself, contains about 4500 inhabitants. These 4500 inhabitants have the honour of promoting science by maintaining a sewage farm upon which to dispose of their drainage. The spot selected for the farm was also one calculated to call into play the resources of the engineer and the miner. It was covered with huge boulders of "sarsen" stone – a stone far harder than granite – nearly the whole of which had to be blown to pieces with dynamite. To convey the sewage to this romantic spot it was necessary to carry a tunnel under the town at a depth of 35 feet. The strict propriety of these proceedings was evident because old Swindon stands upon a hill with sharp fall in every direction but that chosen; and the soil surrounding it is free from such boulders except in and around this one particular place. The expenditure upon this farm during last year amounts to 1446L., and the receipts were 842L., leaving a clear loss of 604L. This is simply the revenue account and does not include the cost of preparing the farm for irrigation. For blowing up the boulders, tunnelling at a depth of 35 feet, etc., the town had to borrow, it is believed, for the figures are not published officially, about 4000L., and in the present year has rejoiced in the payment of 3s. per pound local board rate. These are large sums for a population of 4500. The vast advantage derived from this expenditure in a sanitary sense is illustrated by the official statement recently made that the death-rate was 16(?) per 1000, and only a few weeks since seven wells and springs were officially declared more or less affected by sewage, and unfit for drinking. These wells and springs represent pretty nearly all the water of the town proper, which thus, notwithstanding its vast expenditure for sanitary purposes upon sewers, sewer tunnels, upon irrigation farms, etc., was found not to have water – the commonest necessity of life – fit to drink, excepting that brought by a company in pipes from a distance of three miles.

The district employs the following list of officials, who are entrusted with the administration of its local taxation:– The union occupies the attention of 24 guardians, besides ex officio guardians (magistrates), a treasurer, and auditor. It employs a chaplain, salary 40L.; a clerk, salary 130L.: a master of the workhouse, salary 75L.: a matron, 50L.; a schoolmaster, 40L.; an 'industrial trainer,' 25L.; a nurse, 25L.; a porter, 25L.; a hospital nurse, 25L.; three relieving officers at salaries of respectively 115L., 130L., and 90L.; four medical officers at respectively 80L., 70L., 57L. 10s., 75L. 10s.; and in addition for medical attendance at the workhouse 35L. Add to this that in the last half year the "officers' rations" came to 84L., and the extra medical fees to 73L. showing a total expenditure upon salaries for one year of 1106*L*., making, plus half a year's rations and fees only, no less a sum than 1263*L*. The highway board cost 286*L*. in salaries, etc. The local board of the old town only employs a clerk, a surveyor, an inspector, a collector, all of whom are paid. The collector of poor rates for the old town only gets 100*L*. per annum. The inequalities of assessment have not been examined here, but they present startling anomalies. Enough has been said, however, to illustrate the proposition that before any arbitrary attempt is made to legislate upon local taxation there should be a searching investigation (and publication) into the working and the expense of the present system. When that is done it will be found that the assessments throughout the country are unfair and unjust, that the distribution of the burden is unequal, that the cost is excessive and alarming, and the results utterly disappointing. The so-called "local taxation" is, in fact, imposed for imperial purposes – even the disposal of sewage is really a national question – and therefore the control of such immense interest ought no longer to be left in the hands of hole and corner cliques. That the question of local taxation is a national one is admitted in point of fact by that party who are now clamouring for assistance from the consolidated Fund. If the nation has to pay the nation must control. The example given above is but one, but how many others are there in the country? The sums expended must equal if not exceed the national revenue. Over the budget there is an annual excitement; but this other national budget really touches all persons much more nearly. – I am faithfully yours, Richard Jefferies[1]

Swindon.

THE SPIRIT OF MODERN AGRICULTURE[2]

NEW QUARTERLY MAGAZINE, JULY 1876

A great and radical change in a social or commercial system is natu-rally accompanied by the introduction of new words and phrases, till, from the continual use of these, the former aspect of the thing under-stood disappears, and a fresh spirit springs up. The rural revolution of the last quarter of a century has been marked by the gradual disuse of

---

1. A misspelling of the name appeared in the original text as 'Jeffries'.
2. Uncollected and not since republished.

the terms, "farmer," "farming," "farm," which have been supplanted by the more polished expressions, "agriculturist," "agriculture," "tenancy." This attests the growing tendency to approach the subject from a more enlightened – a more *educated* standpoint – and exhibits a desire for a broader treatment. In fact, as well as in phrase, agriculture is rapidly superseding farming; the old narrow and contracted method is giving place to an expanded system of culture. The old spirit of farming was the most contracted that could be imagined, the policy of the farmer was bounded by his double-mounds; while now, as the whole world enters into agricultural competition, so the spirit of agriculture becomes hourly more cosmopolitan. The one idea of the farmer of former times was economy – his true husbandry was nothing else but economy, elaborated to the smallest detail, so that as he sat by his fire of logs and old poles, grown in his own hedges, he would carefully extract the crooked, red-hot nails from the glowing wood, and preserve them with care; nor would he pass a cast-off horse-shoe in the field without picking it up. His farm was a world in itself, his one object to make that world self-supporting without extraneous aid – above all without expending hard cash. The bread he ate was made from the wheat grown in his own fields, some sacks of the less profitable sort kept back from the market, and despatched to the miller. The hogs in the sty supplied bacon, beef fed on the farm was salted down, the dairy yielded cheese, the orchard cider, beer was brewed upon the premises, and small indeed was the sum annually expended in the shops of tradesmen. Out of doors, beyond the household, the same idea was paramount. The cattle required were bred upon the place, the seed sown preserved from last year's crop, and the whole tenor of leases was to the effect that whatever was taken out of the soil must be put back into it again. Arable farmers were bound down to a specified rotation of crops with this object; pasture farmers were, and often still are, prohibited from selling hay. These restrictions, excellent in their day, though mainly worse than useless now, evidence a spirit opposed to commercial circulation, a desire to make the farm all in all to itself.

The entire drift of modern circumstance, the pressure of events domestic and foreign, has been to sweep away the system, and to substitute for it its very antithesis. Instead of being self-supporting, the farm new is perhaps the business of all others which depends upon outward aid and extraneous demands – the most complicated, and the one that employs the largest variety of tradespeople and manufacturers. Visitors to the Agricultural Hall during the annual cattle show cannot fail to be impressed with the monster collection of machinery then exhibited. Scarcer any single operation of agriculture remains which is not gone through by steel and steam. Steam ploughs the fallows, threshes the corn, and lately traction-engines have drawn heavy loads of wheat or produce along the roads to market or to the railway-station. The seed is sewn by the drill, the roots sliced by machinery, the straw or boy is carried up to the top of the rick by the "elevator," grass is mown and the yellow corn reaped by the aid of rattling wheels and cogs. A simple catalogue of the endless implements of husbandry now employed would make a large volume.*

Apart from the great change which this fact alone indicates in the character of farming itself, there must also be considered the very extensive effect produced upon the iron trade, the consumption of coal, and in the multiplication of factories employing thousands of artisans. Irrespective of the great firms, whose names are almost household words, there is hardly a town of moderate size in the rural counties which does not contain a factory of this kind, and the aggregate of the business thus transacted must be something enormous. It has often been alleged that agriculture does less than any other trade for the material prosperity of the kingdom. Men, whose object it has been to elicit the sympathies of the purely mechanic class, accuse agriculture of requiring less labour, of circulating scarcely any coin, and even of partially depopulating those tracts where it is practised. A more fallacious statement could not be made, for the exact converse is the truth. The mere iron used in the construction of machines for tilling the land represents the labour and, consequently, the maintenance of thousands. Iron cannot be produced without coal, coal again employs miners, and the use of steam for ploughing and threshing, chair-cutting, etc, also causes a direct consumption of coal in agriculture.

The entire tendency of modern agriculture – the practice – is in complete accord with the interests and the views of the manufacturing class. The two have now a mutual interest, for the agriculturist could not flourish without the mechanic. The use of guano necessitates transhipment, and has a direct effect upon commerce. Artificial manures are manufactured upon a truly gigantic scale, and the innumerable factories for its production employ large numbers of men, both in the actual work of the factory and indirectly. The transit of machinery, coal, guano, manures – imports upon the farm – and of corn, stock, and general produce-exports from the farm – represents the expenditure of heavy sums, swelling the incomes of railway companies, and filtering into the pockets of their employés. In this sense modern agriculture comes into the closest contact with commerce and manufacture.

Descending from the more general term manufacturer to the less pretentious, but more important, factor in the social life of the age – the shop

* New developments constantly arise. In the Agricultural Department of the Centennial Exhibition at Philadelphia, is shown "the automatic binder, with which the farmer drives around his field, leaving the grain behind him, not only cut, but put up in sheaves, and laid out neatly in rows."

and the tradesman – how many trades are supported in great measure by agriculture, which in its turn depends upon them for the distribution of its produce. The butcher, the baker, the grocer, confectioner, even the chemist (for articles consumed in the nursery) all go to the agriculturist, and indirectly through them the farm gives employment to hundreds upon hundreds. No longer self-supporting, and at the same time, so to say, selfish in its aim, the farm cannot be carried on without the assistance of the manufacturer and the tradesmen; while on the other hand it supplies them with a market for their goods and labour. It is a system of exchange – the true commercial system. The farmer living isolated upon his fields, his horizon bounded by the double-mound hedge, is gone. The modern agriculturist gives and takes with the manufacturer and the trader.

It is difficult to draw a line of distinction between the rising generation of agriculturists and the commercial man. In matters of business their courses almost entirely coincide. The practice of disposing of stock by auction, instead of exposing it for sale in the open market, has done much to familiarize the farmer with the recognized resources of the avowed trader. Sales by auction now take place in almost every market town, once or even twice a week, of cattle, sheep, and horses, and occasionally of implements. These sales have, in many instances, superseded the ancient open market, established by charter, and usually held in the street. Instead of keeping his fat stock in the street waiting all day for a customer, they are driven into the auction-yard, and await their turn under the hammer. Simple as these auctions appear – they are now so universal as to be passed over without a thought – yet in reality the introduction of the system exercised a powerful influence in modifying the habits of the farmer. Credit was made known to him with all its ways and secrets.

The auctioneer often stands much in the position of a banker, and his profits do not so much arise from the percentage upon sales, as the discount for the accommodation he affords. The dealer or the butcher to whose bid the animals are knocked down, pays only partially in cash or cheque, the remainder, and perhaps the heaviest portion, is represented by a bill of exchange, which the auctioneer may back; and on the other hand, the vendor accepts a bill from the auctioneer. The auctioneer is ready to advance the vendor cash on loan to meet his heavy expenses – "the capital invested in improvements" – upon the security of his stock; so that when these animals come to the auction yard the farmer cannot insist upon receiving cash for them. In this way an immense amount of business is transacted at the various county banks. How many farmers of the olden time understood what was meant by a bill of exchange, or guessed at the secrets of discount and accommodation? The modern agriculturist has an extensive acquaintance with paper; and his dealings with it in no way differ from those of the commercial man. Something of the same system extends into the Corn Exchange, where the agriculturist meets the dealer every market day. Transactions in wheat and barley often reach very heavy amounts, and the dealer cannot pay for the goods in coin. He therefore gives a bill payable at a certain date, and the vendor usually discounts it. The dealer may perhaps attend two or even three markets in one day, assisted by the ramifications of the railway, and at each market find a slight difference in the price at which he can purchase, arising from local peculiarities. Upon a dexterous manipulation of these, and upon the rise or fall of the general market, he depends for his profits, and, in order to avail himself of a rise, he must have a certain margin of time, which time is afforded by the bill. The practice of the Stock Exchange is, in fact, closely imitated in the corn market, and really, if not nominally, the dealer frequently buys "for the account."

This reacts upon the agriculturist, who gradually grows sensitively alive to the fluctuations of the market, and becomes himself to some extent a speculator, watching carefully the prices in the journals, eagerly inquiring what was done on the corn exchanges of neighbouring towns, and sometimes perhaps a little anxious about the "paper" he has accepted. His calculations are not even confined to his native country – he reads with intense interest the returns from France, Austria, and America, endeavouring to foresee whether the yield in those distant lands will rise above or fall below the average; for according as the importations increase or decrease, so must he sell or withhold his produce. He scans the money article in the daily papers for the first intimations of tightness in the money market, so as to know when to discount the bills he holds to the best advantage. In what particular do these proceedings differ from those of the commercial man?

To go farther – probably there never was a time when so much borrowed capital was employed in agriculture. It was not unusual in former days for a farmer who was pinched as rent day drew near, to "take up," as it was called, a hundred or two from a fellow-agriculturist. The county banks, if they chose, could tell an extraordinary story of the amount of money in use on loan by the agriculturists of the period. It could hardly be otherwise. In the first place, money circulates so much more freely than it used to do in rural districts – it is turned over more rapidly – credit is shorter. The outlay upon machinery is large, the price of labour higher, the system of culture more expensive. The old prejudice against borrowed capital has almost wholly disappeared. No man feels himself lowered in self-esteem by the fact that his steam-plough is driven with the aid of a banker's money. The agriculture of the past was economy, the agriculture of today is outlay – outlay to produce heavier crops and finer cattle. The ancient farmer looked upon money as something sacred, something to be hoarded in the oaken chest, and hidden in deep pouches, to be handled reverently, parted with grudgingly – as an article utterly distinct from all other commodities. The idea of money, as now understood in the money market – as a species of goods, like wool or iron – never entered his mind. The modern agriculturist rises almost to the money market conception of coin, and unhesitatingly employs it to extend his operations. What is the practical distinction between cash advanced upon the security of stock or produce, and the cash or goods advanced upon a bill of sale to the tradesmen? The commercial spirit permeates modern agriculture in all its branches.

In dealing with produce, agriculture daily approaches more closely to manufacture. To the mind of the farmer of a former time, no greater heresy could have been thought of than sending away the milk yielded by his cows off the farm. The idea would have been opposed to his most cherished convictions. Now hundreds of dairy farmers despatch all the milk from their cattle twice a day to London, there to be retailed from street to street. The churn is set on one side, the cheese-tub discarded, the dairymaid dismissed, barely enough milk is kept back for the use of the family. A stranger walking through a rich dairy country may call in vain for a glass of fresh milk at a dozen farm-houses in succession, and would not get butter in many places at any price. This habit again brings agriculture into connection with railways, most of which have their milk trains daily running into the metropolis. The old farmer, with his breeches and gaiters, his ashen staff and dangling seals, would have turned aghast at the idea of the pure milk from his beloved cows being rattled along at forty miles an hour to be cried in the dirty, smoky streets of " Lun-uun." A disused cheese-tub, a discarded churn, rows of empty vats, would have seemed to him a world turned upside down. All the care taken in building the dairy – cool, half underground, paved with stone flags, and window to the north – wasted and thrown away. The elder bushes planted about to secure an atmosphere clear and pure – to keep dust and smoke from the delicious pats of golden butter – useless, except for firewood. The farm thus approaches to the idea of a manufactory in quick and constant communication with the customers of the town.

Still further, actual factories for the conversion of agricultural produce start up at every turn. Condensed milk factories increase in numbers, and absorb the yield from the neighbouring dairies. Some of them have been very successful, and are paying large dividends to the shareholders – agricultural shareholders! Factories for the manufacture of cheese are rapidly spreading, and here again the joint-stock principle, the true commercial spirit, appears in all its vigour. The cheese-factory is usually situated near a railway, in the midst of a dairy district, and the farmers send their milk to the factory, and receive in return a proportioned share of the profits. It is as if fifty dairies all cast their milk into one common cheese-tub. Now nothing could be more opposed to the feelings of the old farmer than such a course as this. He always had the most perfect confidence, the most implicit belief in the milk, and butter, and cheese made from that milk, of his own dairy. No neighbour could turn out such cheese – let it be ever so good there was always a smack about it, something "hot" or unpleasant. The rivalry to get the longest price at the cheese-market was intense. The fact that several score of farmers can be persuaded to contribute the milk from their dairies to one common cheese-tub, there to be mixed and mingled, is indeed to those who know the class, a sufficiently strong proof of the mighty change that has come over the spirit of agriculture.

Where now are the pig-styes – the hogs and sows, and porkers, grunting as the hour of feeding drew near, hunting for acorns in the ditches as the autumn arrived? The hog vault was principally supplied from the refuse of the dairy, consequently when the dairy is closed, the pig-styes soon become empty. Few farmers now care to breed pigs, the result is a rise in the price of bacon, till good smoke-dried is actually as dear as beef or mutton. Each farmer formerly killed his own pig, and cured it; now the pigs that are kept, like the milk, go to factories to be converted into food. Vast bacon factories may be found doing an immense trade all the year round, killing thousands upon thousands of pigs, and employing every artificial aid in the curing, from cartloads of sawdust to give the smoky flavour, to ship-loads of Norwegian or American ice to insure the proper cooling of the carcase. One reason why milk is despatched to London, or deposited in factories, is a growing appreciation among the agriculturists of the advantage of smaller profits but quick returns – the true tradesman's view. Cheese made at home gives a large profit, but a slow return – it takes time to mature. The arable agriculturist exhibits the same tendency, forced thereto by the circumstances of the times. Barley is becoming far more important than wheat, especially the finer sorts, and barley goes to the manufacturer of beer.

The agriculturist looks more and more daily in the direction of manufactures. Lately experiments have been made upon a large scale on certain estates as to the practicability of producing sugar and spirits from mangolds. The experiment did not at first succeed, from a lack of technical knowledge only however, and there can be little doubt that the distillery and the refinery will even yet raise their tall chimneys upon the farm. Imagine a factory chimney in the midst of the yellow wheat and scarlet poppies!

With this tendency there has arisen a marked inclination for new forms of investment. The old farmer was conservative in all things, particularly in his business; the modem agriculturist, whatever his political opinions may be, is ready to adopt fresh plans, and invest in anything that promises to be popular. If a new root or a new cereal were to be discovered which held out promise of profit, it would be eagerly accepted. In the past the idea of feeding fat cattle upon anything else but hay would have been looked upon with horror; now cake is universally used. Scarcely any practice and belief of the old race of farmers which has not been reversed. Agriculture gravitates towards special-ization like all other occupations in this age of intense competition. The orig-inal farm produced something of everything, and was rarely devoted to any one particular yield. Large numbers of dairy farms, as already pointed out, are now nothing else but manufactories of milk to be sent to London, or to the factory. Twenty years ago, or less, the same farm would have made butter and cheese, fatted pigs, grazed and fatted a few Christmas beasts, and bred up a nag or two from foals. At this day they are really specialized as milk farms, and the leading idea of the occupier is therefore to secure the class of cow which will yield the largest amount of milk. Then there is an increasing number of farms whose speciality is some particular breed of cattle, or sheep, and a few where thoroughbreds and hunters are raised. There are two or three instances at least in which agriculturists have specialized their tenancies as wheat farms; they grow nothing else but wheat, year after year in succession, defying the old rules of rotation of crops, by the aid of deep steam cultivation and artificial manure.

All these are efforts to fall into accord with the spirit of the age, which at the same time that it believes in the division of labour, believes also in the division of production. It is very probable that as time goes on this practice will increase, particularly in the neighbourhood of great cities, or where there is good railway accommodation. The influence of such great cities, with their hungry population, and at the same time their wealth and demand for luxuries, has been almost incalculable upon agriculture. They have shut up the dairy, and absorbed the milk; they have consumed such vast quantities of liquor that barley becomes of more importance than wheat. They will and they must have meat; the immediate result is that everything is made subservient to the production of stock, and the indirect result is the establishment of specialized farms where the one object is the evolution of a superior animal. The middle classes of these cities who can-not provide themselves from their own gardens and glasshouses, still insist upon being supplied with the luxury of early vegetables. Naturally there-fore, in places where the soil or the climate is specially suitable, as in the Scilly Islands, attention is turned to this branch, for the railway abolishes the restrictions of distance.

So thoroughly is the agricultural mind imbued with the necessity of marching with the age, and obtaining profit by a judicious investment in what is demanded by the cities, that the one great desideratum in rural dis-tricts is now quicker communication. The number of light railways and tramways that have been lately laid down in purely agricultural places is an obvious proof of this disposition. Every year sees an additional number of bills for the incorporation of railway companies to construct short lines, taken to the House. Most of these are really agricultural lines, supported by landowners, and tenant farmers – many have been made, and others are now making, entirely with agricultural money, without any "financing" whatever. They run over rich arable or pasture land, where there are no towns of any size, nothing but farms and villages, and join some great through-route of rail. Even the open and sparsely populated downs are anxious now to connect themselves by light tramways with the cities. These local companies acknowledge openly that they neither desire nor expect large dividends from the line, they are satisfied if it pays its working expenses; the real dividend is obtained in an indirect manner – by the landlords through the increased value of property, the tenants profit by the easier and cheaper access to the markets. These local railways, these village lines, are striking instances of the change which has come over the spirit of agriculture.

The old farmer prided himself above all things on being a practical man, a man of experience, learned only in the knowledge acquired through generations of cultivation. The modern agriculturist is a theorist, a student – book-learned. He is ever ready to make experiments. He sends his son to an agricultural college, he reads and ponders over the discoveries of agricultural professors, he lends plots of ground for the purpose of comparing the advantages of various methods of culture. The meaning of the words geology, botany, even entomology, is well known to him. He analyzes the soil, the water, the crops, and is familiar with the phraseology of the chemical laboratory. Hardly a science but is pressed into the service of agriculture. Geology, botany, entomology, meteorology, chemistry, natural history, and biology – the list might be extended indefinitely, to say nothing of mechanics and engineering. The engineer indeed is indispensable to the modern agriculturist – to drain his fields, to irrigate others, to construct reservoirs, roads, and lastly, tramways. The mechanic finds constant employment in repairing the steam plough and tackle, the threshing machine, the endless implements employed.

Does all this read like farming? Is it not clear that agriculture is a distinct occupation, a business – a business of the present and the future, almost totally severed from the past? It is true that only the larger agriculturists as yet can go to these lengths; but this spirit has filtered down into the minds of the smaller men, who go as far as they can in the same direction. Those who cannot afford to purchase the expensive steam-ploughing tackle hire it of agricultural machinists, who are now to be found almost everywhere, or of companies started to let out such engines. Even small farmers resort to draining, and use as much artificial manure as they can afford to purchase. The spirit of enterprise and speculation has seized upon them also, but their sphere of operation being limited, its results are not so immediately apparent.

A broader, more cosmopolitan feeling amongst agriculturalists has been fostered by the great shows of stock and implements. To these exhibitions men flock from all parts of the kingdom, eagerly comparing the cattle shown with their own, curiously inquiring how such results were attained, examining the new machinery, exchanging ideas with others. By these assemblages much of the old local spirit has been effaced – men who have once ventured from the homestead fifty or a hundred miles, and have seen what their brother agriculturists have accomplished, can no longer pin their faith upon the traditionary usages of their native dales.* Their prejudices are shaken, the facts they have seen cannot be got over – farmers are a class particularly amenable to visible, tangible results. It may not be for years afterwards, but sooner or later, when opportunity offers, they will attempt to accomplish similar things.

Nor must the vast flow of agricultural literature which has set in of late years be left out of account. The mere number of newspapers, journals, and magazines, devoted to farming and matters connected with the land, now published is very considerable. Some of these are edited with great care, and possess a staff of clever contributors, able to throw the light of science and research upon the agricultural topics of the day. They have a large circulation, but their influence does not end with that. No agricultural district now is without its local paper, and these papers reproduce the materials of the high-class journals, so that a new discovery or a better method of treatment once published in London, is immediately disseminated over the length and breadth of the agricultural world. The effect of this literature is very powerful; it has been slowly educating the mass of agriculturists for years, and the generation now growing up is impregnated with ideas derived originally from these journals.

Agriculture is perhaps fortunate in possessing more experimental men than any other calling; men who have expended fortunes in the endeavour to push on the culture of the land, who have, in many cases, reduced themselves to all but ruin, but the benefit of whose experience is now utilized on every farm in England. Such men led the van in the introduction of artificial manures, guano, and super-phosphates, proved the value of drainage, and at a vast expenditure of time and money perfected the steam plough. Scattered here and there all over the country, each has acted as a focus into which was drawn the attention of the neighbouring agriculturists, till in more than one

---

* Fifty years ago an agricultural writer recommended farmers to take rides of twenty or thirty miles, and note the methods followed in other localities. They carry out the spirit of this advice now by railway.

instance, a world-wide fame has been the result. But undoubtedly the great cause of the immense progress that has been achieved, was the pressure consequent upon the repeal of the Corn Laws. From that hour, the agriculturist has had to encounter a constantly increasing host of competitors. The whole world has risen up to compete against him. Wheat flowed in from the Continent, from America, wool from Australia, and latterly preserved meat has come into the market in sufficient quantities to cause an appreciable effect. Slowly the farmer awoke to the altered condition of affairs, and roused himself to vigorous efforts in accord with the times.

Had there been nothing to compensate this competition, it would have been impossible for him to have stood his ground. But at the same time the population increased, increased in numbers, and multiplied its demands for luxuries, for rich, succulent meats. The flow of wealth permitted of higher prices, or rather caused them, and the more rapid circulation of money compensated the farmer for the loss of the old system of profit. Yet it is questionable, even now, as the pressure of competition is made heavier by the rise in the cost of labour, whether a sufficient return or percentage can be got out of the land with the limited capital invested in it. As I suggested three years ago, the direction of events seems to point irresistibly to the conclusion that at no distant date joint-stock farming will have to be resorted to. With the sole exception of the novelty of the thing, there is practically no obstacle. It is a safer outlet at all events for capital than loans to foreign states which repudiate the interest. A certain amount of difficulty has been already found in letting large arable farms. To work them with any prospect of profit a heavy outlay is necessary – such an outlay as few men are prepared, upon their sole responsibility, to incur. By the union of a small band of capitalists, the difficulty would be overcome, and at the same time the land would be made to produce the utmost possible yield, for a company or syndicate could employ every means science can suggest.

If any one had reviewed the position of agriculture a generation ago, they would have described it as a calm, quiet calling, far from the turmoil of trade and the din of manufacture, reposing from year to year among flowery meadows and beautiful cornfields. At this hour there is presented the spectacle of a mass of restless, educated, intelligent men, struggling – seething as it were – pushing forward and adopting the resources of commerce and of science. The contrast is intense. The spirit exhibited in modern practical agriculture is one of vigorous enterprise, speculation, progress. The change has been accompanied with striking modifications in the position and habits of the people engaged.

To commence at the foundation with the labourers – the change that has come over that class is obvious and unmistakable. It must, however, be distinctly understood that the purpose of this article is to trace out and define the spirit of agriculture; it is no part of its design to argue on one side or the other; but simply to approach, as nearly as possible, to an estimate of actual existing facts, whether they relate to labourer, tenant, or landlord. Among the causes which led up to the labourer movement must be reckoned the repeal of the Corn Laws, and the inflow of foreign wheat, which in a measure placed the labourer in an independent position. Then the introduction of a new system of poor relief had its effect, and the vast impetus given to labour by the railways – their construction and maintenance – must not be forgotten.

It is common to ascribe the agitation amongst the agricultural labourers to the violent speeches and defective organization of a few clever men; and it is equally the habit to assert that now those men have failed in their immediate endeavours, the movement is at an end. Neither of these assertions is accurate. The above causes and many others had been at work for years previously to the outbreak of unionism; at this day other causes are at work whose effect will tend much in the same direction. The truly gigantic emigration that has been going on for years, is still proceeding; the colonies, Australia, New Zealand, Canada, and the United States, are still absorbing the very flower and strength of the labouring population. History stands confounded, and withholds her assent in doubt, to the record of the enormous numbers of men who followed Xerxes into Greece. But what are these numbers – the wonder of the world for centuries – compared with the emigration to America, and the colonies? The United States are this year celebrating their centennial. The land was discovered before; but practically their country is just a century old. Our country, reckoning only from the Conquest is eight centuries old; yet their population is larger than ours, and the vast majority speak English.

In addition to the direct effect of this emigration, there must be remembered the indirect reaction – incalculably great – of American ideas upon the lower orders in England. Somehow they have become disseminated – it is needless now to inquire how. This indirect effect increases annually, as the labourers become more educated, and read of their brethren across the Atlantic. The exact "how" is difficult to define, but certain it is that a common feeling at this moment animates the workmen of all western countries. They are *en rapport* with each other. Independent of literature, or even organization, there exists a mysterious communication; a movement at a distance is propagated like a wave along the ranks of labour. It is one of the most striking phenomena of modern social life; a phenomenon becoming more visible, tangible, and powerful year by year. Without any doubt the enforced education of the future will intensify this tendency; for if ignorant, prejudiced men can combine for a common end, it is absurd to suppose that the same men when educated will not be more ready to act in concert.

With education there always comes a certain sense of self-importance; the best of us who have acquired superior knowledge are not free from this weakness, how much more may it not be expected from men whose ancestors for centuries have laboured in the darkest ignorance. It is a mistake to view the movement among the agricultural labourers in any other light than that which has been fermenting for years in other classes of workmen. The only difference is that it has come last, and therefore has yet to pass through stages which the others have already completed. It is a part of the great labour movement, a movement going on all over the world, and cannot be separated from it, and arrested by petty local treatment. In truth, that movement is one which the hand of man cannot stay. It owed its origin to a variety of causes out of his control; those causes and others are still at work.

Leaving the more general question to estimate the present position of the labourer with relation to the two classes above him, landlord and tenant, it may be summed up in one sentence – the old semi-feudal relations are totally extinguished. The old local spirit is gone. There is a familiar phrase asserting that the interests of the landlord, tenant, and labourer are identical. Looked at from a general point of view this is an incontrovertible truth, but like other generalizations, in practice it is precisely the reverse. For all practical purposes the interests of the labourer and the tenant are exactly opposed to each other. The labourer's one great object is to obtain the maximum of wages with the minimum of work; the tenant's object – like that of all employers – is to get the best labour at the lowest price. Apart from all sentimental considerations this is the root of the matter. It resolves itself into pounds, shillings, and pence. There was at one time a certain amount of common interest between the labourer and tenant, but at present their position is the same as the employers in a factory. At all events the labourers themselves in thought, word, and deed do their best to make this the position. They are determined to exact the uttermost penny from the employer; in doing so they are simply acting in accordance with the spirit of the age, and there is no reason to exclaim against their conduct as outrageous. Especially tenants must not so exclaim, for of late they have exhibited a similar resolution to force the most advantageous terms from their landlords. It is but another phase of social pressure extending from the lowest to the highest rank.

Admitting this fact honestly, and making no attempt to gloss it over, there remains the question how far can the tenant endure the pressure of the labour movement, in other words how high will wages rise? There are good reasons for the belief that we have not yet seen the topmost price. In a very few years agricultural wages have gone up fully fifty per cent.; instances might be adduced of one hundred per cent. Yet still the men are not satisfied – the complaint is general that although paid so much more, they are less and less inclined to exert themselves in the field. There is a distinct muttering of a demand for shorter hours, for over-time payment, and a most decided spirit of sullen insubordination abroad. Although the nominal strike is over, the real strike is still in progress – it is not confined to one district, it extends to every parish where the plough is at work.

Last season it was often the case if a farmer threatened to discharge one of his labourers that the rest would convey their determination to leave him in a body if he did. Now, this fact alone speaks volumes for the altered spirit prevailing at this hour amongst the men, especially as it occurred time after time in districts nearly two hundred miles from the scene of the great strike, and where no union organization exists.

The union itself is under a cloud; but its spirit is alive and vigorous. We hear of gentlemen who have farmed one tenancy for forty years, and their forefathers before them, retiring from the business altogether, saying that they could not submit to be dictated to by their men. The men say, "You have had us under your thumb, master, for a long time; now we have got you under our thumbs." These very words have been heard more than once in the field.

The labourer used to be placed under an obligation to the farmer by the winter, when wages were low and work scarce. But emigration abroad and migration inland to the neighbourhood of great works and factories, have so thinned the ranks of labour that work is really never scarce now, winter or summer. Neither do wages fall to the extent that used to be the case. It has so happened that with a decreasing number of labourers, an increasing demand, and higher wages, there has also arisen superior cottage accommodation. The number and the quality of cottages has immensely improved of late – many were built out of a genuine desire to create an attachment between the labourer and employer, and to eradicate the wandering habits of the former. But the precisely opposite result has occurred; for the labourer feels that he is no longer obliged to be civil for fear of forfeiting his cottage and garden – there are plenty of cottages and gardens elsewhere.

The labourer knows that his value has increased, and acts accordingly. The boys and youths, the rising generation, full of eager spirits and untamed by experience, cast the altered condition of affairs in their employers' teeth in a way extremely irritating, and often cause an ill-will that would not otherwise have been felt by the latter. Under these circumstances it is not to be expected that the cost of labour will stand still; it must advance, unless any great check occurs to the prosperity of the country at large.

The agricultural labourer day by day identifies himself with the mechanic and the navvy. Whatever course is taken by the mass of workmen will sooner or later be followed by him. When the agricultural labourer is educated, as he will very soon be now that schools are in energetic action over the whole country, he will more readily and quickly respond to the motions of his organised brethren in trade and manufacture. Those who deny this can only do so by shutting their eyes to obvious facts. While on this subject it may not be out of place to make a suggestion in reference to the education of the agricultural labourer. At present there is plenty of provision for the education of youth, but all who have thought upon the subject know well that true education does not end there. In towns the workmen have their Mechanics Institutes, their reading-rooms, free libraries, classes for every species of learning, and no one is surprised to hear that the son of a mechanic has obtained a prize from South Kensington. It is wonderful to watch the vast audiences composed of intelligent workmen who assemble to listen to the lectures of scientific men.

Now, so soon as the agricultural boy leaves the elementary school, he simply runs wild; he forgets what he has learnt; he is left with a certain pride and self-importance only, believing that he knows as much as his employer. What is wanted is an education for the grown-up man, something to awaken the brain, to soften the asperities of an uncultivated mind. Owing to the scattered population, an establishment resembling the Mechanics' Institute – an Agricultural Labourers' Institute – is hardly feasible in rural districts. But the lecture, with its interesting experiment, is possible, and would be crowded with labourers. Why should not lecturers so pass from village to village, illustrating in the schoolroom the theories of light and heat, or the physiology of plants and animals – things which the labourer constantly associates with, or describing with the aid of pictures the progress of a Livingstone or a Franklin? Though the audiences would not approach those of towns, one gratification the lecturer would feel – he would be really teaching, and his every word would be listened to with intense eagerness. The suggestion may be thought extravagant. What does a ploughman need to know of such things? But the hour approaches when the ploughman will vote and his voice will sway the State. Though postponed, there is no doubt the franchise must at last be extended to the agricultural labourer. His influence will then be directly felt. Candidates for Parliament must then shape their addresses so as to obtain his support. It is very, very desirable that, before such a state of things arrives, the labourer should receive some additional education than can be imparted before the age of thirteen years. It has been objected that education makes the young agricultural labourer insubordinate: it is partially true, but this is an unworthy view to take. A fuller education would have an opposite effect. The higher class of mechanics are now well educated, they are not insubordinate; clerks are well educated, they do not bully their employers.

Briefly summed up, the spirit of the agricultural labourer at this hour is restless, changeable, unsettled, pushing forward to an indefinite end, commercial in the sense of exacting the utmost value for work done, sullenly independent, and sometimes menacing. It is time, quite time, that something was done upon a large scale, as I suggested in a paper which appeared in this magazine,* to meet the labourer half-way. It is worth doing, for there is good honest material to work upon, a material which has proved itself for centuries to be the back-bone of the country.

Although the labour movement has greatly embarrassed the tenant farmer, it has also advanced his cause, for the additional pressure upon him forced out the Agricultural Holdings Act. The spirit animating the modern farmer has been already amply illustrated by reviewing the practice of agriculture, but there yet remains to be considered the change in his personal habits. Excepting the smallest holders, whose position is little above that of the agricultural labourer, the life of the farmer approaches more nearly now to that of the townsman. The old custom of early rising, early breakfasts, early dinners, and early retirement is going out of date. There are agriculturists now whose breakfast-tables are not cleared till what their forefathers would have called luncheon time, if not noon, and who regularly dine at six, with several courses. These are men of capital, of course; but at the same time the contrast of habit is equally great, for men of large wealth but a few years ago would have stared aghast at the wines, cigars, waggonettes, pianos, hunters in stable, and even footmen of the period. The middle class of agriculturists have also altered their household ways after a similar fashion, though not to such extremes. Bacon was once the staple food – fat bacon, too; now beef and mutton and veal are general. Almost all keep at least one good nag, and a respectable dog-trap or conveyance. In social matters they are less isolated, less village-like, more refined in speech and manners.

A more gentlemanly tone prevails; the old rude abruptness is disappearing. Daughters well educated at good schools, sons who have been sent to large towns to colleges and grammar-schools as they grow up, and read and converse with better [sic] class of people, gradually introduce more civilized manners into old-fashioned households. The very furniture changes – the stone floors are taken up and planking substituted; carpets are put down in rooms long bare; more comfortable, modern chairs and sofas take the place of the old angular, stiff-backed seats. Tin sconces and ancient brass candlesticks are replaced by the paraffin-lamp; plated forks and spoons are introduced instead of the old two-pronged steel fork; the carving-knife with the bucks-horn handle is put out of sight. The upright eight-day clock, with brazen dial and slow ponderous pendulum, is concealed in the

---

* "Village Organisation."

lumber-room, and a modern time-piece is placed upon the mantel-shelf. The sons no longer work in smock frocks and huge boots, the daughters do not milk, and yet somehow both seem to be fully employed. With this change of habits, old evil customs of hard drinking have disappeared. The daily newspaper is read, and the supply of books is frequently renewed. The conversation is not confined to beeves and corn; the modern agriculturist is a man of wide general information, who can discuss questions far removed from his farm. It is much better that it should be so.

With broader views, higher education, and that species of knowledge which is acquired by travelling occasionally, old local prejudices are no longer believed in; a more liberal spirit arises, which can make allowances for others. Had it not been so, the conflict between labourer and tenant would have been marked with violence, whereas it is admitted on all sides that the conduct of the employers has on the whole been conciliatory. The Chambers of Agriculture, if they have done nothing else, have at last opened the tenant's lips. He stands forward boldly new, fearless of landlord or agent, and proclaims his views with voice and pen. The awkward game question is a case in point. Here the tenant comes into direct conflict with the landlord, but he does not hesitate to state aloud his dislike of ground game. There has, in fact, gradually grown up an agricultural popular opinion; if the tenant feels that that opinion is with him, he knows that, say what he will, he is safe. The old farmers were a silent race; grin and bear it, was said of them, and we all know the tavern-sign where John Bull, in farmer's dress, pays for all, king, divine, lawyer, without demur. The modern agriculturist is a speaker and a public writer, who does not conceal his grievances, but proclaims them from the housetop. They also begin to know their own value, to realize the fact that they represent an enormous amount of property, and to act in concert with the object of attaining a corresponding power. They are fast learning the meaning of the word organization. The existence of the Central Chamber has shown how a direct influence may be brought to bear upon the Government. The spirit of the tenant farmers, in a political sense, is decidedly aggressive. Socially, there is an immense improvement exhibiting itself in a more gentlemanly manner, a power of speaking and writing with ease, and refined household habits.

The landlords are between two millstones – the labourers below, grinding them for cottages, gardens, allotments, schools; the tenants above, grinding them for compensation, new farm-buildings, drainage, improvements generally. Their position is less distinctly defined than hitherto – it is in a state of transition, hence their attitude is somewhat uncertain, and they appear to lack cohesion amongst themselves, so that there are instances of landowners going to either extreme, of harshness and of liberality. On the one hand, some few are said to exhibit an irritation, not unnatural at the changes of late years, and to be disposed to exact the letter of the law. On the other, accounts are constantly coming to hand of landlords who have far exceeded the utmost wishes of tenants, who erect new buildings, drain land, offer assistance in purchasing expensive tackle, and give fair notice, and liberal compensation. Still farther there were many who after the disastrous floods and weather of last season, remitted a heavy percentage of their rents. On the whole there is an impression that landowners are disposed to a generous course, and are ready to fall in with the march of events. There is also an impression, whether ill-founded or not, that there would be little bickering between landlord and tenant could their intercourse be conducted without the assistance of agents. That is, however, impossible until the laws relating to land are simplified.

The old scandals rumoured about of interference by landlords with their tenant's freedom of conscience are heard no more. Such stories as that which relates how a gentleman addicted to shooting ordered his tenants to vote blue in order to secure the return of a candidate who promised him a moor, and again at the next election commanded that a yellow candidate should be supported for the same reason, are no longer afloat, and if they were would not be credited. With a view to prevent misconceptions, more than one great landowner at the last election issued a notice particularly cautioning tenants not to believe any agents who called upon them to influence their votes; but to act exactly as their own wishes dictated. Gentlemen of prominently Conservative politics, and staunch Church of England men do not refuse to receive tenants of precisely opposite opinions. It may be affirmed that with very rare exceptions, the tenant has now absolute liberty of political or social action.

There still remains one source of difficulty between landlord and tenant; it is the antiquated form of the lease or covenant. The provisions, or rather the restrictions, of the ancient lease were well calculated to protect the estate from injury in the old times when the farm was understood to be self-supporting. But at the present moment, were these rules to be insisted on, an enterprising tenant would be clogged at every step; and, as a matter of fact, in many instances they are passed over and openly violated by tacit consent of the owner, who yet insists upon retaining the clauses. Landowners feel a natural hesitation to give up those safeguards which appear to have preserved their estates for generations from depreciation. But even in this matter there are signs of progress. Model leases and covenants have been drawn up, and adopted by many.

There are landlords, and some of them very large ones, who are in the van of civilized agriculture, and their influence upon the body of owners in ameliorating former rigid contracts is highly beneficial. There lingers an ill-defined dread of a tendency towards the partition of land, of Irish tenant-right, of an undue recognition of the tenant at the expense of the landlord, and this causes many to hesitate who would otherwise lead the way. But this is a dread without foundation – such ideas are repugnant to the spirit of agriculturists, and have acquired no hold upon their minds. Such a measure would be repudiated by them, as un-English. It is a fact that the landlord and the tenant are on better terms, taken on the whole, than the tenant and the labourer.

There are in the House of Commons, and in the House of Lords, numerous members and peers owning immense tracts of land, and belonging to both parties. Till recently the tenants of Liberals and Conservatives sitting in Parliament, have left them to follow the dictates of party, without any attempt to sway their decisions, or to introduce agricultural measures to their notice. But of late years there has grown up an agricultural popular opinion, and an agricultural political party, bent upon forcing forward measures for their relief or benefit. When, at last, these bills come to be discussed, a singular phenomenon happens. Those members who represent landed property, upon whichever side of the house they sit, suddenly find themselves to have a common interest, apart from party considerations. Examining these measures they discover that their interests are involved, and may be forwarded; the result is that after a show of resistance for appearance's sake, both Liberals and Conservatives vote on the same side. Indications of something of this kind have increased lately, and must increase still further as the agricultural party pushes itself forward.

Perhaps nothing is more remarkable in recent political history than the rapid rise to power of the party representing modern agricultural interests. "Modern" advisedly; for so many ancient landmarks have disappeared, so many rallying cries have lost their significance, that the present policy of agriculture may fairly be described as new. It is still old in the sense of an undeviating adherence to constitutional forms and principles. It is strikingly new in its development of fundamental ideas, in the shapes they have assumed, and the means by which it is sought to carry them into effect. There was once a "young England" party; there is now a "young Agriculture" party, as patriotic as the old, but fulfilling itself in novel ways. It has lost that old blind confidence in a party or a leader which once distinguished it, and does not hesitate to make decided protests when its desires are passed over. The retirement of Mr. C. S. Read from the Ministry was a potent instance of the restive character of "young Agriculture." The independent spirit which animates it has entered even into the minds of men the whole course of whose lives has indicated their party feelings. At the close of last session, gentlemen who declared that they had been sturdy Tories for fifty or sixty years were heard publicly declaiming against the action of a Tory Government, and applauding the conduct of Mr. Read. Members whose chance of political distinction depended entirely upon the favour of their chiefs were not afraid to criticise those chiefs severely, conscious that their agricultural constituencies would support them.

The "young Agriculture" party has this immense advantage – the measures proposed are such that every tenant, every agriculturist, sees are for his benefit, and therefore so ardently supports, irrespective of old cries. A powerful machinery has sprung into existence, an organisation extending itself over the width of the land, and of late showing signs of firm consolidation. The Chambers of Agriculture in every rural district collect the opinions of the residents, and these opinions come to a focus in the Central Chamber, which is in direct and frequent communication with the Government. The strangest part of all is, that this organization is professedly non-political, and, as a matter of fact, strictly excludes the terms Liberal or Conservative. It is as if they said, "We decline any longer to divide ourselves into two opposing camps – to weaken our natural strength by internal struggles. We will henceforth form ourselves into one vast firm, a joint-stock company. We recognize the fact that our interests are identical, and we combine to see that they are attended to." This is, briefly, the attitude of modern agriculture.

That attitude is largely owing to the extraordinary change in the practice of agriculture, and to the abolition of the belief that the Manchester man and the farmer must of necessity be antagonistic. Instead of exhibiting a rampant opposition to commerce and manufacture, or to those measures which provided for their extension, agriculture is at this day one of the firmest supporters of manufacture, and one of the largest customers of commerce. Vast factories for the production of implements of husbandry attest the influence of agriculture upon the iron trade. The farm, once self-supporting, now draws its supplies from almost every source, and gives rise to an enormous traffic. It requires coal for the household and cottage, coal for the threshing-engine and steam-plough. It requires iron, brass, copper, steel, etc., for those engines, and the machinery which they drive. Multitudes find employment in constructing these machines, in mining the coal, in smelting the iron. The locomotive rushes over the country in the service of the soil, the swift steamer skims the sea, and the busy brains of the speculator are for ever intent upon the agricultural supply and demand.

A thoughtful agriculturist who observes all this can entertain no prejudice against commerce or manufacture. There exists an appreciable community of interest between the agriculturalist and the commercial man, and with it, necessarily, a certain reciprocity of sentiment. The sharp distinction drawn between the farmer and the manufacturer, and between the labourer and the mechanic, melts away daily and hourly as their interests become commingled. At the same time, the pressure of circumstances has tended to supplant the old race of farmers, pledged to traditional customs, by a fresh colony, as it were, untrammelled, and with no reputation for unvarying consistency to maintain. The typical agriculturist of the day is a man who knows books as well as bullocks, science as well as sheep; a man quick to discern possible advantages, eager to seize them, and willing to lay out his money rather than to hoard it. He has sacrificed sentiment to utility. He has cut down injurious trees, grubbed up rambling hedges, swept away picturesque thatched sheds, and replaced them with slated, comfortable stalls. But he has also abolished the midden before the door, and utilized its precious constituents to increase the fertility of the soil.

It is natural that, with such altered conditions, there should have grown up a new spirit – a spirit no longer determined upon isolation and immutable permanency, but assimilating itself to the wants and interests of others, and ready to endorse reasonable change. The remarkable prominence of the agricultural party at the present time, and the influence they exercise over events, is mainly due to this elasticity, and the vigour with which it is accompanied. No more restricted by stiff precedents, and deep-worn grooves of conduct, they throw the whole weight of their ranks into the struggle for measures which recommend themselves to their intellects, apart from considerations of a traditionary policy. And yet they do still retain the principle of that traditionary policy, insomuch that these powerful efforts are conducted with an admirable moderation, and a fixed veneration for constitutional procedure.

The policy of agriculture has become aggressive and agglutinative, absorbing in itself ideas not always originated by its own leaders. The stubborn, slow, waiting game is exchanged for a pushing organization, not yet complete, but rapidly approaching maturity. A marked difference might be observed if anyone were to compare the speeches of representative men made only a short time since with those now uttered by the leaders of the landed interest. In the place of legendary watchwords, the iteration of party cries, and loud assertion, there are now heard careful arguments, apt illustrations, and well-digested statistics. The speaker knows that he is addressing an educated and intelligent class, and, further, that his words will be weighed by a large and growing public, outside pure agriculture, but closely connected with it.

The leaders of the party are also fast learning that political dexterity which can only be acquired by experience in the manipulation of men and contact with the centre of government. They understand when to press their demands, when to let them remain in abeyance, how to manoeuvre their forces, and gain allies from unpromising quarters. In the most outlying districts the wave of opinion, passing over, has left behind it a firm conviction that united action is the one thing needful; so that when the standard is unfurled, and the word to advance given, the whole agricultural army thrills to the call. After all, perhaps it is the character of the demands rather than the method of making them which has led to so much progress. Measures founded upon sound reason, recommended by the sense of natural justice, and put forth in a moderate way, are sure of public approval. The "young Agriculture" party asks for nothing subversive of the existing order of things, contemplates no spoliation of any class, and carefully avoids extravagant pretensions. Its leading ideas are founded upon reason rather than sentiment, and are therefore suitable to the temperament of the times.

As the changes and vast improvements effected in the practice of farming have been accompanied by the formation of a new platform, so it is very probable that, in the future modifications and extensions of practice may occasion a still broader political front. Alterations in the method of cultivating land eventually lead to legislative enactments, and cause parties to assume a corresponding aspect. It is within the bounds of probability, that before many years are gone by the irresistible march of circumstances will compel agriculture to look to a very different source for returns upon investment than has been the case. The primary idea of farming is a business occupied in providing the simple necessaries of life. To speak of a farm is at once to call up visions of wheat, the staff of life; of meat, and wool for clothing. But there are symptoms tending to show that in the future, the business of the farm will not so much lay with necessaries as with luxuries. If the present current of events flows on without serious disturbance, the agriculturist will ere long look for profit to the production of luxuries.

Already it is so in a measure. The complaint is loud that wheat – a simple plain necessity of life – does not pay, the importations from abroad are so large.* The last two seasons have been singularly bad for the producer of wheat. One gave an exceptionally great yield, but prices were so low that cattle were fatted and pigs fed upon it. The other was below the average, but the market remained equally dull. The few who maintain that wheat pays, are either rented easily, or else till their own land. The true reasons why it is still grown appears [sic] to be, first, that it is a product which leases and covenants permit to pass at once off the farm and to be converted into cash – cash which business men often find it necessary to handle, even at a sacrifice; and secondly, because such agreements prescribe a certain routine, and to alter it would indeed be expensive. Year by year the import increases, and the foreign cultivation improves; unless, therefore, any complications, such as a war, interfere, it is clear that the agriculturist will be forced more and more to abandon the cultivation of

* Recently Calcutta has entered the market, and wheat from India competes with English produce.

necessaries, and turn his attention to luxuries. He has indeed already done so in a measure.

What are the vast quantities of primest beef and mutton, the meat of special strains of cattle, but luxuries, and an indication on the part of the population of cities that it is luxuries which they expect from agriculturists. They must and will have the very best of meat. The result is that, year by year, the number of farmers engaged in improving the breed of cattle or sheep, at an enormous expenditure, increases, and will increase. At a glance it is obvious that animals for which fancy prices have been paid, would not recoup the butcher if slaughtered – that is not the point; the object is to obtain the finest meat at any cost, and a name for the finest meat. Meat is, in fact, treated as a luxury. See the enormous consumption of lamb and veal as a proof. The milk sent to London and other large cities is not only consumed as a necessity, but as a luxury – in pastry and confectionery, by invalids – and what is condensed milk but a luxury? Let any one calculate the area required to supply the metropolis alone with early greens, Brussel-sprouts, and similar vegetables.

It may be objected that this is market gardening, not agriculture; but then the fact is that agriculture is gradually becoming market-gardening upon a gigantic scale. So far, therefore, as it is possible to predict the spirit that will animate the agriculture of the future, it appears that it will discard the old reliance upon necessaries, and depend principally upon luxuries. Only by the production of articles which will command a high and increasing price, can the social pressure be met by agriculturists. With heavy rents, heavy outlay upon machinery, artificial manure, and labour, it is evident that the old system cannot long endure.

Never before probably in the history of the world has agriculture made such giant efforts. Not only England, but France, Italy, Austria, Russia, even India, have been moving. Our agricultural implement factories having satisfied the first keen edge of the appetite at home for machinery, are now constructing traction-engines, thrashing-engines, and similar tackle to go abroad. Even the wide plains of distant Russia have heard the hum of English engines. Everywhere agriculturists are musing themselves and coming to the front. The associated farmers of America, under the name of Grangers, exercise immense influence in their country.

The change in the system of cultivation of English farms, like most other changes, though beneficial in the mass, has caused much individual suffering. Men of small capital and limited enterprise, unable to expand their views to meet the times, have been, in many cases, driven from their tenancies. Hence arises an artificial demand for small farms, which are shaven of refuge to the non-enterprising man. Here he can potter on as of yore, at least for awhile. There may yet come a sharp trial for agriculture generally, as the new system forces itself in before all are prepared. But so long as the country at large remains prosperous, and agriculture accommodates itself to the altered demands of the population, there will be a bright future before it.

To meet that future the young Agriculture party are stepping forward boldly, and to all appearance wisely. One thing only they must not forget, it is the higher education of the labourer. Sooner or later he must have the franchise, and will then wield an enormous power. If after thirteen years of age he is left to the dull plough and to the public-house, what can be expected? – simply another proof of the adage that a little knowledge is a dangerous thing. If, on the other hand, due care be taken to provide for the enlargement of his at present very narrow and contracted views, he will become the strength of the rising party.

What that party now mainly wants, is a chief, a leader of leaders. It has already men of energy, intellect, organizing powers; it lacks the man who can combine, who can fuse jarring elements into one, who will proclaim the spirit of modern agriculture in boldest colours and striking outline.

JOINT-STOCK AGRICULTURE[1]

PALL MALL GAZETTE, 16 MARCH 1877

A proposal to cultivate land and breed cattle by a joint-stock company or syndicate will not, under the present state of affairs, meet with the same amount of disapproval it would have called forth before the importation of dead meat from America, and before wheat from distant India placed so great a pressure upon English farmers. Already there has arisen a cry for the reduction of rents, in order that the tenant-farmer may meet his Yankee competitor, who is usually a freeholder, upon more equal terms. Nor have there been wanting signs that the selling value of agricultural land has considerably depreciated, in some cases to the extent of two years' purchase. It is clear, therefore, that the owners of large estates, and the prospective heirs to them, are deeply interested in the question whether farming can

---

1. Miller and Matthews, p. 41, list 'Joint-Stock Agriculture' as Jefferies' first contribution to the *Pall Mall Gazette*.

still be made to pay. The leading authorities are well agreed that the chief desideratum is the investment of capital; that land must now be worked by men who come to it with capital in their pockets, and not by men who start with next to nothing, hoping to accumulate a fortune. These latter have no chance; but to the capitalist land still offers a fair and even high rate of interest as a return for intelligent cultivation. That the joint-stock principle is not entirely inapplicable to agriculture may reasonably be concluded from the success of such concerns as the Aylesbury Milk Company, of the various cheese factories scattered over the country; and lastly, but not least, the stud companies, whose operation has almost wholly superseded the desultory rearing of hunters by tenant-farmers. There can be no absolute necessity in the nature of things for agriculture to be conducted on the responsibility of one person to the utter exclusion of cooperation. Why should not a farm be carried on by a firm, or "Co.," as well as any other business? By adopting so many commercial practices agriculture has lost its former special character, and has become assimilated to "business"; and it is hardly possible that this last step can be much longer delayed.

The idea in its broad outline is simple enough. A band of gentlemen, say fifty, combine and agree to subscribe £1,000 a piece, representing a capital of £50,000, a sum small indeed compared with the millions sunk yearly in shaky foreign mines and loans. A call of about a fifth would enable their executive committee to commence work by leasing 3,000 acres of fairly good land. Of this two-thirds might be arable at a rent of £1 10S. per acre, and the remainder grass at £2, making a total rental of £5,000. They should be careful not to expend the whole of their paid-up capital upon experiments immediately. They would find it better to confine their attention in the beginning to some 300 or 400 acres, placing this section in a high state of cultivation, and to the erection of suitable buildings. The remaining and larger portion of the estate should be carried on in the ordinary way, and by degrees brought into an equally high condition. By this judicious method of procedure it would be so arranged that the expenditure from the very first should yield a small percentage, and should not all be sunk in scientific experiments, which would not bring forth fruit for some time. No capital need be laid out in drainage and similar heavy and unremunerative works. There are corporations of perfect respectability and solidity which, under the protection of special Acts of Parliament, are prepared to advance money for such purposes, repayable – principal and interest – by instalments extending over twenty-five years. Farm buildings may in like manner be erected in an advantageous manner, thereby liberating the larger portion of the company's capital to be employed upon more immediate matters. Neither need heavy expenditure take place upon such items as steam-ploughing machinery, which is now let out for use upon moderate terms. The executive committee should rather be prepared to lay the foundation of a first-class short-horn herd, purchasing the best strain, even at fancy prices, as certain to become remunerative. Their sheep should also be of a character to achieve a reputation; and they might perhaps venture upon the rearing of carthorses, some breeds of which are growing extremely valuable. They would find no lack of practical men to advise them as to the desirability or not of including the sale of milk in their scheme; being guarded to some extent by the class of farmers in the vicinity. Whatever discussion might arise upon that point, there could be no division of opinion as to the general directions which the company's efforts should take. They should look more to the production of luxuries than to the sale of necessaries of life for their profits. Experience has shown that necessaries of the coarser kind, such as wheat and flesh meat, can be imported in increasing quantities from abroad. The meat, therefore, they must produce must be of an exceptional description and achieve a special name; and the same holds good of every other product. The poultry-yard must form a conspicuous feature upon their premises; nor must they neglect market-gardening upon a great scale. Wheat is a non-profitable crop, but vegetables are always saleable in the London markets; and if at any time an abundant season should lower their value, the company's cattle would readily consume excess quantities. There is a very wide opening in this direction alone, and other ideas would speedily suggest themselves – ideas which the ordinary tenant-farmer cannot carry out, but which the aggregate capital of several gentlemen might bring to a profitable result. The relations of such a company with its landlord must necessarily differ slightly from the time-honoured contracts now in force, but not to his disadvantage. The company must possess absolute freedom of cropping, and certainty of tenure for a given number of years; but on the other hand, may be rigidly bound down to leave the land in a condition not inferior to that in which they found it. In consideration of freedom of cropping and general liberty of action, and also on the principle at fair play, the landlord should receive a progressive rent. When the audited returns of the company showed an increase of income, the landlord should be entitled to an additional percentage per acre. If such a company could be satisfied in the commencement with a 5 or 6 per cent dividend, there seems to us no reason why in process of time the dividend might not rise far above that level, with an almost absolute safety for the principal invested.

THE LANDOWNERS' DIFFICULTIES[1]

PALL MALL GAZETTE, 29 MARCH 1877

SIR,– If a colliery is closed, or a number of iron-furnaces blown out, the loss to trade, and indirectly to the public, is at once palpable to every one, because in such places industry is centralized, and the blow is felt by large numbers at the same time. Losses in agriculture appeal less forcibly to popular notice, being diffused over a wide area, and it is therefore possible for considerable pressure to exist without any noise. It is true that the importation of American meat has not sensibly affected the general cost of living to the consumer, but it is equally certain that it has materially depreciated the value of cattle in the market. That is to say, while the meat salesmen and butchers contrive to keep up the retail price of beef, the farmer who sells his animals to them is forced to receive less money. When agriculture became assimilated to manufacture, it also became as sensitive to outward influences as the latter. Hence the very dread that the retail price of meat would fall has lowered the wholesale value. The terror of rinderpest now shown in every rural district illustrates the nervousness of modern farming. A fall of 2d. per pound in the price of meat is about equivalent to a drop of 10 per cent. in the letting value of land. In other words, a landlord must reduce his rents at that rate, or be prepared to see his tenants leave him.

No one is more envied than the possessor of a great estate, and yet the residents in "the stately homes of England" have for some time past been labouring under a constantly increasing pressure. They have been ground not merely between two but three millstones. First, the labourers demanded higher wages, which, however just in itself, caused much trouble to the tenant and reacted upon the owner. Then enormous expense (in the aggregate) was incurred in the erection of cottages on sanitary principles. It is hardly

---

1. Letter to the editor, signed 'J.'. 'J.' was used by Jefferies elsewhere. The letter has been previously noted by Matthews and Trietel, p. 85. The opening lines – 'If a colliery is closed, or a number of iron-furnaces blown out, the loss to trade, and indirectly to the public, is at once palpable to every one, because in such places industry is centralized, and the blow is felt by large numbers at the same time. Losses in agriculture appeal less forcibly to popular notice, being diffused over a wide area' – echo a similar observation in 'The Wiltshire Labourer' (1883): 'When a factory shuts its doors, the fact is patent to all who pass. The hum of machinery is stopped, and smoke no longer floats from the chimney; the building itself, large and regular – a sort of emphasized plainness of architecture – cannot be overlooked. It is evident to everyone that work has ceased, and the least reflection shows that hundreds of men, perhaps hundreds of families, are reduced from former comparative prosperity. But when ten thousand acres of land fall out of cultivation, the fact is scarcely noticed.'

too much to say that in the last ten years 30 per cent. of the farmers' work-men have been re-housed. For this the landowners have paid. The shilling or so a week rent returned by the labourer represents about 2 per cent. on the capital sunk in a good cottage. The tenant passes this on to the landlord who thus has the pleasure of investing money at 2 per cent. which he cannot borrow under 4 per cent.[1] Parliament insisted that the ploughboy should be educated. New schools were accordingly built in every village. The chief landowners presented the sites and found the larger share of the money in the hope that, by avoiding a school board, the annual charge would be less. As a matter of fact, whenever parishes were split up into numerous freeholds, having no great landlord to find the capital, endless squabblings have resulted in inefficient teaching; till lately the central authorities have been compelled to interfere and order the formation of boards. No matter which system is adopted, the tangible result is a heavy charge on land. After the labourer had been well housed and educated the next thing was to promote habits of economy by friendly societies, and to provide innocent amusement in the shape of fêtes, cottage flower-shows, &c. Without the landlord's cheque nothing could be done in this way either. The most recent scheme he will be called upon to support is an improved system of village drainage, water supply, scavenging, &c.

The second millstone is turned by the tenant-farmer, and he is a miller who, in the words of the old Greek proverb, "if he grinds late grinds very fine." His cattle, of a delicate breed, are no longer able to shelter them-selves behind a hedge or in a tumble-down shed half a century old. They must have ranges of stalls, well-built, weather-proof, warm and comfort-able, which the landowner has to find, because the tenant declares his expenditure upon steam ploughing machinery, artificial manures, and skilled labour is already more than he can bear. Then the whole place must be drained, which also being a permanent improvement, the landlord pays for. The tenant, a man of some refinement and no longer a rude boor, is not satisfied with the ancient and picturesque but draughty and uncomfortable homestead. The landlord has to add new rooms, to replace the thatch with slate, and rebuild the offices. Upon some of this expenditure the tenant pays 2 1/2 per cent. per annum – a truly profitable interest – and the owner has the satisfaction of knowing that he has got his money's worth, only unfortunately it is buried in bricks and draining-tiles, and he cannot walk up Pall-mall with it in his pocket. In return for these advantages the ten-ant agitates for compensation on leaving his farm. Presently there comes a very wet season, the ground is so interlaced with drains that the water cannot sink in, but runs off quickly and causes a flood, towards the losses

---

1. Word is illegible in the text.

sustained by which the landlords are asked to subscribe. Or there comes a very dry season, roots won't grow, sheep get nothing to eat, there is much lamentation, and either way, wet or dry, the landlords have to concede a remission of rent. Announcements of such remissions, ranging from 10 to 25 per cent. have been made now every half-year for three seasons. The owner hopes, perhaps, to replace this by the sale of the rabbits and hares in his preserves. Vain thought! A deputation waits upon him to assure him of the damage they cause to crops; either the ground game must be exterminated or the farms lie empty. Winged game is not so objectionable; but everybody knows that a pheasant costs about three times as much to breed as you can sell him for. Finally comes the American beef, the depreciation of the home cattle-market, and the terror of the cattle-plague – fresh and powerful reasons why the tenant should not be pressed for that little matter of rent. The present difficulty of reletting a large arable farm when once empty is notoriously owing to the low price of wheat; and as the eastern half of the country is mainly corn land, its aggregate depreciation must be serious. It is a mistake to suppose that the landowner's receipts have risen: his income is practically fixed; for although the nominal rental of farms has been raised, the extra expenditure already indicated about balances it.

The third millstone is composed of miscellaneous social demands. The great landowner is expected to do everything. The parish church-yard becomes full, and further interments are impossible; he is asked to present a slice of ground, or, if a village cemetery is decided upon, to give the land and contribute heavily towards the chapels. The church is out of repair; the vicar determines upon thorough restoration, and the landowner has to head the subscriptions. Of the cost of supporting the hunt and subscribing towards various county associations of a private character nothing need be said; nor of the enormous cost of the annual visit to London.

The millowners, the colliery proprietors, the ironmasters, and the merchants combine, and to a certain extent assist each other by agreeing upon rates and tariffs and the way the market shall be managed. But landowners either cannot or will not – at all events, they do not combine; and indeed it is not easy to understand how they could. The proprietor of a colliery has a direct control over his workmen and over the output of his mine. The landowner has none whatever over the labourer, nor can he regulate the production, or in the most distant manner influence the market price of anything sent forth from his estates. He can only sit still and take things as they come. *Noblesse oblige*; he has not even the luxury of complaining, for a man of long descent and high social rank cannot put himself in the pitiful position of publicly proclaiming his discontent. Meantime he is the observed of all observers and the butt of satire and malice. A great landowner is of necessity a public character. The party he adheres to, the speeches he makes, every step he takes – all and everything concerning him is severely criticised, for somehow or other there is a rooted jealousy of the possessors of land.

Any one who will look down the long list of mansions to let in the country will be surprised to find so many of them belong to families which, if not titled, or in common parlance noble, are of ancient descent – families which one would think would hardly care to see a stranger, if only for a term, in the halls that have been theirs for generations. Is it because the difficulties and pressure described above render it necessary for them, however reluctantly, to seek some compensation for loss of income? –

Yours, etc,

March 27. J.

THE AGRICULTURAL LABOURER'S VOTE[1]

PALL MALL GAZETTE, 24 MAY 1877

In the present agitation to so extend the county franchise as to include the agricultural labourer it appears to have been overlooked that there is already at least one large district where the labourer has voted in very considerable numbers. It is true their votes were given under the borough franchise, but at such a distance from any great town as to assimilate the circumstances to county voting in the closest manner. The district alluded to is the borough and hundreds of Cricklade in North Wiltshire, now represented in the House of Commons by Sir Daniel Gooch, the chairman of the Great Western Railway Company, and Mr. Goddard, both of whom belong to the Conservative party. Previous to the general election of 1874 the representation was equally divided between the Liberals and Conservatives. The borough and hundreds are of a very exceptional character, and cover an unwieldy space of country. Measuring the longer axis, from Inglesham to Draycott Cerne, it must reach almost twenty miles as the crow flies, and would of course be farther if the roads were followed. The shorter axis, from Somerford Keynes to Chiseldon, cannot be less than fourteen miles

---

1. Newly identified and not since republished.

in length in a straight line. So that it is at once apparent that the conditions of voting must approximate very nearly to the county franchise now
desired. The employment of the inhabitants is distinctly agricultural, with
the solitary exception of the town of Swindon, where the factories of the
Great Western Railway are situated. There are three other small towns,
Cricklade, Highworth, and Wootton Bassett; but they stand, as it were, in
the fields; they are supported by agriculture, and contain no manufactories.
The exports of the district are cattle, butter, cheese, and milk, of which
latter article immense quantities are daily forwarded to London, and the
fact of the establishment at Swindon station of a depot of the Aylesbury
Dairy Company is a clear proof of the general character of the country.
Excluding the above-named towns, there remain no fewer than forty-five
villages and hamlets, all unequivocally agricultural, all within the borough
and hundreds, and the inhabitants of which are entitled to vote under the
borough franchise. It would be hard to find a more thoroughly rural district.
In these villages and hamlets almost every full-grown agricultural labourer
has a vote – almost every cottage occupier not disqualified by the receipt
of parochial relief is, and was, on the register. So that to all intents and purposes the borough and hundreds of Cricklade (outside Swindon) may justly
be termed an agricultural labourer's constituency. Any undue influence of
the farmers and landowners was in 1874 of necessity prevented – first, by
the numbers of labourers voting, and, secondly, by the operation of the
ballot. It would not, therefore, be too much to say that in the action of the
voters at that election some notion may be formed of the way in which an
agricultural labourers' constituency is likely to behave.

    The National Agricultural Labourers' Union had previous to the elec-
tion made very considerable progress in the district. There were branches
of the union with local secretaries in every village and hamlet. The name of
Mr. Arch was well known, and he had himself addressed an audience of at
least 2,000 people in the Corn Hall at Swindon. No strike had occurred, for
the simple reason that the large demand for labour at the works of the Great
Western Railway had already raised the rate of wages in the neighbourhood. But the union had got a firm hold of the labourers, and the boast has
been made that through its beneficial action, by raising wages and assisting
emigration, the board of guardians were enabled to reduce their expenditure by £2,000 in one year. Nor were the labourers without the advantage
of their own particular candidate for parliamentary honours. The editor of a
local newspaper which had identified itself with the union movement came
forward as a working man's candidate independent of either party. A retired
manufacturer, a Nonconformist, also appeared in the field, supported by
the Liberal party as their second candidate, and it was supposed that he
would obtain the suffrages of many of the labourers. They are known

to chiefly frequent the various Dissenting chapels, and the gentleman in question had contributed somewhat largely to the chapel funds, and was naturally looked up to as their leader. There then remained the first Liberal candidate, the late member, and the two Conservative candidates, besides a brewer, who as he did not obtain fifty votes may be left out of the question. As the writ was made returnable in a very short time, there was no possibility of anything like a systematic canvass; and this fact again told in favour of the liberty of the agricultural labourers, since in such a brief space there was no opportunity of bringing any influence to bear upon them. When the polling day arrived the spectacle might have been witnessed of hedgers and ditchers, labourers fresh from the field, driving in flys to the polling-booths. The shepherd was fetched straight from his flock, the ploughman left his team standing still in charge of his boy while he went and recorded his vote free from the observation of farmers or landowners. When the votes were counted it was found that two Conservatives had been returned, and one of these a large local landowner – the very class the unionists appear to dislike most. The lowest number of votes recorded (excepting the brewer's forty odd) were in favour of the "working man's" candidate, who, however, had received a respectable percentage of "plumpers." Viewed in connection with the present agitation for the extension of the franchise to labourers, this may be considered a somewhat instructive result. At the same time the Nonconformist candidate polled many votes and would in all probability have been returned had he not destroyed his popularity with the mechanics and artisans of Swindon by announcing his support of the Permissive Bill. This gentleman is on the commission of the peace, and is therefore a practical refutation, in so far as that district is concerned, of Mr. Bright's insinuation that Dissenters were excluded from the magisterial bench. Of course, under the provisions of the Ballot Act there were no means of ascertaining the precise truth of the supposition; but there was a general impression that he had received the suffrages of the majority of the labourers who had voted on the Liberal side. On the other hand, he is also a tolerably large landowner and employer of agricultural labour. There could be no doubt whatever that one at least of the successful Conservative candidates had been returned by the agricultural vote.

These facts appear to show that the agricultural labourers, where they have the franchise, are inclined to give their votes in favour of the landowner, Liberal or Conservative, in preference to a professed "working man's" candidate.

UNEQUAL AGRICULTURE[1]

FRASER'S MAGAZINE, MAY 1877

In the way of sheer, downright force few effects of machinery are more striking than a steam-ploughing engine dragging the shares across a wide expanse of stiff clay. The huge engines used in our ironclad vessels work with a graceful ease which deceives the eye; the ponderous cranks revolve so smoothly, and shine so brightly with oil and polish, that the mind is apt to underrate the work performed. But these ploughing engines stand out solitary and apart from other machinery, and their shape itself suggests crude force, such force as may have existed in the mastodon or other unwieldy monster of the prehistoric ages. The broad wheels sink into the earth under the pressure; the steam hissing from the escape valves is carried by the breeze through the hawthorn hedge, hiding the red berries with a strange, unwonted cloud; the thick dark brown smoke, rising from the funnel as the stoker casts its food of coal into the fiery mouth of the beast, falls again and floats heavily over the yellow stubble, smothering and driving away the partridges and hares. There is a smell of oil, and cotton-waste, and gas, and steam, and smoke, which overcomes the fresh, sweet odour of the earth and green things after a shower. Stray lumps of coal crush the delicate pimpernel and creeping convolvulus. A shrill, short scream rushes forth and echoes back from an adjacent rick – puff! the fly-wheel revolves, and the drum underneath tightens its hold upon the wire rope. Across yonder a curious, shapeless thing, with a man riding upon it, comes jerking forward, tearing its way through stubble and clay, dragging its iron teeth with sheer strength deep through the solid earth. The thick wire rope stretches and strains as if it would snap and curl up like a tortured snake; the engine pants loudly and quick; the plough now glides forward, now pauses, and, as it were, eats its way through a tougher place, then glides again, and presently there is a pause, and behold the long furrow with the upturned subsoil is completed. A brief pause, and back it travels again, this time drawn from the other side, where a twin monster puffs and pants and belches smoke, while the one that has done its work uncoils its metal sinews. When the furrows run up and down a slope, the savage force, the fierce, remorseless energy of the engine pulling the plough upwards, gives an idea of power which cannot but impress the mind.

1. This article has been previously collected in *HV*. It is a companion piece to 'Patchwork Agriculture', included in this volume, and 'High Pressure Agriculture' (1876, *LL*).

This is what is going on upon one side of the hedge. These engines cost as much as the fee-simple of a small farm; they consume expensive coal, and water that on the hills has to be brought long distances; they require skilled workmen to attend to them, and they do the work with a thoroughness which leaves little to be desired. Each puff and pant echoing from the ricks, each shrill whistle rolling along from hill to hill, proclaims as loudly as iron and steel can shout, 'Progress! Onwards!' Now step through this gap in the hedge and see what is going on in the next field.

It is a smaller ground, of irregular shape and uneven surface. Steam-ploughs mean *plains* rather than fields – broad, square expanses of land without awkward corners – and as level as possible, with mounds that may have been tumuli worked down, rising places smoothed away, old ditch-like drains filled up, and fairly good roads. This field may be triangular or some indescribable figure, with narrow corners where the high hedges come close together, with deep furrows to carry away the water, rising here and sinking there into curious hollows, entered by a narrow gateway leading from a muddy lane where the ruts are a foot deep. The plough is at work here also, such a plough as was used when the Corn Laws were in existence, chiefly made of wood – yes, actually wood, in this age of iron – bound and strengthened with metal, but principally made from the tree – the tree which furnishes the African savage at this day with the crooked branch with which to scratch the earth, which furnished the ancient agri-culturists of the Nile Valley with their primitive implements. It is drawn by dull, patient oxen, plodding onwards now just as they were depicted upon the tombs and temples, the graves and worshipping places, of races who had their being three thousand years ago. Think of the suns that have shone since then; of the summers and the bronzed grain waving in the wind, of the human teeth that have ground that grain, and are now hidden in the abyss of earth; yet still the oxen plod on, like slow Time itself, here this day in our land of steam and telegraph. Are not these striking pictures, remarkable contrasts? On the one side steam, on the other the oxen of the Egyptians, only a few thorn-bushes between dividing the nineteenth century B.C. from the nineteenth century A.D. After these oxen follows an aged man, slow like themselves, sowing the seed. A basket is at his side, from which at every stride, regular as machinery, he takes a handful of that corn round which so many mysteries have gathered from the time of Ceres to the hallowed words of the great Teacher, taking His parable from the sower. He throws it with a peculiar *steady* jerk, so to say, and the grains, impelled with the exact force and skill, which can only be attained by long practice, scatter in an even shower. Listen! On the other side of the hedge the rattle of the complicated drill resounds as it drops the seed in regular rows – and, perhaps, manures it at the same time – so that the plants can be easily thinned out, or the weeds removed, after the magical influence of the despised clods has brought on the miracle of vegetation.

These are not extreme and isolated instances; no one will need to walk far afield to witness similar contrasts. There is a medium between the two – a third class – an intermediate agriculture. The pride of this farm is in its horses, its teams of magnificent animals, sleek and glossy of skin, which the carters spend hours in feeding lest they should lose their appetites – more hours than ever they spend in feeding their own children. These noble creatures, whose walk is power and whose step is strength, work a few hours daily, stopping early in the afternoon, taking also an ample margin for lunch. They pull the plough also like the oxen, but it is a modern implement, of iron, light, and with all the latest improvements. It is typical of the system itself – half and half – neither the old oxen nor the new steam, but midway, a compromise. The fields are small and irregular in shape, but the hedges are cut, and the mounds partially grubbed and reduced to the thinnest of banks, the trees thrown, and some draining done. Some improvements have been adopted, others have been omitted.

Upon those broad acres where the steam-plough was at work, what tons of artificial manure, superphosphate, and guano, liquid and solid, have been sown by the progressive tenant! Lavishly and yet judiciously, not once only, but many times, have the fertilizing elements been restored to the soil, and more than restored – added to it, till the earth itself has grown richer and stronger. The scarifier and the deep plough have turned up the subsoil and exposed the hard, stiff under-clods to the crumbling action of the air and the mysterious influence of light. Never before since Nature deposited those earthy atoms there in the slow process of some geological change has the sunshine fallen on them, or their latent power been called forth. Well-made and judiciously laid drains carry away the flow of water from the winter rains and floods – no longer does there remain a species of reservoir at a certain depth, chilling the tender roots of the plants as they strike downwards, lowering the entire temperature of the field. Mounds have been levelled, good roads laid down, nothing left undone that can facilitate operations or aid in the production of strong, succulent vegetation. Large flocks of well-fed sheep, folded on the corn-lands, assist the artificial manure, and perhaps even surpass it. When at last the plant comes to maturity and turns colour under the scorching sun, behold a widespread ocean of wheat, an English gold-field, a veritable Yellow Sea, bowing in waves before the southern breeze – a sight full of peaceful poetry. The stalk is tall and strong, good in colour, fit for all purposes. The ear is full, large; the increase is truly a hundredfold. Or it may be roots. By these means the progressive agriculturist has produced a crop of swedes or mangolds which in individual size and collective weight per acre would seem to an old-fashioned farmer perfectly fabulous. Now, here are many great benefits. First, the tenant himself reaps his reward, and justly adds to his private store. Next, the property of the landlord is improved, and increases in value. The labourer gets better house accommodation, gardens, and higher wages. The country at large is supplied with finer qualities and greater quantities of food, and those who are engaged in trade and manufactures, and even in commerce, feel an increased vitality in their various occupations.

On the other side of the hedge, where the oxen were at plough, the earth is forced to be self-supporting – to restore to itself how it can the elements carried away in wheat and straw and root. Except a few ill-fed sheep, except some small quantities of manure from the cattle-yards, no human aid, so to say, reaches the much-abused soil. A crop of green mustard is sometimes ploughed in to decompose and fertilize, but as it had to be grown first the advantage is doubtful. The one object is to spend as little as possible upon the soil, and to get as much out of it as may be. Granted that in numbers of cases no trickery be practised, that the old rotation of crops is honestly followed, and no evil meant, yet even then, in course of time, a soil just scratched on the surface, never fairly manured, and always in use, must of necessity deteriorate. Then, when such an effect is too patent to be any longer overlooked, when the decline of the produce begins to alarm him, the farmer, perhaps, buys a few hundredweight of artificial manure, and frugally scatters it abroad. This causes 'a flash in the pan'; it acts as a momentary stimulus; it is like endeavouring to repair a worn-out constitution with doses of strong cordial; there springs up a vigorous vegetation one year, and the next the earth is more exhausted than before. Soils cannot be made highly fertile all at once even by superphosphates; it is the inability to discern this fact which leads many to still argue in the face of experience that artificial manures are of no avail. The slow oxen, the lumbering wooden plough, the equally lumbering heavy waggon, the primitive bush-harrow, made simply of a bush cut down and dragged at a horse's tail – these are symbols of a standstill policy utterly at variance with the times. Then this man loudly complains that things are not as they used to be – that wheat is so low in price it will not yield any profit, that labour is so high and everything so dear; and, truly, it is easy to conceive that the present age, with its competition and eagerness to advance, must really press very seriously upon him.

Most persons have been interested enough, however little connected with agriculture, to at least once in their lives walk round an agricultural show, and to express their astonishment at the size and rotundity of the cattle exhibited. How easy, judging from such a passing view of the finest products of the country centred in one spot, to go away with the idea that under

every hawthorn hedge a prize bullock of enormous girth is peacefully grazing! Should the same person ever go across country, through gaps and over
brooks, taking an Asmodeus-like glance into every field, how marvellously
would he find that he had been deceived! He might travel miles, and fly
over scores of fields, and find no such animals, nor anything approaching
to them. By making inquiries he would perhaps discover in most districts
one spot where something of the kind could be seen – an oasis in the midst
of a desert. On the farm he would see a long range of handsome outhouses,
tiled or slated, with comfortable stalls and every means of removing litter
and manure, tanks for liquid manure, skilled attendants busy in feeding,
in preparing food, storehouses full of cake. A steam-engine in one of the
sheds – perhaps a portable engine, used also for threshing – drives the
machinery which slices up or pulps roots, cuts up chaff, pumps up water,
and performs a score of other useful functions. The yards are dry, well
paved, and clean; everything smells clean; there are no foul heaps of decay-
ing matter breeding loathsome things and fungi; yet nothing is wasted, not
even the rain that falls upon the slates and drops from the eaves. The stock
within are worthy to compare with those magnificent beasts seen at the
show. It is from these places that the prize animals are drawn; it is here
that the beef which makes England famous is fattened; it is from here that
splendid creatures are sent abroad to America or the Colonies, to improve
the breed in those distant countries. Now step forth again over the hedge,
down yonder in the meadows.

This is a cow-pen, one of the old-fashioned style; in the dairy and pasture counties you may find them by hundreds still. It is pitched by the side
of a tall hedge, or in an angle of two hedges, which themselves form two
walls of the enclosure. The third is the cow-house and shedding itself; the
fourth is made of willow rods. These rods are placed upright, confined
between horizontal poles, and when new this simple contrivance is not
wholly to be despised; but when the rods decay, as they do quickly, then
gaps are formed, through which the rain and sleet and bitter wind penetrate with ease. Inside this willow paling is a lower hedge, so to say, two
feet distant from the other, made of willow work twisted – like a continuous hurdle. Into this rude manger, when the yard is full of cattle, the fodder is thrown. Here and there about the yard, also, stand cumbrous cribs
for fodder, at which two cows can feed at once. In one corner there is
a small pond, muddy, stagnant, covered with duckweed, perhaps reached
by a steep, 'pitched' descent, slippery, and difficult for the cattle to get
down. They foul the very water they drink. The cow-house, as it is called,
is really merely adapted for one or two cows at a time, at the period of
calving – dark, narrow, awkward. The skilling, or open house where the
cows lie and chew the cud in winter, is built of boards or slabs at the back,

and in front supported upon oaken posts standing on stones. The roof is of thatch, green with moss; in wet weather the water drips steadily from the eaves, making one long gutter. In the eaves the wrens make their nests in the spring, and roost there in winter. The floor here is hard, certainly, and dry; the yard itself is a sea of muck. Never properly stoned or pitched, and without a drain, the loose stones cannot keep the mud down, and it works up under the hoofs of the cattle in a filthy mass. Over this there is litter and manure a foot deep; or, if the fogger does clean up the manure, he leaves it in great heaps scattered about, and on the huge dunghill just outside the yard he will show you a fine crop of mushrooms cunningly hidden under a light layer of litter. It is his boast that the cow-pen was built in the three sevens; on one ancient beam, worm-eaten and cracked, there may perhaps be seen the inscription '1777' cut deep into the wood. Over all, at the back of the cow-pen, stands a row of tall elm-trees, dripping in wet weather upon the thatch, in the autumn showering their yellow leaves into the hay, in a gale dropping dead branches into the yard. The tenant seems to think even this shelter effeminate, and speaks regretfully of the old hardy breed which stood all weathers, and wanted no more cover than was afforded by a hawthorn bush. From here a few calves find their way to the butcher, and towards Christmas one or two moderately fat beasts.

Near by lives a dairy farmer, who, without going to the length of the famous stock-breeder whose stalls are the pride of the district, yet fills his meadows with a handsome herd of productive shorthorns, giving splendid results in butter, milk, and cheese, and who sends to the market a succession of animals which, if not equal to the gigantic prize beasts, are nevertheless valuable to the consumer. This tenant does good work, both for himself and for the labourers, the landlord, and the country. His meadows are a sight in themselves to the experienced eye – well drained, great double mounds thinned out, but the supply of wood not quite destroyed – not a rush, a 'bullpoll,' a thistle, or a 'rattle,' those yellow pests of mowing grass, to be seen. They have been weeded out as carefully as the arable farmer weeds his plants. Where broad deep furrows used to breed those aquatic grasses which the cattle left, drains have been put in and soil thrown over till the level was brought up to the rest of the field. The manure carts have evidently been at work here, perhaps the liquid manure tank also, and some artificial aid in places where required, both of seed and manure. The number of stock kept is the fullest tale the land will bear, and he does not hesitate to help the hay with cake in the fattening stalls. For there are stalls, not so elaborately furnished as those of the famous stock-breeder, but comfortable, clean, and healthy. Nothing is wasted here either. So far as practicable the fields have been enlarged by throwing two or three smaller enclosures together. He does not require so much machinery as the great arable farmer, but here are mowing machines, haymaking machines, horse-rakes, chain harrows, chaff-cutters, light carts instead of heavy waggons – every labour-saving appliance. Without any noise or puff this man is doing good work, and silently reaping his reward. Glance for a moment at an adjacent field: it is an old 'leaze' or ground not mown, but used for grazing. It has the appearance of a desert, a wilderness. The high, thick hedges encroach upon the land; the ditches are quite arched over by the brambles and briars which trail out far into the grass. Broad deep furrows are full of tough, grey aquatic grass, 'bullpolls,' and short brown rushes; in winter they are so many small brooks. Tall bennets from last year and thistle abound – half the growth is useless for cattle; in autumn the air here is white with the clouds of thistle-down. It is a tolerably large field, but the meadows held by the same tenant are small, with double mounds and trees, rows of spreading oaks and tall elms; these meadows run up into the strangest nooks and corners. Sometimes, where they follow the course of a brook which winds and turns, actually an area equal to about half the available field is occupied by the hedges. Into this brook the liquid sewage from the cow-pens filtrates, or, worse still, accumulates in a hollow, making a pond, disgusting to look at, but which liquid, if properly applied, is worth almost its weight in gold. The very gateways of the fields in winter are a Slough of Despond, where the wheels sink in up to the axles, and in summer great ruts jolt the loads almost off the waggons.

Where the steam-plough is kept, where first-class stock are bred, there the labourer is well housed, and his complaints are few and faint. There cottages with decent and even really capital accommodation for the families spring up, and are provided with extensive gardens. It is not easy, in the absence of statistics, to compare the difference in the amount of money put in circulation by these contrasted farms, but it must be something extraordinary. First comes the capital expenditure upon machinery – ploughs, engines, drills, what not – then the annual expenditure upon labour, which, despite the employment of machinery, is as great or greater upon a progressive farm as upon one conducted on stagnant principle. Add to this the cost of artificial manure, of cake and feeding-stuffs, etc., and the total will be something very heavy. Now, all this expenditure, this circulation of coin, means not only gain to the individual, but gain to the country at large. Whenever in a town a great manufactory is opened and gives employment to several hundred hands, at the same time increasing the production of a valuable material, the profit – the *outside* profit, so to say – is as great to others as to the proprietors. But these half-cultivated lands, these tons upon tons of wasted manure, these broad hedges and weed-grown fields, represent upon the other hand an equal loss. The labouring classes in the rural districts are eager for more work. They may popularly be supposed to look with suspicion upon change, but such an idea is a mistaken one. They anxiously wait the approach of such works as new railways or extension of old ones in the hope of additional employment. Work is their gold-mine, and the best mine of all. The capitalist, therefore, who sets himself to improve his holding is the very man they most desire to see. What scope is there for work upon a stagnant dairy farm of one hundred and fifty acres? A couple of foggers and milkers, a hedger and ditcher, two or three women at times, and there is the end. And such work! – mere animal labour, leading to so little result. The effect of constant, of lifelong application in such labour cannot but be deteriorating to the mind. The master himself must feel the dull routine. The steam-plough teaches the labourer who works near it something; the sight must react upon him, utterly opposed as it is to all the traditions of the past. The enterprise of the master must convey some small spirit of energy into the mind of the man. Where the cottages are built of wattle and daub, low and thatched – mere sheds, in fact – where the gardens are small, and the allotments, if any, far distant, and where the men wear a sullen, apathetic look, be sure the agriculture of the district is at a low ebb.

Are not these few pictures sufficient to show beyond a cavil that the agriculture of this country exhibits the strangest inequalities? Anyone who chooses can verify the facts stated, and may perhaps discover more curious anomalies still. The spirit of science is undoubtedly abroad in the homes of the English farmers, and immense are the strides that have been taken; but still greater is the work that remains to be done. Suppose anyone had a garden, and carefully manured, and dug over and over again, and raked, and broke up all the larger clods, and well watered one particular section of it, leaving all the rest to follow the dictates of wild nature, could he possibly expect the same amount of produce from those portions which, practically speaking, took care of themselves? Here are men of intellect and energy employing every possible means to develop the latent powers of the soil, and producing extraordinary results in grain and meat. Here also are others who, in so far as circumstances permit, follow in their footsteps. But there remains a large area in the great garden of England which, practically speaking, takes care of itself. The grass grows, the seed sprouts and germinates, very much how they may, with little or no aid from man. It does not require much penetration to arrive at the obvious conclusion that the yield does not nearly approach the possible production. Neither in meat nor corn is the tale equal to what it well might be. All due allowance must be made for barren soils of sand or chalk with thinnest layers of earth; yet then there is an enormous area, where the soil is good and fertile, not properly productive. It would be extremely unfair to cast the blame wholly upon the tenants. They have achieved wonders in the past twenty years;

they have made gigantic efforts and bestirred themselves right manfully. But a man may wander over his farm and note with discontented eye the many things he would like to do – the drains he would like to lay down, the manure he would like to spread abroad, the new stalls he would gladly build, the machine he so much wants – and then, shrugging his shoulders, reflect that he has not got the capital to do it with. Almost to a man they are sincerely desirous of progress; those who cannot follow in great things do in little. Science and invention have done almost all that they can be expected to do; chemistry and research have supplied powerful fertilizers. Machinery has been made to do work which at first sight seems incapable of being carried on by wheels and cranks. Science and invention may rest awhile: what is wanted is the universal application of their improvements by the aid of more capital. We want the great garden equally highly culti-vated everywhere.

THE PROSPECTS OF FARMING[1]

PALL MALL GAZETTE, 19 JULY 1877

I

Agriculture in England is passing through a crisis. There is great alarm and no inconsiderable amount of suffering. Many farmers of late years have been ruined, many farms are vacant, and there is great difficulty in finding tenants. In some districts the difficulty amounts to impossibility, and land-owners have been forced to become farmers themselves and to cultivate their own land. Nay, there are not a few cases in which the offer to give a farm rent free for some years fails to bribe any one to undertake to pay a moderate rent at a future period. The leaders among the tenant farmers recommend their brethren to bring up their children to any trade but that of agriculture. These are symptoms of a change of which no one can confidently predict the issue, but which in any case must certainly be momentous. If it means a permanent depreciation in the value of land, it means a social, and perhaps a political, revolution. If it means only that

1. Newly identified and not since republished. In two parts (19 July and 23 July). The second part was presented with the additional title of [Second Article].

new conditions are calling for new developments of capital and skill, it still means that old systems are dying, and that hence-forth there will be new relations between the various classes who are interested in "the land".

One thing is at least clear, that this disturbance in the established order of things is not due to any temporary or accidental cause. We have had two deficient harvests, but they followed upon one which was very abundant, and even 1875 and 1876 were not to be classed with many black years that have been known. Nor is it any novelty to farmers that a couple of bad seasons should come together. Such events as these are the ordinary incidents of their occupation, and if in any case they have been the last drop that made the bucket overflow, it must have been already full of misfortune from some other source. Nor has the loss of cattle by disease, heavy as it has been in individual instances, been sufficient to account for widespread distress. The importation of fresh meat from America has been a scare, but as yet it has been nothing more. In short, neither have the seasons nor the prices been yet so diverse as to explain the losses and depression which have come upon the farming interest. Nor, again, do we find in the history of former periods of gloomy anticipation anything that exactly parallels the present case. During the time of the corn laws, and on their abolition, it was always a fall in prices that gave alarm. These laws were devised to maintain a fixed value of wheat, and it was the fact that the actual value never reached that which the law had promised that led to the periodical outcry of ruin from the farming interests. When at last these laws were abolished, it was expected that wheat could no more be grown in England. But several circumstances conspired to falsify this prediction. Wheat fell for a year or two, but the first bad season sent it up again; or it was discovered that, in spite of the competition from Europe and America, it was still the English harvest that regulated prices: and the low price, when it did occur, was not only compensated by the large crop, but by an increase beyond what was ever known before. The extension of drainage and the introduction of foreign manures and feeding stuffs brought up the average returns from the soil to a pitch they had never previously reached. At the same time, the extraordinary development in trade and manufactures raised wages in the manufacturing districts and carried meat and wool to prices unheard of. These influences in combination not only delivered the British farmer from anticipated ruin, but gave him a prosperity he had never before attained – a result which involved the consequence that rents during the quarter of a century between 1848 and 1873 not only did not fall, but unquestionably tended to rise.

But in every one of the elements of this prosperity there has now occurred a check. Competition from abroad still assumes new phases. Wheat comes not only from Russia and the Atlantic seaboard, but from India, Australia, and California. Meat itself is now imported from America, and even if this should not be on a scale to depress prices, it will probably, at least, prevent any further rise. But, in addition to these old sources of apprehension, the farmer has now to encounter a totally new burden. The cost necessary for production has immensely increased. More labour is needed under the new system of farming than under the old, and the wages of labour have, as a consequence of the movement of which the strikes were only a symptom, risen on an average at least 30 per cent. Machinery has indeed been largely introduced; but machines, too, are very costly. Again, foreign manures, which are now so much depended on to augment the bulk in the rickyard, are, considering deterioration of quality, 50 per cent. dearer than they used to be. The position on the whole is this – that though produce and prices do not as yet fall off, yet to produce involves a much greater outlay, while there seems no longer any room for expecting that prices will go higher. Therefore matters look very black for those who only think of farming as farming used to be. For such persons there is only one element of the outlay that can be reduced, and that element is the rent. To spend less on labour means to grow more weeds; to spend less on artificial manures means to grow less corn; to spend less on machines means to get the work worse done; and therefore there is nothing for it but to spend less in the hire of the land.

It is remarkable, however, that this gloom, with its practical consequences, is confined only to certain districts, one might almost say to certain classes of individuals. Nay, outside these districts there are even some who say that farming is now more profitable than ever. Were it not for occasional visitations of disease this might, in fact, be asserted at least of all classes of dairy farms. The demand of the towns for milk and butter of good quality is insatiable, and the introduction of cheese factories has enabled us successfully to meet American competition in the only branch in which it is possible. In Scotland also it may be safely said that there is no agricultural depression. A good many farms have certainly been thrown up, but these have generally been in cases where the practice of letting by open tender, fostered by the peculiarities of the law of "hypothec," had previously forced rents to an exorbitant amount. On all fairly rented farms there has been no fall, and for average holdings there is no difficulty in finding tenants at reasonable rents. Over large districts of England, even in the corn-growing counties, the same may be said. The farmers grumble, say they cannot go on long, ask for reductions of rent, and are not very eager to enter upon new undertakings. But they do not give up their farms, and, if pressed closely, they admit that they have not as yet exactly suffered losses, and even that, one thing with another, the year's balance-sheet has shown its usual figure of profits. They are frightened, but not yet hurt.

THE PROSPECTS OF FARMING

PALL MALL GAZETTE, 23 JULY 1877

II

To understand under what circumstances it is still possible for farming to be remunerative, it will be best to glance at some practical instances, and we may first select Scotland. In that country the point that immediately strikes the observer is that the farmer understands his business and sticks to it. He knows at least the leading principles by which his daily practice is guided, and therefore he is prompt to see advantage and to avoid error in novel methods. Probably he may have some little idea of chemistry and of mechanics; almost certainly he reads an agricultural paper or attends discussions in the local club, where science in its relation to practice is often the topic of argument. But, above all, he gives his whole attention to his work. He does not hunt, or shoot, or linger over market ordinaries; he rises at six, and is all day in the fields giving orders and seeing that they are executed. He watches not merely the rise and fall of markets, but studies what crops give the best profits, and seizes every advantage offered by locality or season. He is handicapped by a climate inferior for wheat to that of England, so that harvest is often spoiled by rain, and the grain never comes within 10*S.* a quarter of the price of the best growth of Essex or Kent. But he has his advantage in potatoes, which all along the eastern half of the country yield a gross return of £20 to £30 per acre; and the cool summer and long days just suit turnips, which average 20 tons an acre, and fatten beasts with little outlay on cake or corn. To raise both these profitable crops he adds to his farm-yard manure (itself made in boxes or stalls) heavy dressings of artificial manure; but the outlay is well repaid, and the land is the better for the following wheat or barley. And the profit on such outlay can be calculated, for the farm is held on a lease of generally about twenty years. Lastly, the soil is drained when requisite, either by the landlord or under special arrangement with him; and the landlord, too, has erected and maintains ample buildings for the profitable feeding of cattle and threshing of the grain. Under these conditions the tenant thrives, and pays, as a rule, a far higher rent than the like quantity of land would fetch in England.

Now let us review the conditions in which in some districts an equal prosperity is achieved in the southern half of the island. It may be taken as a safe proposition that the first of these is the holding under a lease, or an equivalent custom of compensation for tenants' unexhausted outlay.

And next it is certain that success nowadays attends only the man who farms intelligently, and closely attends to the daily work of the farm. Given such elements, the further conditions of profit vary with the locality. Round large towns, as far as a radius of one hundred miles, milk and butter are highly remunerative. As far as a radius of fifty miles, what may be called market-garden crops – peas, cabbages, turnips, and the like – are often cultivated to great advantage. Hay and straw pay very well, when leave can be obtained to sell them. Indeed, of late the straw of a crop is often worth almost as much as the grain, and therefore it is a cruel injustice to the farmer to prohibit him from selling. The old idea was that if there was no straw there could be no manure, but chemistry has shown that the ingredients which the straw furnishes may be obtained from other sources at one-tenth the price of straw. Mr. Lawes, by his admirable series of experiments, and two other land-owners, one in Herts the other in Oxfordshire, have proved by systematic farming on a large scale that crops of grain and straw may year after year be removed from the land, while its fertility is maintained unabated by a proper supply of nitrogen, phosphorus, and potash, contained in "artificial manures." And the aid which steam gives to all operations on a large scale must not be left out of computation. A steam-engine consumes coals to do the work for which a horse consumes oats and a man beef; and though the animal engine is so perfect that it can extract more work from its fuel than any iron engine yet constructed, nevertheless the comparison of food to fuel is not unfair, because flesh and blood must eat even while resting, while steel and steam cost nothing except when actually at work. But to manage an engine to profit needs some skill and more common-sense, therefore it is that this potent auxiliary comes but slowly into use.

If now we try to bring together the sources of success under such variety of circumstances, we may be able to penetrate the secret of future gain or loss in farming. Obviously it does not lie in any one method. Rather it seems to be found in the adaptation of methods to circumstances. Local circumstances have more than ever to be considered. If the neighbourhood of a manufacturing town sets up a good market for vegetables, or fruit, for milk or eggs, the man who devotes a few acres to green peas or plum-trees, or establishes a connection with a milk or egg dealer, will thrive, while his neighbour, who grows wheat and fattens oxen as his father did will fail. If land is found to be good for potatoes, potatoes well manured will always pay. If leave can be got to sell straw, a tenant will be able to pay his rent, while if it is denied he must give up the farm. The adaptation of crop to soil admits also of considerable increase of profits. There are heavy-land farmers who never dream of the value of cabbages as food for stock, there are light-land farmers who know nothing of how kohl rabi grows in periods of drought that are fatal to turnips or even to mangels. Gorse and lupine, so precious to the Continental cultivator, would save many an acre of sand and gravel from going out of cultivation. But while all these resources afford means of making more from the ground than has been made hitherto, there are some indispensable conditions common to all situations. Suitable buildings must be provided; security must be given in some shape that capital invested shall be repaid; skill and knowledge must be invoked, and strict attention given to every detail of management.

If we could suppose that these requirements could be met, there seems, then, no reason to despair of the future of farming. But they unquestionably imply a change, which may be very gradual, but is inevitable, in the character of the English farmer and the relation between him and his landlord; for at the basis of any chance of progress there lies the indispensable element that the farmer of the future must be a better educated man and a richer man. His education must go beyond the study of the clouds and the soil as they appear to the eye; he must have book-learning and be an acute man of business, as wide in survey and as prompt in action as a manufacturer or trader; and both he and the landlord must be prepared to put more capital into the business. The landlord ought to execute all permanent improvements; but if he cannot, the tenant must invest (doubtless securing good interest) all the more himself. If it seems a risk to venture more where what is invested does not pay, let it be remembered that in farming there are a number of fixed outlays which must be met first of all. There are the rent and rates, the seed, the cost of manure and labour necessary to secure the minimum of crops. It is only on the manure and labour which raise crops above the minimum that net profit begins to accrue; but when that point is passed every outlay (within reasonable limits) brings in a percentage which restores the balance of gain and loss on the whole capital to the right side. High authorities have said that better farming would double the produce of English land, but to farm properly it is certain that the capital invested in the business ought in general to be increased by a half. It is, however, plain that if such hypothetical suggestions are sound a double return on a capital that is only a half larger would make all the difference between a business that does not pay and one that does.

Such changes as these are inevitable, but they cannot be rapid. Capital and education will flow in by degrees, but a generation must pass before the void is fully filled. Meantime, a landlord has only two courses open to him – to farm his land himself or concede the conditions which will induce competent men to farm it and pay rent. The first alternative cannot be generally adopted. To supply both landlord's and tenant's capital would involve raising a sum which cannot be set at less than £15 per acre. Nor have many landowners either the skill or the inclination necessary to make such an investment profitable. The alternative is, therefore, that which must generally be resorted to. But in adopting it the landlords of England will have to overcome some prejudices. The well-educated and sharp capitalist whom they must invite to hold under them will be a very different person from the typical farmer of the past. If he treats his landlord with respect, he certainly will not look up to him with reverence. He will require mercantile security for every penny he invests, liberty to make profit in any way he can; and in any matter outside the business relation he will hold himself quite independent of the squire. Yet in the change, frankly embraced as the inevitable should be, there may not after all be found much to regret. Truth to say, the British farmer has fallen behind his age. Nobody can deny his good qualities, for they are those which are natural to the unsophisticated Englishman. But nobody can deny that he would be all the better if he had been sent to a good school, and travelled and thought outside his fields, his parish, or his country a little more. Nor certainly need the introduction of new business relations between landlord and tenant, farmer and labourer, prevent the maintenance of bonds of kindly interest and regard. For the farmer who is the best master will always have the best workmen, and the landlord who is the most liberal in bargaining and most large-minded in intercourse will secure the best tenants and the highest rents.

MILK SUPPLY[1]

PALL MALL GAZETTE, 26 DECEMBER 1877

We noticed briefly a few days since the formal opening of a cluster of model dwellings attached to the premises of the Aylesbury Dairy company at Bayswater. But the erection of these dwellings in St. Petersburgh place is only the last touch of an organization which may fairly stand as a model for similar enterprises.

   Milk is, of course, one of the most important items in the food supply of any great population. It is the sole food of a large number of hand-fed infants, the main element in the dietary of all young children, and for the population generally, whether in health or in sickness, it is of the most

---

1. Newly identified and not since republished.

serious moment that the milk supply should be not only of good quality and safe from deterioration, but also free from contact with those particles of contagion by which modern sanitary science has shown it to be peculiarly liable to contamination. Until a very recent date the milk trade had received little of the advantages which capital and scientific skill can bestow. It was for the most part in the hands of small tradesmen, and prior to the year of the cattle-plague, when London was studded with small cowsheds, the arrangements of the small dairies at London retained something of old-world simplicity, and were accepted with little questioning as belonging to a traditional type. When, however, cows were swept away by the rinderpest and cowsheds abolished, London had to supply itself from the surrounding counties. About the same time the inquiring analysts began to discover, not only that the cow with the iron tail had more than its fair share of the business, but that, in spite of all that laws could ordain or magistrates could enforce, there were no means of securing with certainty, by the agency of the police-court, a really pure milk supply, as the law could never compel milk-men to sell milk above the minimum standard of a supposed invalid cow whose milk does not contain more than 10 per cent. of solids, although the experience of all who have investigated the subject shows that honest average milk has a standard of "11.50 per cent. of solids." At about the same time Dr. Ballard, by the investigation of an epidemic of typhoid at Islington, showed that the use of contaminated water in some way or other mixed with milk, which he did not venture to pronounce adulterated, was capable of spreading disease; and subsequent experience in Marylebone, at Eagley, at Penrith, and a dozen other places, told the same tale.

Taught by these facts, and profiting by an experience of some few years gained by Mr. G. Mander Allender (a Berkshire farmer who had successfully commenced a system of supplying pure milk from his own and contiguous farms direct to Londoners through a depot established at Bayswater), the Aylesbury Dairy Company have gradually developed a system of milk supply which, under the direction of scientific experts, has been ingeniously surrounded by a great number of precautions and safe-guards.

The first precautions, we note, are taken at the farms. All of these are surveyed and inspected as to their drainage and water supply; the method of cleansing the milk-pails, of cooling the milk, &c. Very stringent conditions are laid down under the advice of the general sanitary superintendent, and maintained by the control of a visiting inspector and sanitary engineer. The collecting sheds of the company at Swindon and the building in which milk is set for cream occupy half an acre of ground, and are of special construction; duly asphalted, thoroughly ventilated, and built so as to be without access of sewer gas. Connected with this is a large cheese factory, where the skimmed milk and surplus milk is converted into different qualities of cheese. This cheese factory is on a large scale, and new models, partly American; and in an adjoining field are erected large model piggeries, where 500 to 600 pigs are constantly fattening on the surplus whey. Thus economy and efficiency and perfection of quality are secured.

The milk from fifty farms is brought to London twice a day in cans specially devised to minimise jolting, which have received the medal of the Society of Arts. In London, again, instead of being brought into some little shop dignified with the title of dairy, but communicating with dwelling-rooms, or into underground cellars with open drains, the milk is received into a spacious and carefully arranged dairy, tiled, paved, cooled, and shut off from all access of sewer-gases, and free from communication with any dwelling-house. Every churn of milk is sampled and tested for cream and specific gravity, and the results recorded in a register. The outgoing churns containing milk are all "plumbed" with a leaden seal, such as that used at the Custom House, and the numbered churns are once more sampled, the quality of the sample being again registered in the office. Finally, perambulating inspectors daily take samples of the milk as it is being delivered at one or another customer's house, and these samples are once more compared with the registered results recorded against the numbered and registered and sealed churns when they were despatched. The accessory operations of the company's business, such as butter-making, are conducted with similar exactness. The latter being churned by machinery daily over ice and with the use of French pressure-mills, which completely free it from extraneous butter-milk and water, of which the excess spoils the quantity of a large proportion of even pure English butter. The apparatus for filling the churns and cleansing them with superheated steam and all the details of the duties of the men have been thought out with care. The erection of dwellings in which the whole of the milk-carriers and their families are housed and kept under sanitary supervision is one of the most important and the last-added element of safety; and these buildings too, which were last week inspected by Mr. Lyon Playfair, Mr. George Goodwin, Surgeon-General Mackinnon, C.B., and others well versed in such matters, are pronounced to be also well worthy of imitation as models of good sanitary dwellings for working-men. Thus to house and to isolate the milk-carriers who enter twice daily so many houses is an obviously useful sanitary precaution.

THE STATE OF FARMING[1]

ST. JAMES'S GAZETTE, AUGUST 1881

I. – Shaken To Pieces

Perhaps the shaking to pieces of agriculture generally has now proceeded sufficiently far to make a survey possible; for while the house is falling no one can tell how far the ruin will extend, but when it has toppled over and lies still the damage may be estimated. There are some signs that the bottom of agricultural depression has been reached – not that that implies much present hope; but upon looking round it is difficult to see how it can go lower. Wheat, stock, produce of all kinds, are down to an unremunerative price. Disease appears at intervals, notwithstanding stringent regular imports of foreign foods of all sorts, from flour to frozen mutton from La Plata, continue to gradually increase in quantity, and their effect upon home prices is now beyond all question. From all sides accounts come in of farms vacant, land to let at any rent almost, land to sell, and no one to buy. It is at last recognized that a good corn harvest alone is not enough to put matters right. And, to sum up, agriculture generally is shaken to pieces; yet it goes on just the same.

This is a curious paradox, of the truth of which any one whose thoughts turn towards green fields may assure himself by journeying forth among them. Though tenants quit and farms are to let, the face of the country is not apparently altered. The arable lands are ploughed and sown and harrowed and rolled; corn is ripening, herds are grazing in the meadows. Farm-yards present the same appearance; there are still ricks, and labourers moving about, cart-horses harnessed, and the very barn-door fowls picking among the chaff. It is hard to believe that everything is really in such decay. Outwardly – and superficially – there is no change. Where are the lands going out of cultivation? They exist, but they are far apart; mere dots upon the map. There is no doubt that the old tenants have in too many cases for ever quitted the homesteads wherein their families have dwelt these hundred years past. Still, somehow or other, the lands are tilled – not so well, but tilled they are. There are cattle about – not so many, nor of such good quality; but there are plenty of cattle. In the case of a factory, when the demand ceases the factory closes, the hands disappear, and there is nothing left but the empty building. It is different with agriculture. Though the demands are low the demand never quite ceases, and the fields can never be quite shut.

---

1. In three parts, and previously collected in *FF*. Collected here in full for the first time.

But while the outward appearances remain much the same, the suffering and loss within the homestead is another matter. The fields are tilled, but not by the same people: the herds graze, but they are not owned by the old folk. Thus the change in agriculture has made itself felt more by the men and women than by the business itself. The fields smile, but there is bitterness under the roof-tree.

The story is the same everywhere. Speak to the bailiff, whom you may find working in the field in order to be near and keep an eye upon the men, and he will point out different farms to you. The tenant of one has lost £300, of another £700; of a third £500; in one case £1,000 has gone. There is no secret about it; you may easily learn names and facts. Now, in agriculture these are large sums, because they represent the slow accumulations of years. A man goes into a farm, and, if he is fortunate, has perhaps sufficient capital to stock it; more often he borrows a part. In seven years, with good fortune, he may pay off part of his loan; in twenty he may have saved a few hundreds; possibly, on large tenancies and where there was money to begin with, a thousand. This money, it must be carefully borne in mind, is not the sudden product of a lucky speculation – money made in an hour out of nothing. It is the product of hard work, exposure, experience, shrewd dealing, foresight, and actual physical labour; especially it is the product of time. In the course of that time the man has grown to his work, to his fields, and homestead. So that when the few hundred pounds are lost, they represent, as it were, flesh and blood. The hope of so many years, the product of continued labour, is gone. Life is not all mechanical: nor can the most resolute of us entirely guide our course by pure reason. Reason may say, "This may be regained;" but the heart is not satisfied: the vacancy, the sense of numbness, left by suffering is not so easily exchanged for an elastic trust in the future. Most tenant-farmers are middle aged men; this today is the future they had looked forward to and strived for. They cannot put their future forward again. Here is the bitterness that has passed over the breadth of the land. It is the people who feel it; the human beings, not the smiling fields. And it will leave its mark behind, no matter what the ultimate result may be; for the old families are thus forced out from the farms, and once out they do not return. The middle-aged and the aged have not the heart, though they may often think that lower rents are offering some chance of profit, and cannot but remember that a few years ago such offers as they can now obtain would have been seized with avidity. The younger men, their sons, in the first place, have not the capitals – farmers' sons never have any capital while their parents live – and in the second, they look to something brisker then farming. They do not like it; they see that the same amount of patience, care, economy, and personal labour required to simply get on at farming, in any other business would bring them a little fortune. If they adhere to agriculture, they emigrate: if not, they gradually find employment in other directions. The race of home-bred tenant farmers is thus by degrees pushed out – those with whom farming is a tradition. Their places are taken for the most part by inferior men, with less capital and less education – men who look to make money not exactly by impoverishing the land, but by avoiding all expenditure upon it – by working on it as labourers, with the labourer's idea and manners. The state of cultivation is thus slowly retrograding. That it is so, an examination of the fields, which at first sight look so smiling, will quickly convince those who take the trouble. Ask the first labourer you meet, he will tell you that not half the labour is expended that there used to be. Half, of course, is a vague term: it is not correct; it is not so much less as that; still the diminution is very perceptible. Both in the tenants and the cultivation the high standard of recent years is lowered.

No matter how depreciated the value of wheat, still wheat when grown can be sold; and, being on the spot, it even now has some slight advantage over that which has to travel several thousand miles. Reduced to a minimum, the advantage, or the possibility of it in good harvests, yet remains, and consequently wheat is still grown. The market for home cattle is low – beaten down at last by imported meat and beasts; yet there is a market, and it must be remembered that all the wool sent hither from the vast Australian sheep-walks has not rendered English sheep-farming altogether unrenumerative. It is difficult to convey the idea –difficult to state the fact in words – but the point is like this: while the man who originally cultivated the field is driven off it – starved off it – the field is yet cultivated (after a fashion), and its produce is still saleable. It is a kind of produce which can never become unsaleable so long as the population continues to increase. To appreciate the actual state of agriculture, it is necessary to separate the tenant from his farm, to look at them apart. The tenant is driven out, but the farm is not valueless. In the extreme, if the worst comes to the worst, grass will grow with very little tending, and cattle can eat it. The farm is not like the factory which when the hands leave is entirely unproductive – merely four walls which of themselves produce nothing. Suppose not one shilling expended upon a farm; suppose it deserted, still grass springs up. This is an extreme illustration – let us hope nothing so miserable will happen in our time – but it may help the realization of the idea that the ruin of the tenant and the losses of the owner do not mean the absolute, downright disappearance of agriculture. Now from this fact, which sounds so harsh and cruel, some hope may perhaps be derived. For the tenant-farmer thus driven out there is little indeed; for the heart, after forty years of labour ending with irretrievable loss, is no longer elastic. But for agriculture there is the hope that arises from the power of endurance. Everything has done its worst by now. The iron trade (the iron trade directly affects agriculture), bad harvests, and weather cannot do more than they have done; foreign imports of fowl will check themselves in some degree, perhaps; everything has about done its worst. Yet agriculture survives; and although a percentage of tenants have left their farms, all farms are not vacant – quite the contrary. All have lost, but not all to such a degree as to compel them to leave.

The question arises whether the depression is not sometimes too much yielded to – whether some have not too readily given way. With rents very considerably lowered, with farms to be had on reasonable terms, with facilities of every kind held out and all kinds of objectionable clauses removed from agreements, ground game handed over, improvements effected, and so on, the question may be seriously entertained whether the present is not the farmer's opportunity. It is no use, of course, to ask the tenant who has lost his hard-earned savings to look at things in this light. No human philosophy could go so far. But to those who have still something left – to those who have youth, or any chance, as it were – the present time has the appearance of an opportunity. The risks have been already incurred and paid for: the blanks have been drawn. Only ten years ago if any one could have had a good farm at the price and upon the advantageous terms at which they are now offered, it would have been deemed a perfect windfall. – J.

THE STATE OF FARMING

II

Some who see that things have now about reached the lowest level may perhaps be waiting in hope that a specific may be discovered to render agriculture remunerative, or that radical changes will be made in the laws relating to land. But, putting aside a return to protection as quite out of the question, and confiscation as equally beside rational discussion, what remedy is there that has not been already tried? Everything yet recommended for the improvement of agriculture has been in practice. Woods and hedges were to be got rid of – grubbed up; marshy lands drained, hill-sides cultivated. This has been done. The woods remaining will be found for the most part to occupy inferior land, and if looked upon from the purely commercial point of view, so much insisted on not long since, perhaps on balance they pay as well as anything. The labour required is not much, and the return nearly certain. Nor do the woods interfere with the tenant-farms. If we suppose a junta of farmers, the tenants on an estate, entrusted with its management, it is certain that they would retain a proportion of wood. Poles, flakes, hurdles, gates, repairs to sheds, posts, and rails are needed upon farms: wood is necessary in a hundred shapes; and if it is not at hand it must be brought from a distance. The grubbing of hedges, which proceeded with such vigour for a time, has received a check from an appreciation of this fact. In go-ahead America farmers are well known to set aside so much of their property for the growth of timber. Iron is not a substitute for everything, and for iron money must be paid. Now at this juncture of circumstances the last thing a farmer wants to do is to pay away ready money. Wood grows for nothing on his mounds: these take up so much space; but rents are lower, and if it is a question between space and coin, the farmer to-day would probably prefer giving a little space. To a very great extent, therefore, it may be assumed that the grubbing of woods has gone as far as it is likely to go. Marshy places have been drained wherever the land was worth the trouble. The sums sunk in draining already cultivated fields throughout the country would amount to something enormous. In places it is even thought it has been overdone; still, there it is. No owner or tenant needs any lecturing nowadays on the value of drainage. Hill-sides have been ploughed up and cultivated, till at last, the soil becoming so thin at the top, it was demonstrated that it was no use to go any further.

Steam ploughing, again, was at one time to do wonders. Steam ploughing has been tried and we are where we are just the same. What can be done with it has been done. Many maintain that the steam plough is responsible for the weeds and the bad state of the soil in some districts. Certain it is that those who had gone to the expense of such tackle suffered as much from the depression as the rest. Any one who has visited an agricultural show must have seen that iron and brass can hardly be twisted into many more shapes. There is machinery for everything, even to tying up the corn as it is cut. If the limit of invention is not reached, the practical limit of what machinery can do appears to have been arrived at. With guano it is the same. Guano has been used, as has every other kind of manure. Guano is of very great value, but guano has not saved the tenant farmer. Root-crops were to be the farmer's great hope; root-crops are to be found wherever a farmer exists. Roots are grown, and will continue to be grown, in vast quantities; but I doubt whether much more can be done with them than has already been done.

The improvement of animal shape was the most promising and fascinating of all the agricultural theories. What volumes have not been written upon it! How many lives have not been devoted to it? And great things, very great things, were accomplished: possibly more success attended these efforts than has followed any other similar pursuit. We have, however, seen the apotheosis of the Short-horn. We have likewise seen the breeds of sheep carried to the utmost perfection. The world has come to us for cattle and sheep: from the ends of the earth men have arrived seeking to improve their stock from ours. Thousands, perhaps, have been expended in this pursuit by owners and tenants together: it is of no use whatever to lecture them any more on that subject.

Cattle are now sheltered far better than ever they were before; sheds, cow-houses, farm-buildings of all kinds, were never so good as at present. Even the tenants' houses – the last thing of all to get attention – have been somewhat improved: less, perhaps, than anything else. Cattle must be properly housed, but any inconvenient house will do for a tenant. Much certainly remains to be done in this way; but it will not make any addition to the tenants' income, as the cattle-sheds possibly may. Far more improvement has been effected in the dwellings of the labourers than of tenant-farmers. The agricultural labourers' habitations have been practically rebuilt in the last twenty years. They are not perfect, nor is the improvement universal; still, no one can deny that substantial progress has been made. Model cottages have not prevented depression. Labour is a vexed question – a dangerous one to touch: probably the price of labour will never be less than it is now. The fact is unmistakable – the rising generation will not be content with the wages that served their fathers' turn. A deduction will simply drive them away: no relief is likely from a fall of wages. What remedies remain? Science? Science has its colleges, professors and students, collections, experiments, and diplomas; but though science is it good thing, it has been tried, and people are still out of pocket. When foods were imported in such quantities, farmers were told, with some show of reason, that they must meet quantity with quality: they must defy competition by sending the primest beef and the sweetest butter to market. But it is found that English beef has no real pre-eminence over the American, and often cannot be distinguished from it. As for butter oleomargarine and similar compounds are authoritatively pronounced more "wholesome" than butter: and, to such an extent have people become used to the manufactured article, that many would now think that the best real butter had a "peculiar taste." The distillation of spirit from mangel-wurzel and the extraction of sugar from beet have both been tried and commercially failed.

The latest resource cried up was the putting of more capital in the soil – the attracting of more capital to the land. The arguments were sound enough; and no doubt it would be a profit to some one. But capital has been put into the soil, or on it, for many generations and in continually increasing amounts, both by tenants and owners. Capitalists of the present day are scarcely likely to be attracted by two per cent. per annum. It used to be considered that £10 per acre was a reasonable capital to stock a farm; "experts" of recent years have pronounced £40, £50, or even more, as nearer the mark. Where are they to find tenants to do that?

It appears, then, that everything that has ever been recommended to owners and tenants has already been tried; there does not remain one single untried remedy; and it is of no avail to wait in hope of some marvellous discovery. Owners and tenants together have, in one way or other, put every plausible recommendation into practice.

THE STATE OF FARMING

III

Most of the denunciations hurled from platforms against the proprietors of land are based upon the assumption that owners are opposed to the increase of the rural population. Traced to their origin, nearly all the arguments heard in or out of the House of Commons on the anti-land side spring from or appeal to a popular belief that the landowner desires to possess the country exclusively. The how and the why of this idea, or whether it had or had not any grounds to go upon in the past, forms no part of the present inquiry, which aims to honestly sketch out the actual existing state of things. At the present moment, then, there is certainly no greater fallacy than this assumption. The truth is precisely the reverse. An increase of the rural population is just the one thing which every estate-owner wishes, not for philanthropic reasons but his own interest. Increase of population means increased income to every one who possesses any property, whether it be stocks and shares, or whether it be land to be built upon or land to let. For the sake of illustration, imagine an estate (there are thousands of them) situated in an outlying district, very picturesque, thinly inhabited, with reasonably good soil, and tenants deeply in debt. The very best thing that could happen to the owner of that estate would be a rush of people – a rush like that which flocks to gold-fields. If he could get five hundred tenants instead of fifty his income would be trebled. He would be only too glad to split every farm up into allotments, and to let every single acre at an allotment rental. If a thousand people applied to him for an acre each, they would get it immediately. The idea is too ravishingly pleasant even to dream of! If any family settlements blocked the way, he would go to Parliament instantly for a private Act. There is nothing that would so delight a land-owner as to deplete a great city of its inhabitants, and to set them down into his hamlet. They would find every facility afforded. Now these town-folk whom the landowner so eagerly desires are the very people who are told that the landowners are only anxious to shut them out from the fields. The people have had all this preached at them for years, but they instinctively know better. They do not care a brass farthing for the land. Peasant proprietors they might become – at least, many of them; but the mechanic who has saved £150 in Leeds is not quite so foolish as to spend it on two acres of agricultural land in Berkshire. He invests it in a little house near Leeds, which will let well when he does not want to live in it and will give his children a certain income after him. Besides, a peasant farmer must do one or two things in this country: he must grow vegetables and be in fact a market-gardener, or he must cultivate in the same way as the present tenant-farmers. In the first case the demand is not large enough nor certain enough to make it remunerative when long distances intervene between the grower and his market. Close round great cities a profit is made out of market gardens; but if much land in the country was turned to market-gardening, there would soon be end to the profit. Some of the farmers in Kent who live near enough to London now grow large quantities of vegetables, send them to market in their own waggons, and bring back loads of manure. In this way they have already undersold the market gardeners close to town who pay thrice as much per acre. A large farmer can always undersell a little one. Nor could peasant-proprietors or tenants keep horses to draw their goods to market; they must accept the prices offered to them by the higglers who came round, and who would not be likely to give more than necessary for the sake of philanthropy. If the peasant proprietor endeavoured to work his plot on the same system as the tenant-farmers now do – a system let it be remembered, not rashly adopted, but the outcome of long experience combined with the teachings of science – they would at once come face to face with the same difficulties which have nearly overwhelmed the ordinary tenant. The difference would be that as the peasant-proprietor would not have a tenth of the resources in capital or labour at command, the peasant-proprietor would suffer ten times more, and it is questionable if he could even exist – even if he were put into possession, as a father might put his son, free of debt, without loans, interest, or rent to pay. I think I may say therefore that no enthusiastic theorist has yet propounded any practical solution of the land question, not even from his own point of view and under the most favourable circumstances. The market is dead against him. No one has or can propound any method of cultivation better than at present followed; and it would be wonderful if they could, for that method is founded upon centuries of experience, guided by science, supported by capital, and assisted by all the power of machinery. But some things may yet be done to enable the farmer to gather from various directions crumbs of profit. And it is difficult for those bred in city traditions to appreciate the value put upon mere crumbs by the farmer. Such large sums are daily handled in cities that people get into a habit of looking with indifference upon the trifling amounts that make all the difference to a tenant-farmer. Hearing of agricultural depression, they are of course interested; but when a cursory examination reveals the fact that all the trouble is over a few fifties in one place or hundreds in another, they fail to see that the crisis is very imminent. To the tenant-farmer the crumbs are everything – £1 here, £5 yonder, 10s. in a third place, make up the substance of his yearly income.

Perhaps the first thing that should be done for him is in the way of taxation. It is admitted that taxation presses heavily upon land. Of course, if the towns paid for the country that would not do. Still, something surely might be done: the lightening of the burden even by a few shillings would make a real difference. Then, freedom of culture is necessary in order to enable him to meet the altered conditions of to-day. Of late years many owners have practically conceded freedom of culture, or something near it; and experiment seems to prove that it can be safely done. But what is needed is something like a public and general recognition of the principle. We may depend upon it, the greater the liberty the landlord gives, and the more he as the seller can encourage confidence in the farmer as the buyer, the more profit there will be got out of the land. This freedom of culture would be another crumb for the farmer. Of course it follows that the owner must receive his land at the expiration of the agreement in as good condition as when it was entered on. Already forms of leases and agreement have been drawn which provide for this. How the new bankruptcy law would affect such cases remains to be seen; but upon the face of it a stricter bankruptcy law should be safeguard to the landowner, and enable him to allow considerably more latitude to the tenant. It was once a common trick of unscrupulous tenant-farmers to work out a farm, go through the court, and go on again and again till they became well off. True, the landowner as first creditor always recovered his rent, but he did not recover the loss caused by the depreciator of his property, and which he had to make up to the incoming tenant.

When the tenant obtains freedom of culture the owner ought to possess freedom of disposal of his property. Easier sale and transfer of land are questions which must force themselves forward in time. In themselves they scarcely concern the tenant, directly or generally; but in some cases it is believed that owners would be glad to lower their rents, but are unable to do so because certain settlements have to be met out of the rental, and they have no power to move. But nothing radical is wanting here: nothing but liberty to the owner to do what he finds profitable with his own.

Railway rates present a good illustration of the value of crumbs to the farmer. A few shillings extra puts a strain upon him in this way. It reduces him to the same position as the distant producer. It takes from him the advantages of his proximity to the home markets. This is a very important crumb in these days of cheap transit. But there can be few crumbs for the farmer without a moderate rent. At present, after successive remissions, rent does not press so heavily as it did; but a remission has its drawback, that it gives no security for the future. The rents of farms now vacant have been considerably reduced. But the question that is asked is, How long will this last? If we now take a seven years' agreement at a reasonable rate, and put our money and our time again into the land, shall we at the expiration of that time find our rent risen upon us? Farming is a business of years, and to succeed in it, a man must look forward a long time. But legislation to regulate rent in England seems out of the question: it certainly would strike at the root of every principle of business. So very delicate is this question that I hesitate to make any suggestion; and, after all, freedom of contract, and the natural adjustment of markets in a country like this, seem to give assurance that as long as the produce of the land brings small profits the rent of the land must be kept at a correspondingly low level.

Thus, upon a review of the state of things, it appears that agriculture is not in a quite hopeless state. No measures of confiscation or protection are needed. No plan hitherto put forth can answer better than the present system. What is chiefly required is some moderate amount of concession leading to a restoration of confidence.

STEAM ON COMMON ROADS[1]

STANDARD, 13 SEPTEMBER 1881

Another damaged harvest irresistibly points to the necessity of some important changes in the present agricultural system. Losses year after year and increasing competition indicate that the crops now grown are not sufficient to support the farmer. When he endeavours, however, to vary his method of culture, and to introduce something new, he is met at the outset by two great difficulties which crush out the possibility of enterprise. The first of these – the extraordinary tithe – has already come into prominent notice; the second is really even more important – it is the deficiency of transit. An extensive use of steam on common roads appears essential to a revival of agricultural prosperity, because without it it is almost impossible for delicate and perishable produce to be quickly and cheaply brought to market. Railways, indeed, now connect nearly every town of any size whatever throughout the country with the large cities or London; but railways are necessarily built as lines of communication between towns, and not in reference to scattered farms. Upon the map the spaces between the various rails do not look very broad, but those white bands when actually examined would be found to be six, eight, ten, or even twenty miles wide. Nor are there stations everywhere, so that a farm which may be only six miles from the metals may be ten from the nearest platform. Goods trains do not, as in the United States, stop to pick up wherever there is material or produce waiting to be loaded; the produce has to be taken where the railway chooses, and not where it would suit the farmer's convenience. When at last the farmer's waggon reaches the station he finds no particular trouble taken to meet his needs; his horse and carters are kept hours and hours, perhaps far into the night, for a mere matter of a ton or two, nor is there any special anxiety shown to deliver his consignment early, though if it should not be moved from the companies' premises demurrage is charged. In short, the railway companies, knowing that the agriculturists until the formation of the 'Farmers' Alliance' were incapable of united action, have used them much as they liked. As for the rates charged, the evidence recently taken, and which is to be continued, shows that they are arbitrary and often excessive. The accommodation is poor in the extreme, the charges high, the speed low, and every condition against the farmer. This, in its turn, drives the farmer more into the hands of the middleman. The latter makes a study of the rail and its awkward ways, and manages to

---

1. Collected in *FH* as 'Steam on Country Roads'.

get the goods through, of course adding to their cost when they reach the public. Without the dealer, under present circumstances, the farmer would often find it practically impossible to get to markets not in his immediate neighbourhood. The rail and its awkward, inconvenient ways actually shut him off. In manufacturing districts the transit of iron and minerals and worked-up metal is managed with considerable ability. There are appointed to manage the goods traffic men who are alert to the conditions of modern requirements and quick to meet them. In agricultural districts the question often arises if there be really any responsible local goods managers at all. It seems to be left to men who are little more than labourers, and who cannot understand the patent fact that times are different now from what they were thirty years since, when they first donned their uniforms. The railways may bring their books and any number of their officers to prove that everything is perfectly satisfactory, but the feeling remains, nevertheless, that it is exactly the contrary.

Look at the map, and place the finger on any of the spaces between the lines of rail. Take, then, the case of a farmer in the midst of that space, not more than five or six miles from the metals, and able at times to hear the distant whistle of the engines, but not less than eight from a station. This present season he finds his wheat damaged by the rain after it was cut, and he comes to the conclusion that he must supplement his ordinary crops by some special culture in order to make his way. On the last occasion he was in a large city he was much struck by the quantity of fruit which he found was imported from abroad. The idea naturally occurs to him of setting aside some ten or twenty acres of his holding of four hundred or five hundred for the culture of fruit. He goes to his landlord, who is only too willing to give him every facility, provided that no injury be done to the soil. He faces the monstrous injustice of the extraordinary tithes, and expends fresh capital in the planting of various kinds of fruit.

In places at that distance from a station labour is dear relative to the low profit on the ordinary style of farming, but very cheap relative to the possible profits on an improved and specialised system. The amount of extra labour he thus employs in the preparation of the ground, the planting, cleaning, picking, and packing, is an inestimable boon to the humbler population. Not only men, but women and children can assist at times, and earn enough to add an appreciable degree of comfort to their homes. In itself this is a valuable result. But now suppose our enterprising farmer has the fortune to have a good season, and to see his twenty acres teeming with produce. He sets as many hands on as possible to get it in; but now what is he to do with it? Send it to London. That is easily said; but trace the process through. The goods, perishable and delicate, must first be carted to the railway station and delivered there, eight miles from the farm, at most inconvenient hours. They must be loaded into slow goods trains, which may not reach town for four-and-twenty hours. There is not the slightest effort to accelerate the transit, and the rates are high. By the time the produce reaches the market its gloss and value are diminished, and the cost of transit has eaten away the profit. The thing has been tried over and over again and demonstrated. One need only go to the nearest greengrocer's to obtain practical proof of it. The apples he sells are American. The farmers in New York State or Massachusetts can grow apples, pack them in barrels, despatch them two thousand eight hundred miles to Liverpool, and they can then be scattered all over the country and still sold cheaper than the fruit from English orchards. This is an extraordinary fact, showing the absolute need of speedy and cheap transit to the English farmer if he is to rise again. Of what value is his proximity to the largest city in the world – of what value is it that he is only ninety miles from London, if it costs him more to send his apples about ninety miles than it does his American kinsman very nearly three thousand?

As we have in this country no great natural waterways like the rivers and lakes of the United States, our best resource is evidently to be found in the development of the excellent common roads which traverse the country, and may be said practically to pass every man's door. Upon these a goods train may be run to every farm, and loaded at the gate of the field. This assertion is not too bold. The thing, indeed, is already done in a manner much more difficult to accomplish than that proposed. Traction engines, weighing many tons – so heavy as to sometimes endanger bridges, and drawing two trucks loaded with tons of coal, chalk, bricks, or other materials – have already been seen on the roads, travelling considerable distances, and in no wise impeded by steep gradients; so little, indeed, that they ascend the downs and supply farms situated in the most elevated positions with fuel. What is this but a goods train, and a goods train of the clumsiest, most awkward, and, consequently, unprofitable description? Yet it is run, and it would not be run were it not to some extent useful. Anything more hideous it would be hard to conceive, yet if the world patiently submits to it for the welfare of the agricultural community, what possible objection can there be to engines so formed as to avoid every one of the annoyances caused by it? It may be asserted without the slightest fear of contradiction that there are at least fifty engineering firms in this country who could send forth a road locomotive very nearly noiseless, very nearly smokeless, certainly sparkless, capable of running up and down hill on our smooth and capital roads, perfectly under control, not in the least alarming to horses, and able to draw two or more trucks or passenger cars round all their devious windings at a speed at least equal to that of a moderate trot – say eight miles an hour. Why, then, do we not see such useful road trains running to and fro? Why, indeed? In the first place, progress in this direction is absolutely stopped by the Acts of Parliament regulating agricultural engines. The Act in question was passed at a time when steam was still imperfectly understood. It was in itself a perfectly judicious Act, which ought to be even more strictly enforced than it is. But it was intended solely and wholly for the regulation of those vast and monstrous-looking engines which it was at once foreseen, if left to run wild, would frighten all horse traffic off the roads. The possibility of road locomotives in the reasonable sense of the term was not even in the minds of the framers. Yet, by a singular perversity, this very Act has shut off steam from one of its most legitimate functions.

It is quite possible that the depression of agriculture may have the effect of drawing attention to this subject, and if so it will be but tardy justice to the rest of society that the very calling whose engines now block the roads should thus in the end open them. We should then see goods trains passing every farm and loading at the gate of the field. Such a road goods train would not, of course, run regularly to and fro in the same stereotyped direction, but would call as previously ordered, and make three or four journeys a day, sometimes loading entirely from one farm, sometimes making up a load from several farms in succession. Besides the quick communication thus opened up with the railway station and the larger towns, the farmer would be enabled to work his tenancy with fewer horses. He would get manures, coal, and all other goods delivered for him instead of fetching them. He would get his produce landed for him instead of sending his own teams, men, and boys. In a short time, as the railways began to awaken to the new state of things, they would see the advantage of accommodating their arrangements, and open their yards and sidings to their competitor. In the case of long journeys, and with some kinds of goods, in order to save the cost of transhipment, it would be possible to transfer the bed of the road truck from its frame on to the frame of the railroad truck, so that the goods, with one loading, might pass direct to London. Our American cousins are quite capable of inventing a transferable truck of this kind. In return, goods loaded in London would never leave the same bottom till unloaded at the farmyard or in the midst of the village. For all long journeys the rails would probably always remain the great carriers, and the road trains serve as their most valuable feeders. When farmers found it possible to communicate with the cities at reasonable rates, and at reasonable speed, they would be encouraged to put forth fresh efforts, to plant vegetables, to grow fruit, to supplement their larger crops with every species of lesser produce. This, in its turn, would bring new traffic to the lines; for instead of one or two crops in the year only, there would be three or four requiring carriage. There would be then speedy results of such improved communication. One would be an increased value of land; the second, an increase in the number of small areas occupied and cultivated; the third, an increase in the rural population. A fourth would be that the incredible amount of money which is now annually transferred to the Continent and America for the purchase of every kind of lesser produce would remain in this country to the multiplication of the accounts at Post Office savings banks. Every one who possibly could would grow or fatten something when he could just put it on a road train, and send it off to market.

Two through passenger road trains a day, one in each direction, carrying light parcels as well, and traversing say forty or fifty miles or less, would probably soon obtain sufficient support, as they ran from village to village and market town to market town. At present, those who live in villages are practically denied locomotion unless they are well enough off to keep a horse and trap and a man to look after them. A person residing in a village must either remain in the village, or walk, or go by carrier. The carrier stops at every inn, and takes a day to get over ten miles. The exposure in the carrier's cart has been the cause of serious illness to many and many a poor woman obliged to travel by it, and sit in the wind and rain for hours and hours together. Unless they ride in this vehicle, or tramp on foot, the villagers are simply shut off from the world. They have neither omnibus, tramway, nor train. Those who have not lived in a village have no idea of the isolation possible even in this nineteenth century, and with the telegraph brought to the local post office. The swift message of the electric wire, and the slow transit of the material person – the speed of the written thought, and the slowness of the bodily presence – are in strange contrast.

When people do not move about freely commerce is practically at a standstill. But if two passenger road trains, travelling at an average speed of not more than eight miles an hour, one going up and the other down, and connecting two or more market towns and lines of railway, passed through the village, how different would be the state of things! Ease of transit multiplies business, and, besides passengers, a large amount of light material could thus be conveyed. There would be depots at the central places, but such trains could stop to pick up travellers at any gate, door, or stile. If the route did not go through every hamlet, it would pass near enough to enable persons to walk to it and join the carriages. No one objects to walk one mile if he can afterwards ride the other ten. Besides these through trains, special trains could run on occasions when numbers of people wanted to go to one spot, such as sheep or cattle fairs and great markets. Large tracts of country look to one town as their central place, not by any means always the nearest market town; to such places, for instance, as Gloucester and Reading, thousands resort in the course of the year from hamlets at a considerable distance. Such road trains as have been described would naturally converge on provincial towns of this kind, and bring them thrice their present trade. Country people only want facilities to travel exactly like city people. It is, indeed, quite possible that when villages thus become accessible many moderately well-to-do people will choose them for their residence, in preference to large towns, for health and cheapness. If any number of such persons took up their residence in villages, the advantage to farmers would of course be that they would have good customers for all minor produce at their doors. It is not too much to say that three parts of England are quite as much in need of opening up as the backwoods of America. When a new railroad track is pushed over prairie and through primeval woods, settlements spring up beside it. When road trains run through remote hamlets those remote hamlets will awake to a new life.

Many country towns of recent years have made superhuman efforts to get the railway to their doors. Some have succeeded, some are still trying; in no case has it been accomplished without an immense expenditure, and for the most part these railroad branches are completely in the control of the main line with which they are connected. In one or two cases progress has been effected by means of tramways, notably one at Wantage – an excellent idea and highly to be commended. All these are signs that by slow degrees matters are tending towards some such scheme as has been here sketched out. While local railroads are extremely expensive, slow in construction, and always dominated by main lines, and while tramways need rails, with the paraphernalia rails require, they have this drawback – they are not flexible. The engines and cars that run upon them must for ever adhere to the track: there may be goods, produce, ricks, cows, fruit, hops, and what not, wanting to be landed only a quarter of a mile distant, but the cars cannot go to the crops. The railroad is rigid, everything must be brought to it. From town to town it answers well, but it cannot suit itself and wind about from village to hamlet, from farm to farm, up hill and down dale. The projected road train is flexible and capable of coming to the crops. It can call at the farmer's door, and wait by the gate of the field for the load. We have lately seen France devote an enormous sum to the laying down of rails in agricultural districts, to the making of canals, and generally to the improvement of internal communication in provinces but thinly populated. The industrious French have recognised that old countries, whose area is limited, can only compete with America, whose area is almost unlimited, by rendering transit easy and cheap. We in England shall ultimately have to apply the same fact.

THE PRESERVATION OF GAME IN ENGLAND[1]

ST. JAMES'S GAZETTE, 25 OCTOBER 1881

Preservers of game have for some time past been labouring under many difficulties, which are now accumulating so fast as to reduce some of them to despair. Here and there they are already turning off their gamekeepers, letting their country houses, and forswearing all intimacy with the fields and copses through which they loved to stroll gun in hand. It would of course be a gross exaggeration to say that this new movement is at all general. But it is to be observed; and it may spread. The difficulties in the protection of game are partly of old standing, but aggravated during these last few years; and partly new. First and foremost among them has always been the great poaching nuisance. There was perhaps as much poaching in England a century ago as there is now, and nearly as much of that morbid communism which regards the trespasser in pursuit of game as a martyr. But the old system of plunder differed in many respects from the new; and particularly in this, that it inflicted a much less severe loss on the landowner. It did not in those days cost nearly so much to keep up till September or October a good head of game; nor, for various reasons, was the game itself when killed of so much value to the proprietor. Each pheasant which is now poached in October represents on the average a sum of little less than a pound out of the pocket of the man on whose property it was reared – plus the value, whatever it may be, of the sport it would have afforded to him and his friends. The illegal slaughter of a single bird is, therefore, no slight robbery, and is a worse injury than if the spoil had been taken out of the owner's larder. Anciently, the cost of pheasants to the owner was comparatively trifling. Few were artificially fed, and still fewer reared at home. The natural resources of the estate were trusted to produce sufficient sport, if only moderately cared for by the vigilance of a keeper and a few watchers. Moreover, the poacher of those days was, generally speaking, a humble and modest being compared with his successor. He walked about in dread of the powers that be; he was regarded with an unkind eye not only by the Magistrates, but by the more respectable of his neighbours; and he had to resort to mean and precarious methods for disposing of his game. The modern plunderer of game preserves has reverted to the best traditions of the Locksley school, and walks with bold and firm step – not upon the woodland glade, but upon the pavement of the East End or through the devious precincts of Seven Dials. Our improved system of communication has freed him from

---

1. Previously identified by Samuel Looker and not since republished.

the inconvenient necessity of carrying on operations in a place where he was more known than respected, and enabled him to organise from a distance regular campaigns; while at the same time it is more easy for him to enter into offensive and defensive alliances with trustworthy "pals." The modern gamekeeper is often powerless against a raid planned on the grand scale not at all uncommon now. He is neither able to anticipate it, nor willing, in many cases to meet it with sufficient vigour. A recent example has shown that burglars, when interrupted in their work, are capable of providing for their own safety by shooting the intruder through the head: and a line of tactics which has proved so successful when followed by burglars can be adopted still more profitably by poachers. These considerations, joined with the fact that there is now not the smallest difficulty in selling stolen game and eggs, make the modern poacher, when he goes about his business in a systematic way, a much more formidable thief than his predecessor.

Many of the facilities and advantages now enjoyed by the poacher are also enjoyed by the dishonest keeper, who, under favourable circumstances, makes a better income out of his gun than out of his salary. It may be said that now-a-days dishonest keepers are more easily detected by any man who has a head on his shoulders, and knows anything about the amount of game there ought to be on his estate. But all men do not know this, and many who are forced to live at a distance from their shooting quarters cannot by any reasonable possibility know it. The bareness of their favourite covers is explained by various ingenious falsehoods, and they either "grin and bear it" or give up game preserving in disgust, dismissing, not without an excellent character, the salaried poacher who has been living in their gamekeeper's lodge.

Of the new difficulties which confront the preserver of game several may be traced to an altered and improved system of agriculture. But the most notable change which has come over the whole art and science of preserving is the operation of the Hares and Rabbits Act. In some districts ground game is fast vanishing, and with it the food of foxes. Foxes must live on pheasants and thus inflict a new loss upon those who preserve them.

To stand out against discouragements while suffering at the same time from a loss of income in the shape of reduced rents, requires a long purse as well as a pretty obstinate love of sport for its own sake. There are doubtless plenty of landowners who will stand their ground for a long while yet, some by taking the fields as well as the woods into their own occupation, and combining a little farming with timber-growing and game-preserving; others by effecting a tacit understanding with farmers whom they know they can trust. But game-preserving in a really effectual way is no longer practicable for a man of moderate means; and one proof of this is to be found in the fact that more shooting parties went out after pheasants on the 1st of October this season than for many years past.

THE BEAUTY OF THE FIELDS[1]

MAGAZINE OF ART, DECEMBER 1881

The earth has a way of absorbing things that are placed upon it, of draw-ing from them their stiff individuality of newness, and throwing over them something of her own antiquity. As the furrow smooths and brightens the share, as the mist eats away the sharpness of the iron angles, so, in a larger manner, the machines sent forth to conquer the soil are conquered by it, become a part of it, and as natural as the old, old scythe and reaping-hook. Thus already the new agriculture has grown hoar.

The oldest of the modern implements is the threshing-machine, which is historic, for it was once the cause of rural war. There are yeomanry men still living who remember how they rode about at night after the rioters, guided by the blazing bonfires kindled to burn the new-fangled things. Much blood – of John Barleycorn – was spilt in that campaign; and there is many a farmer yet hearty who recollects the ale-barrels being rolled up into the rickyards and there broached in cans and buck-ets, that the rebels, propitiated with plentiful liquor, might forbear to set fire to the ricks or sack the homestead. Such memories read strange to the present generation, proving thereby that the threshing-machine has already grown old. It is so accepted that the fields would seem to lack something if it were absent. It is as natural as the ricks: things grow old so soon in the fields.

On the fitful autumn breeze, with brown leaves whirling and grey grass rustling in the hedges, the hum of the fly-wheel sounds afar, travelling through the mist which hides the hills. Sometimes the ricks are in the open stubble, up the Down side, where the wind comes in a long, strong rush, like a tide, carrying away the smoke from the funnel in a sweeping trail; while the brown canvas, stretched as a screen, flaps and tears, and the folk at work can scarce hear each other speak, any more than you can by the side of the sea. Vast atmospheric curtains – what else can you call them? – roll away, opening a view of the stage of hills a moment, and, closing again, reach from heaven to earth around. The dark sky thickens and low-ers as if it were gathering thunder, as women glean wheatears in their laps. It is not thunder; it is as if the wind grew solid and hurled itself – as a man might throw out his clenched fist – at the hill. The inclined plane of the mist-clouds again reflects a grey light, and, as if swept up by the

---

1. This item was last published under this title in *Land* (1881). The text was included by Jefferies in *LF* as the first part of 'Notes on Landscape Painting'.

fierce gale, a beam of sunshine comes. You see it first long, as it is at an
angle; then overhead it shortens, and again lengthens after it has passed,
somewhat like the spoke of a wheel. In the second of its presence a red
handkerchief a woman wears on the ricks stands out, the brass on the
engine glows, the water in the butt gleams, men's faces brighten, the
cart-horse's coat looks glossy, the straw a pleasant yellow. It is gone, and
lights up the backs of the sheep yonder as it runs up the hill swifter than
a hare. Swish! The north wind darkens the sky, and the fly-wheel moans
in the gloom; the wood-pigeons go a mile a minute on the wind, hardly
using their wings; the brown woods below huddle together, rounding their
shoulders to the blast; a great air-shadow, not mist, a shadow of thickness
in the air looms behind a tiled roof in the valley. The vast profound is full
of the rushing air.

These are days of autumn; but earlier than this, when the wheat that is
now being threshed was ripe, the reaping-machine went round and round
the field, beginning at the outside by the hedges. Red arms, not unlike
a travelling windmill on a small scale, sweep the corn as it is cut and
leave it spread on the ground. The bright red fans, the white jacket of
the man driving, the brown and iron-grey horses, and yellow wheat are
toned – melted together at their edges – with warm sunlight. The machine
is lost in the corn, and nothing is visible but the colours, and the fact
that it is the reaping, the time of harvest, dear to man these how many
thousand years! There is nothing new in it; it is all old as the hills. The
straw covers over the knives, the rims of the wheels sink into pimpernel,
convolvulus, veronica; the dry earth powders them, and so all beneath is
concealed. Above the sunlight (and once now and then the shadow of a
tree) throws its mantle over, and, like the hand of an enchanter softly waving, surrounds it with a charm. So the cranks, and wheels, and knives, and
mechanism do not exist – it was a machine in the workshop, but it is not a
machine in the wheat-field. For the wheat-field you see is very, very old,
and the air is of old time, and the shadow, the flowers, and the sunlight,
and that which moves among them becomes of them. The solitary reaper
alone in the great field goes round and round, the red fans striking beside
him, alone with the sunlight, and the blue sky, and the distant hills; and he
and his reaper are as much of the corn-field as the long-forgotten sickle or
the reaping-hook.

The sharp rattle of the mowing-machine disturbs the corncrake in the
meadow. Crake! crake! for many a long day since the grass began to grow
fast in April till the cowslips flowered, and white parsley flourished like
a thicket, blue scabious came up, and yonder the apple trees drop their
bloom. Crake! crake! nearly day and night; but now the rattle begins,
and the bird must take refuge in the corn. Like the reaper, the mowing-

machine is buried under the swathe it cuts, and flowers fall over it – broad ox-eye daisies and red sorrel. Upon the hedge June roses bloom; blackbirds whistle in the oaks; now and again come the soft hollow notes of the cuckoo. Angles and wheels, cranks and cogs, where are they? They are lost; it is not these we see, but the flowers and the pollen on the grass. There is an odour of new-made hay; there is the song of birds, and the trees are beautiful.

As for the drill in spring-time, it is ancient indeed, and ancients follow it – aged men stepping after over the clods, and watching it as if it were a living thing, that the grains may fall each in its appointed place. Their faces, their gait, nay, the very planting of their heavy shoes' stamp on the earth, are full of the importance of this matter. On this the year depends, and the harvest, and all our lives, that the sowing be accomplished in good order, as is meet. Therefore they are in earnest, and do not turn aside to gaze at strangers, like those do who hoe, being of no account. This is a serious matter, needing men of days, little of speech, but long of experience. So the heavy drill, with its hanging rows of funnels, travels across the field well tended, and there is not one who notes the deep azure of the March sky above the elms.

Still another step, tracing the seasons backwards, brings in the steam-plough. When the spotted arum leaves unfold on the bank, before the violets or the first celandine, while the "pussies" hang on the hazel, the engines roll into the field, pressing the earth into barred ruts. The massive wheels leave their imprint, the footsteps of steam, behind them. By the hedges they stand, one on either side, and they hold the field between them with their rope of iron. Like the claws of some prehistoric monster, the shares rout up the ground; the solid ground is helpless before them; they tear and rend it. One engine is under an oak, dark yet with leafless boughs, up through which the black smoke rises; the other overtops a low hedge, and is in full profile. By the panting, and the humming, and the clanking as the drum revolves, by the smoke hanging in the still air, by the trembling of the monster as it strains and tugs, by the sense of heat, and effort, and pent-up energy bubbling over in jets of steam that struggle through crevices somewhere, by the straightened rope and the jerking of the plough as it comes, you know how mighty is the power that thus in narrow space works its will upon the earth. Planted broadside, its four limbs – the massive wheels – hold the ground like a wrestler drawing to him the unwilling opponent. Humming, panting, trembling, with stretched but irresistible muscles, the iron creature conquers, and the plough approaches. All the field for the minute seems concentrated in this thing of power. There are acres and acres, scores of acres around, but they are surface only. This is the central spot: they are nothing, mere matter. This is force – Thor in another form. If you are near you cannot take your eyes off the sentient iron, the wrestler straining. But now the plough has come over, and the signal given reverses its way. The lazy monotonous clanking as the drum unwinds on this side, the rustling of the rope as it is dragged forth over the clods, the quiet rotation of the fly-wheel – these sounds let the excited thought down as the rotating fly-wheel works off the maddened steam. The combat over, you can look round.

It is the February summer that comes, and lasts a week or so between the January frosts and the east winds that rush through the thorns. Some little green is even now visible along the mound where seed-leaves are springing up. The sun is warm, and the still air genial, the sky only dotted with a few white clouds. Wood-pigeons are busy in the elms, where the ivy is thick with ripe berries. There is a feeling of spring and of growth; in a day or two we shall find violets; and listen, how sweetly the larks are singing! Some chase each other, and then hover fluttering above the hedge. The stubble, whitened by exposure to the weather, looks lighter in the sunshine, and the distant view is softened by haze. A water-tank approaches, and the cart-horse steps in the pride of strength. The carter's lad goes to look at the engine and to wonder at the uses of the gauge. All the brazen parts gleam in the bright sun, and the driver presses some waste against the piston now it works slowly, till it shines like polished silver. The red glow within, as the furnace-door is opened, lights up the lad's studious face beneath like sunset. A few brown leaves yet cling to one bough of the oak, and the rooks come over cawing happily in the unwonted warmth. The low hum and the monotonous clanking, the rustling of the wire rope, give a sense of quiet. Let us wander along the hedge, and look for signs of spring. This is to-day. To-morrow, if we come, the engines are half hidden from afar by driving sleet and scattered snow-flakes fleeting aslant the field. Still sternly they labour in the cold and gloom. A third time you may find them, in September or bright October, with acorns dropping from the oaks, the distant sound of the gun, and perhaps a pheasant looking out from the corner. If the moon be full and bright they work on an hour or so by her light, and the vast shadows of the engines are thrown upon the stubble.

THE WILTSHIRE LABOURER[1]

LONGMAN'S MAGAZINE, NOVEMBER 1883

Ten years have passed away, and the Wiltshire labourers have only moved in two things – education and discontent. I had the pleasure then of pointing out in 'Fraser' that there were causes at work promising a considerable advance in the labourers' condition. I regret to say now that the advance, which in a measure did take place, has been checkmated by other circumstances, and there they remain much as I left them, except in book-learning and mental restlessness. They possess certain permanent improvements – unexhausted improvements in agricultural language – but these, in some way or other, do not seem now so valuable as they looked. Ten years since important steps were being taken for the material benefit of the labouring class. Landowners had awakened to the advantage of attaching the peasantry to the soil, and were spending large sums of money building cottages. Everywhere cottages were put up on sanitary principles, so that to-day few farms on great estates are without homes for the men. This substantial improvement remains, and cannot fade away. Much building, too, was progressing about the farmsteads; the cattle-sheds were undergoing renovation, and this to some degree concerned the labourer, who now began to do more of his work under cover. The efforts of every writer and speaker in the country had not been without effect, and allotments, or large gardens, were added to most cottage homes. The movement, however, was slow, and promised more than it performed, so that there are still cottages which have not shared in it. But, on the whole, an advance in this respect did occur, and the aggregate acreage of gardens and allotments must be very considerably larger now than formerly. These are solid considerations to quote on the favourable side. I have been thinking to see if I could find anything else. I cannot call to mind anything tangible, but there is certainly more liberty, an air of freedom and independence – something more of the 'do as I please' feeling exhibited. Then the sum ends. At that time experiments were being tried on an extended scale in the field: such as draining, the enlargement of fields by removing hedges, the formation of private roads, the buildings already mentioned, and new systems of agriculture, so that there was a general stir and bustle which meant not only better wages but wages for more persons. The latter is of the utmost importance to the tenant-labourer, by which I mean a man who is settled, because it keeps his sons at home. Common experience all over the world has always

1. Signed 'Richard Jefferies'. Collected in *HV*.

shown that three or four or more people can mess together, as in camps, at a cheaper rate than they can live separately. If the father of the family can find work for his boys within a reasonable distance of home, with their united contributions they can furnish a very comfortable table, one to which no one could object to sit down, and then still have a sum over and above with which to purchase clothes, and even to indulge personal fancies. Such a pleasant state of things requires that work should be plentiful in the neighbourhood. Work at that time was plentiful, and contented and even prosperous homes of this kind could be found. Here is just where the difficulty arises. From a variety of causes the work has subsided. The father of the family – the settled man, the tenant-labourer – keeps on as of yore, but the boys cannot get employment near home. They have to seek it afar, one here, one yonder – all apart, and the wages each separately receives do but just keep them in food among strangers. It is this scarcity of work which in part seems to have counterbalanced the improvements which promised so well. Instead of the progress naturally to be expected you find the same insolvency, the same wearisome monotony of existence in debt, the same hopeless countenances and conversation.

There has been a contraction of enterprise everywhere, and a consequent diminution of employment. When a factory shuts its doors, the fact is patent to all who pass. The hum of machinery is stopped, and smoke no longer floats from the chimney; the building itself, large and regular – a sort of emphasized plainness of architecture – cannot be overlooked. It is evident to everyone that work has ceased, and the least reflection shows that hundreds of men, perhaps hundreds of families, are reduced from former comparative prosperity. But when ten thousand acres of land fall out of cultivation, the fact is scarcely noticed. There the land is just the same, and perhaps some effort is still made to keep it from becoming altogether foul, so that a glance detects no difference. The village feels it, but the world does not see it. The farmer has left, and the money he paid over as wages once a week is no longer forthcoming. Each man's separate portion of that sum was not much in comparison with the earnings of fortunate artisans, but it was money. Ten, twelve, or as much as fifteen shillings a week made a home; but just sufficient to purchase food and meet other requirements, such as clothes; yet still a home. On the cessation of the twelve shillings where is the labourer to find a substitute for it? Our country is limited in extent, and it has long been settled to its utmost capacity. Under present circumstances there is no room anywhere for more than the existing labouring population. It is questionable if a district could be found where, under these present circumstances, room could be found for ten more farmers' men. Only so many men can live as can be employed; in each district there are only so many farmers; they cannot enlarge their territories; and thus it is that every agricultural parish is full to its utmost. Some places among meadows appear almost empty. No one is at work in the fields as you pass; there are cattle swishing their tails in the shadow of the elms, but not a single visible person; acres upon acres of grass, and no human being. Towards the latter part of the afternoon, if the visitor has patience to wait, there will be a sound of shouting, which the cattle understand, and begin in their slow way to obey by moving in its direction. Milking time has come, and one or two men come out to fetch in the cows. That over, for the rest of the evening and till milking time in the morning the meadows will be vacant. Naturally it would be supposed that there is room here for a great number of people. Whole crowds might migrate into these grassy fields, put up shanties, and set to work. But set to work at what? That is just the difficulty. Whole crowds could come here and find plenty of room to walk about – and starve! Cattle require but few to look after them. Milch cattle need most, but grazing beasts practically no one, for one can look after so many. Upon inquiry it would be found that this empty parish is really quite full. Very likely there are empty cottages, and yet it is quite full. A cottage is of no use unless the occupier can obtain regular weekly wages. The farmers are already paying as many as they can find work for, and not one extra hand is wanted; except, of course, in the press of hay-harvest, but no one can settle on one month's work out of twelve. When ten or fifteen thousand acres of land fall out of cultivation, and farmers leave, what is to become of the labouring families they kept? What has become of them?

It is useless blinking the fact that what a man wants in our time is good wages, constant wages, and a chance of increasing wages. Labouring men more and more think simply of work and wages. They do not want kindness – they want coin. In this they are not altogether influenced by self-interest; they are driven rather than go of their own movement. The world pushes hard on their heels, and they must go on like the rest. A man cannot drift up into a corner of some green lane, and stay in his cottage out of the tide of life, as was once the case. The tide comes to him. He must find money somehow; the parish will not keep him on out-relief if he has no work; the rate-collector calls at his door; his children must go to school decently clad with pennies in each little hand. He must have wages. You may give him a better cottage, you may give him a large allotment, you may treat him as an equal, and all is of no avail. Circumstance – the push of the world – forces him to ask you for wages. The farmer replies that he has only work for just so many and no more. The land is full of people. Men reply in effect, 'We cannot stay if a chance offers us to receive wages from any railway, factory, or enterprise; if wages are offered to us in the United States, there we must go.' If they heard that in a town fifty miles distant twenty shillings could be had for labour, how many of the hale men do you suppose would stay in the village? Off they would rush to receive the twenty shillings per week, and the farmers might have the land to themselves if they liked. Eighteen shillings to a pound a week would draw off every man from agriculture, and leave every village empty. If a vast industrial combination announced regular wages of that amount for all who came, there would not be a man left in the fields out of the two millions or more who now till them.

A plan to get more wages out of the land would indeed be a wonderful success. As previously explained, it is not so much the amount paid to one individual as the paying of many individuals that is so much to be desired. Depression in agriculture has not materially diminished the sum given to a particular labourer, but it has most materially diminished the sum distributed among the numbers. One of the remarkable features of agricultural difficulties is, indeed, that the quotation of wages is nominally the same as in the past years of plenty. But then not nearly so many receive them. The father of the family gets his weekly money the same now as ten years since. At that date his sons found work at home. At the present date they have to move on. Some farmer is likely to exclaim, 'How can this be, when I cannot get enough men when I want them?' Exactly so, but the question is not when you want *them*, but when they want you. You cannot employ them, as of old, all the year round, therefore they migrate, or move to and fro, and at harvest time may be the other side of the county.

The general aspect of country life was changing fast enough before the depression came. Since then it has continued to alter at an increasing rate – a rate accelerated by education; for I think education increases the struggle for more wages. As a man grows in social stature so he feels the want of little things which it is impossible to enumerate, but which in the aggregate represent a considerable sum. Knowledge adds to a man's social stature, and he immediately becomes desirous of innumerable trifles which, in ancient days, would have been deemed luxuries, but which now seem very commonplace. He wants somewhat more fashionable clothes, and I use the word fashion in association with the ploughman purposely, for he and his children do follow the fashion now in as far as they can, once a week at least. He wants a newspaper – only a penny a week, but a penny is a penny. He thinks of an excursion like the artisan in towns. He wants his boots to shine as workmen's boots shine in towns, and must buy blacking. Very likely you laugh at the fancy of shoe-blacking having anything to do with the farm labourer and agriculture. But I can assure you it means a good deal. He is no longer satisfied with the grease his forefathers applied to their boots; he wants them to shine and reflect. For that he must, too, have lighter boots, not the heavy, old, clod-hopping watertights made in the village. If he retains these for week-days, he likes a shiny pair for Sundays. Here is the cost, then, of an additional pair of shoes; this is one of the many trifles the want of which accompanies civilization. Once now and then he writes a letter, and must have pen, ink, and paper; only a pennyworth, but then a penny is a coin when the income is twelve or fourteen shillings a week. He likes a change of hats – a felt at least for Sunday. He is not happy till he has a watch. Many more such little wants will occur to anyone who will think about them, and they are the necessary attendants upon an increase of social stature. To obtain them the young man must have money – coins, shillings, and pence. His thoughts, therefore, are bent on wages; he must get wages somewhere, not merely to live, for bread, but for these social necessaries. That he can live at home with his family, that in time he may get a cottage of his own, that cottages are better now, large gardens given, that the labourer is more independent – all these and twenty other considerations – all these are nothing to him, because they are not to be depended on. Wages paid weekly are his aim, and thus it is that education increases the value of a weekly stipend, and increases the struggle for it by sending so many more into the ranks of competitors. I cannot see myself why, in the course of a little time, we may not see the sons of ploughmen competing for clerkships, situations in offices of various kinds, the numerous employments not of a manual character. So good is the education they receive, that, if only their personal manners happen to be pleasant, they have as fair a chance of getting such work as others.

Ceaseless effort to obtain wages causes a drifting about of the agricultural population. The hamlets and villages, though they seem so thinly inhabited, are really full, and every extra man and youth, finding himself unable to get the weekly stipend at home, travels away. Some go but a little distance, some across the width of the country, a few emigrate, though not so many as would be expected. Some float up and down continually, coming home to their native parish for a few weeks, and then leaving it again. A restlessness permeates the ranks; few but those with families will hire for the year. They would rather do anything than that. Family men must do so because they require cottages, and four out of six cottages belong to the landowners and are part and parcel of the farms. The activity in cottage building, to which reference has been made, as prevailing ten or twelve years since, was solely on the part of the landowners. There were no independent builders; I mean the cottages were not built by the labouring class. They are let by farmers to those labourers who engage for the year, and if they quit this employment they quit their houses. Hence it is that even the labourers who have families are not settled men in the full sense, but are liable to be ordered on if they do not give satisfaction, or if cause of quarrel arises. The only settled men – the only fixed population in villages and hamlets at the present day – are that small proportion who possess cottages of their own. This proportion varies, of course, but it is always small. Of old times, when it was the custom for men to stay all their lives in one district, and to work for one farmer quite as much for payment in kind as for the actual wages, this made little difference. Very few men once settled in regular employment moved again; they and their families remained for many years as stationary as if the cottage was their property, and frequently their sons succeeded to the place and work. Now in these days the custom of long service has rapidly disappeared. There are many reasons, the most potent, perhaps, the altered tone of the entire country. It boots little to inquire into the causes. The fact is, then, that no men, not even with families, will endure what once they did. If the conditions are arbitrary, or they consider they are not well used, or they hear of better terms elsewhere, they will risk it and go. So, too, farmers are more given to changing their men than was once the case, and no longer retain the hereditary faces about them. The result is that the fixed population may be said to decline every year. The total population is probably the same, but half of it is nomad. It is nomad for two reasons – because it has no home, and because it must find wages.

Farmers can only pay so much in wages and no more; they are at the present moment really giving higher wages than previously, though nominally the same in amount. The wages are higher judged in relation to the price of wheat; that is, to their profits. If coal falls in price, the wages of coal-miners are reduced. Now, wheat has fallen heavily in price, but the wages of the labourer remain the same, so that he is, individually, when he has employment, receiving a larger sum. Probably, if farming accounts were strictly balanced, and farming like any other business, that sum would be found to be more than the business would bear. No trace of oppression in wages can be found. The farmer gets allowances from his landlord, and he allows something to his labourers, and so the whole system is kept up by mutual understanding. Except under a very important rise in wheat, or a favourable change in the condition of agriculture altogether, it is not possible for the farmers to add another sixpence either to the sum paid to the individual or to the sum paid in the aggregate to the village.

Therefore, as education increases – and it increases rapidly – as the push of the world reaches the hamlet; as the labouring class increase in social stature, and twenty new wants are found; as they come to look forth upon matters in a very different manner to their stolid forefathers; it is evident that some important problems will arise in the country. The question will have to be asked: Is it better for this population to be practically nomad or settled? How is livelihood – *i.e.*, wages – to be found for it? Can anything be substituted for wages? Or must we devise a gigantic system of emigration, and in a twelvemonth (if the people took it up) have every farmer crying out that he was ruined, he could never get his harvest in. I do not think myself that the people could be induced to go under any temptation. They like England in despite of their troubles. If the farmer could by any happy means find out some new plant to cultivate, and so obtain a better profit and be able to give wages to more hands, the nomad population would settle itself somehow, if in mud huts. No chance of that is in sight at present, so we are forced round to the consideration of a substitute for wages.

Now, ten or twelve years since, when much activity prevailed in all things agricultural, it was proposed to fix the labouring population to the soil by building better cottages, giving them large gardens and allotments, and various other privileges. This was done; and in 'Fraser' I did not forget to credit the good intent of those who did it. Yet now we see, ten years afterwards, that instead of fixing the population, the population becomes more wandering. Why is this? Why have not these cottages and allotments produced their expected effect? There seems but one answer – that it is the lack of fixity of tenure. All these cottages and allotments have only been held on sufferance, on good behaviour, and hence they have failed. For even for material profit in the independent nineteenth century men do not care to be held on their good behaviour. A contract must be free and equal on both sides to be respected. To illustrate the case, suppose that some large banking institution in London gave out as a law that all the employés must live in villas belonging to the bank, say at Norwood. There they could have very good villas, and gardens attached, and on payment even paddocks, and there they could dwell so long as they remained in the office. But the instant any cause of disagreement arose they must quit not only the office but their homes. What an outcry would be raised against bank managers' tyranny were such a custom to be introduced! The extreme hardship of having to leave the house on which so much trouble had been expended, the garden carefully kept up and planted, the paddock; to leave the neighbourhood where friends had been found, and which suited the constitution, and where the family were healthy. Fancy the stir there would be, and the public meetings to denounce the harsh interference with liberty! Yet, with the exception that the clerk might have £300 a year, and the labourer 12s. or 14s. a week, the cases would be exactly parallel. The labourer has no fixity of tenure. He does not particularly care to lay himself out to do his best in the field or for his master, because he is aware that service is no inheritance, and at any moment circumstances may arise which may lead to his eviction. For it is really eviction, though unaccompanied by the suffering associated with the word – I was going to write 'abroad' for in Ireland. So that all the sanitary cottages erected at such expense, and all the large gardens and the allotments offered, have failed to produce a contented and settled working population. Most people are familiar by this time with the demand of the tenant farmers for some exalted kind of compensation, which in effect is equivalent to tenant-right, *i.e.*, to fixity of tenure. Without this, we have all been pretty well informed by now, it is impossible for farmers to flourish, since they cannot expend capital unless they feel certain of getting it back again. This is precisely the case with the labourer. His labour is his capital, and he cannot expend it in one district unless he is assured of his cottage and garden – that is, of his homestead and farm. You cannot have a fixed population unless it has a home, and the labouring population is practically homeless. There appears no possibility of any real amelioration of their condition until they possess settled places of abode. Till then they must move to and fro, and increase in restlessness and discontent. Till then they must live in debt, from hand to mouth, and without hope of growth in material comfort. A race for ever trembling on the verge of the workhouse cannot progress and lay up for itself any saving against old age. Such a race is feeble and lacks cohesion, and does not afford that backbone an agricultural population should afford to the country at large. At the last, it is to the countryman, to the ploughman, and 'the farmer's boy,' that a land in difficulty looks for help. They are the last line of defence – the reserve, the rampart of the nation. Our last line at present is all unsettled and broken up, and has lost its firm and solid front. Without homes, how can its ranks ever become firm and solid again?

An agricultural labourer entering on a cottage and garden with his family, we will suppose, is informed that so long as he pays his rent he will not be disturbed. He then sets to work in his off hours to cultivate his garden and his allotment; he plants fruit-trees; he trains a creeper over his porch. His boys and girls have a home whenever out of service, and when they are at home they can assist in cultivating their father's little property. The family has a home and a centre, and there it will remain for generations. Such is certainly the case wherever a labourer has a cottage of his own. The family inherit it for generations; it would not be difficult to find cases in which occupation has endured for a hundred years. There is no danger now of the younger members of the family staying too much at home. The pressure of circumstances is too strong, as already explained; all the tendencies of the time are such as would force them from home in search of wages. There is no going back, they must push forwards.

The cottage-tenure, like the farm-tenure, must come from the landlord, of course. All movements must fall on the landlord unless they are made imperial questions. It is always the landowner who has to bear the burden in the end. As the cottages belong to the landowners, fixity or certainty of tenure is like taking their rights from them. But not more so than in the case of the exalted compensation called tenant-right. Indeed, I think I shall show that the change would be quite trifling beside measures which deal with whole properties at once, of five, ten, or twenty thousand acres, as the case may be. For, in the first place, let note be taken of a most important circumstance, which is that at the present time these cottages let on sufferance do not bring in one shilling to the landlord. They are not the least profit to him. He does not receive the nominal rent, and if he did, of what value would be so insignificant a sum, the whole of which for a year would not pay a tenth part of the losses sustained by the failure of one tenant farmer. As a fact, then, the cottages are of no money value to the landowner. A change, therefore, in the mode of tenure could not affect the owner like a change in the tenure of a great farm, say at a rental of £1,500. Not having received any profit from the previous tenure of cottages, he suffers no loss if the tenure be varied. The advantage the landowner is supposed to enjoy from the possession of cottages scattered about his farms is that the tenants thereby secure men to do their work. This advantage would be much better secured by a resident and settled population. Take away the conventional veil with which the truth is usually flimsily hidden, and the fact is that the only objection to a certain degree of fixity in cottage tenure is that it would remove from the farmer the arbitrary power he now possesses of eviction. What loss there would be in this way it is not easy to see, since, as explained, the men must have wages, and can only get them from farmers, to whom therefore they must resort. But then the man knows the power to give such notice is there, and it does not agree with the feelings of the nineteenth century. No loss whatever would accrue either to landowner or tenant from a fixed population. A farmer may say, 'But suppose the man who has my cottage will not work for me?' To this I reply, that if the district is so short of cottages that it is possible for a farmer to be short of hands, the sooner pressure is applied in some way, and others built, the better for landowner, tenant, and labourer. If there is sufficient habitation for the number of men necessary for cultivating the land, there will be no difficulty, because one particular labourer will not work for one particular farmer. That labourer must then do one of two things, he must starve or work for some other farmer, where his services would dispossess another labourer, who would immediately take the vacant place. The system of employing men on sufferance, and keeping them, however mildly, under the thumb, is a system totally at variance with the tenets of our time. It is a most expensive system, and ruinous to true self-respect, insomuch as it tends to teach the labourer's children that the only way they can show the independence of their thought is by impertinent language. How much better for a labourer to be perfectly free – how much better for an employer to have a man to work for him quite outside any suspicion of sufferance, or of being under his thumb! I should not like men under my thumb; I should like to pay them for their work, and there let the contract end, as it ends in all other businesses. As more wages cannot be paid, the next best thing, perhaps the absolutely necessary thing, is a fixed home.

I think it would pay any landowner to let all the cottages upon his property to the labourers themselves direct, exactly as farms are let, giving them security of tenure, so long as rent was forthcoming, with each cottage to add a large garden, or allotment, up to, say, two acres, at an agricultural, and not an accommodation, rent. Most gardens and allotments are let as a favour at a rent about three times, and in some cases even six times, the agricultural rent of the same soil in the adjoining fields. Cottagers do not look upon such tenancies – held, too, on sufferance – as a favour or kindness, and feel no gratitude nor any attachment to those who permit them to dig and delve at thrice the charge the farmer pays. Add to these cottages gardens, not necessarily adjoining them, but as near as circumstances allow, up to two acres at a purely agricultural rental. If, in addition, facilities were to be given for the gradual purchase of the freehold by the labourer on the same terms as are now frequently held out by building societies, it would be still better. I think it would turn out for the advantage of landowner, tenant, and the country at large to have a settled agricultural population.

The limit of two acres I mention, not that there is any especial virtue in that extent of land, but because I do not think the labourer would profit by having more, since he must then spend his whole time cultivating his plot. Experience has proved over and over again that for a man in England to live by spade-husbandry on four or five acres of land is the most miserable existence possible. He can but just scrape a living, he is always failing, his children are in rags, and debt ultimately consumes him. He is of no good either to himself or to others or to the country. For in our country agriculture, whether by plough or spade, is confined to three things, to grass, corn, or cattle, and there is no plant like the vine by which a small proprietor may prosper. Wet seasons come, and see – even the broad acres cultivated at such an expense of money produce nothing, and the farmer comes to the verge of ruin. But this verge of ruin to the small proprietor who sees his four acres of crops destroyed means simple extinction. So that the amount of land to be of advantage is that amount which the cottager can cultivate without giving his entire time to it; so that, in fact, he may also earn wages.

To landowner and farmer the value of a fixed population like this, fixed and independent, and looking only for payment for what was actually done, and not for eleemosynary earnings, would be, I think, very great. There would be a constant supply of first-class labour available all the year round. A supply of labour on an estate is like water-power in America – indispensable. But if you have no resident supply you face two evils – you must pay extra to keep men there when you have no real work for them to do, or you must offer fancy wages in harvest. Now, I think a resident population would do the same work if not at less wages at the time of the work, yet for less money, taking the year through.

I should be in hopes that such a plan would soon breed a race of men of the sturdiest order, the true and natural countrymen; men standing upright in the face of all, without one particle of servility; paying their rates, and paying their rents; absolutely civil and pleasant-mannered, because, being really independent, they would need no impudence of tongue to assert what they did not feel; men giving a full day's work for a full day's wages (which is now seldom seen); men demanding to be paid in full for full work, but refusing favours and petty assistance to be recouped hereafter; able to give their children a fixed home to come back to; able even to push them in life if they wish to leave employment on the land; men with the franchise, voting under the protection of the ballot, and voting first and foremost for the demolition of the infernal poor-law and workhouse system.

The men are there. This is no imaginary class to be created, they are there, and they only require homes to become the finest body in the world, a rampart to the nation, a support not only to agriculture but to every industry that needs the help of labour. For physique they have ever been noted, and if it is not valued at home it is estimated at its true value in the colonies. From Australia, America, all countries desiring sinews and strength, come earnest persuasions to these men to emigrate. They are desired above all others as the very foundation of stability. It is only at home that the agricultural labourer is despised. If ever there were grounds for that contempt in his illiterate condition they have disappeared. I have always maintained that intelligence exists outside education, that men who can neither read nor write often possess good natural parts. The labourer at large possesses such parts, but until quite lately he has had no opportunity of displaying them. Of recent years he or his children have had an opportunity of displaying their natural ability, since education was brought within reach of them all. Their natural power has at once shown itself, and all the young men and young women are now solidly educated. The reproach of being illiterate can no longer be hurled at them. They never were illiterate mentally; they are now no more illiterate in the partial sense of book-knowledge. A young agricultural labourer to-day can speak almost as well as the son of a gentleman. There is, of course, a little of the country accent remaining, and some few technical words are in use. Why should they not be? Do not gentlemen on the Exchange use techni-cal terms? I cannot see myself that 'contango' is any better English, or 'backwardation' more indicative of intelligence, than the terms used in the field. The labourer of to-day reads, and thinks about what he reads. The young, being educated, have brought education to their parents, the old have caught the new tone from the young. It is acknowledged that the farm labourer is the most peaceful of all men, the least given to agitation for agitation's sake. Permit him to live and he is satisfied. He has no class ill-feeling, either against farmer or landowner, and he resists all attempts to introduce ill-feeling. He maintains a steady and manly attitude, calm, and considering, without a trace of hasty revolutionary sentiments. I say that such a race of men are not to be despised; I say that they are the very foundation of a nation's stability. I say that in common justice they deserve settled homes; and further, that as a matter of sound policy they should be provided with them.

ONE OF THE NEW VOTERS[1]

MANCHESTER GUARDIAN, 24 JANUARY 1885

I

If any one were to get up about half-past five on an August morning and look out of an eastern window in the country, he would see the distant trees almost hidden by a white mist. The tops of the larger groups of elms would appear above it, and by these the line of the hedgerows could be traced. Tier after tier they stretch along, rising by degrees on a gentle slope, the space between filled with haze. Whether there were corn-fields or meadows under this white cloud he could not tell – a cloud that might have come down from the sky, leaving it a clear azure. This morning haze means intense heat in the day. It is hot already, very hot, for the sun is shining with all his strength, and if you wish the house to be cool it is time to set the sunblinds.

Roger, the reaper, had slept all night in the cowhouse, lying on the raised platform of narrow planks put up for cleanliness when the cattle were there. He had set the wooden window wide open and left the door ajar when he came stumbling in overnight, long after the late swallows had settled in their nests in the beams, and the bats had wearied of moth catching. One of the swallows twittered a little, as much as to say to his mate, "my love, it is only a reaper, we need not be afraid," and all was silence and darkness. Roger did not so much as take off his boots, but flung himself on the boards crash, curled himself up hedgehog fashion with some old sacks,

---

1. Collected in *OA*.

and immediately began to breathe heavily. He had no difficulty in sleeping, first because his muscles had been tried to the utmost, and next because his skin was full to the brim, not of jolly "good ale and old" but of the very smallest and poorest of wish-washy beer. In his own words, it "blowed him up till he very nigh bust." Now the great authorities on dyspepsia, so eagerly studied by the wealthy folk whose stomachs are deranged, tell us that a very little flatulence will make the heart beat irregularly and cause the most distressing symptoms.

Roger had swallowed at least a gallon of a liquid chemically designed, one might say, on purpose to utterly upset the internal economy. Harvest beer is probably the vilest drink in the world. The men say it is made by pouring muddy water into empty casks returned sour from use, and then brushing them round and round inside with a besom. This liquid leaves a stickiness on the tongue and a harsh feeling at the back of the mouth which soon turns to thirst, so that having once drunk a pint the drinker must go on drinking. The peculiar dryness caused by this beer is not like any other throat drought – worse than dust, or heat, or thirst from work; there is no satisfying it. With it there go down the germs of fermentation, a sour, yeasty, and, as it were, secondary fermentation; not that kind which is necessary to make beer, but the kind that unmakes and spoils beer. It is beer rotting and decomposing in the stomach. Violent diarrhoea often follows, and then the exhaustion thus caused induces the men to drink more in order to regain the strength necessary to do their work. The great heat of the sun and the heat of hard labour, the strain and perspiration, of course try the body and weaken the digestion. To distend the stomach with half a gallon of this liquor, expressly compounded to ferment, is about the most murderous thing a man could do – murderous because it exposes him to the risk of sunstroke. So vile a drink there is not elsewhere in the world; arrack, and potato-spirit, and all the other killing extracts of the distiller are not equal to it. Upon this abominable mess the golden harvest of English fields is gathered in.

Some people have in consequence endeavoured to induce the harvesters to accept a money payment in place of beer, and to a certain extent successfully. Even then, however, they must drink something. Many manage on weak tea after a fashion, but not so well as the abstainers would have us think. Others have brewed for their men a miserable stuff in buckets, an infusion of oatmeal, and got a few to drink it; but English labourers will never drink oatmeal-water unless they are paid to do it. If they are paid extra beer-money and oatmeal water is made for them gratis, some will, of course, imbibe it, especially if they see that thereby they may obtain little favours from their employer by yielding to his fad. By drinking the crotchet perhaps they may get a present now and then - food for themselves, cast-off clothes for their families, and so on. For it is a remarkable feature of human natural history, the desire to proselytise. The spectacle of John Bull – jovial John Bull – offering his men a bucket of oatmeal liquor is not a pleasant one. Such a John Bull ought to be ashamed of himself.

The truth is the English farmer's man was and is, and will be, a drinker of beer. Neither tea, nor oatmeal, nor vinegar and water (coolly recommended by indoor folk) will do for him. His natural constitution rebels against such "peevish" drink. In winter he wants beer against the cold and the frosty rime and the heavy raw mist that hangs about the hollows; in spring and autumn against the rain, and in summer to support him under the pressure of additional work and prolonged hours. Those who really wish well to the labourer cannot do better than see that he really has beer to drink – real beer, genuine brew of malt and hops, a moderate quantity of which will supply force to his thews and sinews, and will not intoxicate or injure. If by giving him a small money payment in lieu of such large quantities you can induce him to be content with a little, so much the better. If an employer followed that plan, and at the same time once or twice a day sent out a moderate supply of genuine beer as a gift to his men, he would do them all the good in the world, and at the same time obtain for himself their goodwill and hearty assistance, that hearty work which is worth so much.

Roger breathed heavily in his sleep in the cowhouse, because the vile stuff he had taken puffed him up and obstructed nature. The tongue in his open mouth became parched and cracked, swollen and dry; he slept indeed, but he did not rest; he groaned heavily at times and rolled aside. Once he awoke choking – he could not swallow, his tongue was so dry and large; he sat up, swore, and again lay down. The rats in the sties had already discovered that a man slept in the cowhouse, a place they rarely visited, as there was nothing there to eat; how they found it out no one knows. They are clever creatures, the despised rats. They came across in the night and looked under his bed, supposing that he might have eaten his bread-and-cheese for supper there, and that fragments might have dropped between the boards. There were none. They mounted the boards and sniffed round him; they would have stolen the food from his very pocket if it had been there. Nor could they find a bundle in a handkerchief, which they would have gnawn through speedily. Not a scrap of food was there to be smelt at, so they left him. Roger had indeed gone supperless, as usual; his supper he had swilled and not eaten. His own fault; he should have exercised self-control. Well, I don't know; let us consider further before we judge.

In houses the difficulty often is to get the servants up in the morning; one cannot wake, and the rest sleep too sound – much the same thing; yet they have clocks and alarums. The reapers are never behind. Roger got off his planks, shook himself, went outside the shed, and tightened his shoelaces in the bright light. His rough hair he just pushed back from his forehead, and that was his toilet. His dry throat sent him to the pump, but he did not swallow much of the water – he washed his mouth out, and that was enough; and so without breakfast he went to his work. Looking down from the stile on the high ground there seemed to be a white cloud resting on the valley, through which the tops of the high trees penetrated; the hedgerows beneath were concealed, and their course could only be traced by the upper branches of the elms. Under this cloud the wheat-fields were blotted out; there seemed neither corn nor grass, work for man nor food for animal; there could be nothing doing there surely. In the stillness of the August morning, without song of bird, the sun, shining brilliantly high above the mist, seemed to be the only living thing, to possess the whole and reign above absolute peace. It is a curious sight to see the early harvest morn – all hushed under the burning sun, a morn that you know is full of life and meaning, yet quiet as if man's foot had never trodden the land. Only the sun is there, rolling on his endless way.

Roger's head was bound with brass, but had it not been he would not have observed anything in the aspect of the earth. Had a brazen band been drawn firmly round his forehead it could not have felt more stupefied. His eyes blinked in the sunlight; every now and then he stopped to save himself from staggering; he was not in a condition to think. It would have mattered not at all if his head had been clear; earth, sky, and sun were nothing to him; he knew the footpath, and saw that the day would be fine and hot, and that was sufficient for him, because his eyes had never been opened.

The reaper had risen early to his labour, but the birds had preceded him hours. Before the sun was up the swallows had left their beams in the cow-shed and twittered out into the air. The rooks and wood-pigeons and doves had gone to the corn, the blackbird to the stream, the finch to the hedgerow, the bees to the heath on the hills, the humble-bees to the clover in the plain. Butterflies rose from the flowers by the footpath, and fluttered before him to and fro and round and back again to the place whence they had been driven. Goldfinches tasting the first thistledown rose from the corner where the thistles grew thickly. A hundred sparrows came rushing up into the hedge, suddenly filling the boughs with brown fruit; they chirped and quarrelled in their talk, and rushed away again back to the corn as he stepped nearer. The boughs were stripped of their winged brown berries as quickly as they had grown. Starlings ran before the cows feeding in the aftermath, so close to their mouths as to seem in danger of being licked up by their broad tongues. All creatures, from the tiniest insect upward, were in reality busy under that curtain of white-heat haze. It looked so still, so quiet, from afar; entering it and passing among the fields, all that lived was found busy at its long day's work. Roger did not interest himself in these things, in the wasps that left the gate as he approached – they were making *papier-maché* [*sic*] from the wood of the top bar, – in the bright poppies brushing against his drab unpolished boots, in the hue of the wheat or the white convolvulus; they were nothing to him.

Why should they be? His life was work without skill or thought, the work of the horse, of the crane that lifts stones and timber. His food was rough, his drink rougher, his lodging dry planks. His books were – none; his picture-gallery a coloured print at the alehouse – a dog, dead, by a barrel, "Trust is dead! Bad Pay killed him." Of thought he thought nothing; of hope his idea was a shilling a week more wages; of any future for himself of comfort such as even a good cottage can give – of any future whatever – he had no more conception than the horse in the shafts of the waggon. A human animal simply in all this, yet if you reckoned upon him as simply an animal – as has been done these centuries – you would now be mistaken. But why should he note the colour of the butterfly, the bright light of the sun, the hue of the wheat? This loveliness gave him no cheese for breakfast; of beauty in itself, for itself, he had no idea. How should he? To many of us the harvest – the summer – is a time of joy in light and colour; to him it was a time for adding yet another crust of hardness to the thick skin of his hands.

Though the haze looked like a mist it was perfectly dry; the wheat was as dry as noon; not a speck of dew, and pimpernels wide open for a burning day. The reaping-machine began to rattle as he came up, and work was ready for him. At breakfast-time his fellows lent him a quarter of a loaf, some young onions, and a drink from their tea. He ate little, and the tea slipped from his hot tongue like water from the bars of a grate; his tongue was like the heated iron the housemaid tries before using it on the linen. As the reaping-machine went about the gradually decreasing square of corn, narrowing it by a broad band each time, the wheat fell flat on the short stubble. Roger stooped, and, gathering sufficient together, took a few straws, knotted them to another handful as you might tie two pieces of string, and twisted the band round the sheaf. He worked stooping to gather the wheat, bending to tie it in sheaves; stooping, bending – stooping, bending, – and so across the field. Upon his head and back the fiery sun poured down the ceaseless and increasing heat of the August day. His face grew red, his neck black; the drought of the dry ground rose up and entered his mouth and nostrils, a warm air seemed to rise from the earth and fill his chest. His body ached from the ferment of the vile beer, his back ached with stooping, his forehead was bound tight with a brazen band. They brought some beer at last; it was like the spring in the desert to him. The vicious liquor – "a hair of the dog that bit him" – sank down his throat grateful and refreshing to his disordered palate as if he had drunk the very shadow of green boughs. Good ale would have seemed nauseous to him at that moment, his taste and stomach destroyed by so many gallons of this. He was "pulled together," and worked easier; the slow hours went on, and it was luncheon. He could have borrowed more food, but he was content instead with a screw of tobacco for his pipe and his allowance of beer.

They sat in the corner of the field. There were no trees for shade; they had been cut down as injurious to corn, but there were a few maple bushes and thin ash sprays, which seemed better than the open. The bushes cast no shade at all, the sun being so nearly overhead, but they formed a kind of enclosure, an open-air home, for men seldom sit down if they can help it on the bare and level plain; they go to the bushes, to the corner, or even to some hollow. It is not really any advantage; it is habit; or shall we not rather say that it is nature? Brought back as it were in the open field to the primitive conditions of life, they resumed the same instincts that controlled man in the ages past. Ancient man sought the shelter of trees and banks, of caves and hollows, and so the labourers under somewhat the same conditions came to the corner where the bushes grew. There they left their coats and slung up their luncheon-bundles to the branches; there the children played and took charge of the infants; there the women had their hearth and hung their kettle over a fire of sticks.

ONE OF THE NEW VOTERS

MANCHESTER GUARDIAN, 31 JANUARY 1885

II

In August the unclouded sun, when there is no wind, shines as fervently in the harvest-field as in Spain. It is doubtful if the Spanish people feel the heat so much as our reapers; they have their siesta; their habits have become attuned to the sun, and it is no special strain upon them. In India our troops are carefully looked after in the hot weather, and everything made as easy for them as possible; without care and special clothing and coverings for the head they could not long endure. The English simoon of heat drops suddenly on the heads of the harvesters and finds them entirely unprepared; they have not so much as a cooling drink ready;

they face it, as it were, unarmed. The sun spares not; it is fire from morn till night. Afar in the town the sun-blinds are up, there is a tent on the lawn in the shade, people drink claret-cup and use ice; ice has never been seen in the harvest-field. Indoors they say they are melting lying on a sofa in a darkened room, made dusky to keep out the heat. The fire falls straight from the sky on the heads of the harvesters – men, women, and children – and the white-hot light beats up again from the dry straw and the hard ground.

The tender flowers endure; the wide petal of the poppy, which withers between the fingers, lies afloat on the air as the lilies on water, afloat and open to the weight of the heat. The red pimpernel looks straight up at the sky from the early morning till its hour of closing in the afternoon. Pale blue speedwell does not fade; the pale blue stands the warmth equally with the scarlet. Far in the thick wheat the streaked convolvulus winds up the stalks, and is not smothered for want of air though wrapped and circled with corn. Beautiful though they are, they are bloodless, not sensitive; we have given to them our feelings, they do not share our pain or pleasure. Heat has gone into the hollow stalks of the wheat and down the yellow tubes to the roots, drying them in the earth. Heat has dried the leaves upon the hedge, and they touch rough – dusty rough, as books touch that have been lying unused; the plants on the bank are drying up and turning white. Heat has gone down into the cracks of the ground; the bar of the stile is so dry and powdery in the crevices that if a reaper chanced to drop a match on it there would seem risk of fire. The still atmosphere is laden with heat, and does not move in the corner of the field between the bushes.

Roger the reaper smoked out his tobacco; the children played round and watched for scraps of food; the women complained of the heat; the men said nothing. It is seldom that a labourer grumbles much at the weather, except as interfering with his work. Let the heat increase, so it would only keep fine. The fire in the sky meant money. Work went on again; Roger had now to go to another field to pitch – that is, help to load the waggon; as a young man, that was one of the jobs allotted to him. This was the reverse. Instead of stooping he had now to strain himself upright and lift sheaves over his head. His stomach empty of everything but small ale did not like this any more than his back had liked the other; but those who work for bare food must not question their employment. Heavily the day drove on; there was more beer, and again more beer, because it was desired to clear some fields that evening. Monotonously pitching the sheaves, Roger laboured by the waggon till the last had been loaded – till the moon was shining. His brazen forehead was unbound now; in spite of the beer the work and the perspiration had driven off the aching. He was weary but well. Nor had he been dull during the day; he had talked and joked – cumbrously in labourers' fashion – with his fellows. His aches, his empty stomach, his labour, and the heat had not overcome the vitality of his spirits. There was life enough left for a little rough play as the group gathered together and passed out through the gateway. Life enough left in him to go with the rest to the alehouse; and what else, oh moralist, would you have done in his place? This, remember, is not a fancy sketch of rural poetry; this is the reaper's real existence.

He had been in the harvest-field fourteen hours, exposed to the intense heat, not even shielded by a pith helmet; he had worked the day through with thew and sinew; he had had for food a little dry bread and a few onions, for drink a little weak tea and a great deal of small beer. The moon was now shining in the sky, still bright with sunset colours. Fourteen hours of sun and labour and hard fare! Now tell him what to do. To go straight to his plank-bed in the cowhouse; to eat a little more dry bread, borrow some cheese or greasy bacon, munch it alone, and sit musing till sleep came – he who had nothing to muse about. I think it would need a very clever man indeed to invent something for him to do, some way for him to spend his evening. Read! To recommend a man to read after fourteen hours' burning sun is indeed a mockery; darn his stockings would be better. There really is nothing whatsoever that the cleverest and most benevolent person could suggest. Before any benevolent or well-meaning suggestions could be effective the preceding circumstances must be changed – the hours and conditions of labour, everything; and can that be done? The world has been working these thousands of years, and still it is the same; with our engines, our electric light, our printing press, still the coarse labour of the mine, the quarry, the field has to be carried out by human hands. While that is so, it is useless to recommend the weary reaper to read. For a man is not a horse: the horse's day's work is over; taken to his stable he is content, his mind goes no deeper than the bottom of his manger, and so long as his nose does not feel the wood, so long as it is met by corn and hay, he will endure happily. But Roger the reaper is not a horse.

Just as his body needed food and drink, so did his mind require recreation, and that chiefly consists of conversation. The drinking and the smoking are in truth but the attributes of the labourer's public-house evening. It is conversation that draws him thither, just as it draws men with money in their pockets to the club and the houses of their friends. Any one can drink or smoke alone; it needs several for conversation, for company. You pass a public-house – the reaper's house – in the summer evening. You see a number of men grouped about trestle-tables out of doors, and others sitting at the open window; there is an odour of tobacco, a chink of glasses and mugs. You can smell the tobacco and see the ale; you cannot see the indefinite power which holds men there – the magnetism of company and conversation. *Their* conversation, not *your* conversation; not the last book, the last play; not saloon conversation; but theirs – talk in which neither you nor any one of your condition could really join. To us there would seem nothing at all in that conversation, vapid and subjectless; to them it means much. We have not been through the same circumstances: our day has been differently spent, and the same words have therefore a varying value. Certain it is, that it is conversation that takes men to the public-house. Had Roger been a horse he would have hastened to borrow some food, and, having eaten that, would have cast himself at once upon his rude bed. Not being an animal, though his life and work were animal, he went with his friends to talk. Let none unjustly condemn him as a blackguard for that – no, not even though they had seen him at ten o'clock unsteadily walking to his shed, and guiding himself occasionally with his hands to save himself from stumbling. He blundered against the door, and the noise set the swallows on the beams twittering. He reached his bedstead, and sat down and tried to unlace his boots, but could not. He threw himself upon the sacks and fell asleep. Such was one twenty-four hours of harvest-time.

The next and the next, for weeks, were almost exactly similar; now a little less beer, now a little more; now tying up, now pitching, now cutting a small field or corner with a fagging-hook. Once now and then there was a great supper at the farm. Once he fell out with another fellow, and they had a fight; Roger, however, had had so much ale, and his opponent so much whisky, that their blows were soft and helpless. They both fell – that is, they stumbled, – they were picked up, there was some more beer, and it was settled. One afternoon Roger became suddenly giddy, and was so ill that he did no more work that day, and very little on the following. It was something like a sunstroke, but fortunately a slight attack; on the third day he resumed his place. Continued labour in the sun, little food and much drink, stomach derangement, in short, accounted for his illness. Though he resumed his place and worked on, he was not so well afterwards; the work was more of an effort to him, and his face lost its fulness, and became drawn and pointed. Still he laboured, and would not miss an hour, for harvest was coming to an end, and the extra wages would soon cease. For the first week or so of haymaking or reaping the men usually get drunk, delighted with the prospect before them, they then settle down fairly well. Towards the end they struggle hard to recover lost time and the money spent in ale.

As the last week approached, Roger went up into the village and ordered the shoemaker to make him a good pair of boots. He paid partly for them then, and the rest next pay-day. This was a tremendous effort. The labourer usually pays a shilling at a time, but Roger mistrusted himself. Harvest was practically over, and after all the labour and the long hours, the exposure to the sun and the rude lodging, he found he should scarcely have thirty shillings. With the utmost ordinary care he could have saved a good lump of money. He was a single man, and his actual keep cost but little. Many married labourers, who had been forced by hard necessity to economy, contrived to put by enough to buy clothes for their families. The single man, with every advantage, hardly had thirty shillings, and even then it showed extraordinary prudence on his part to go and purchase a pair of boots for the winter. Very few in his place would have been as thoughtful as that; they would have got boots somehow in the end, but not beforehand. This life of animal labour does not grow the spirit of economy. Not only in farming, but in navvy work, in the rougher work of factories and mines, the same fact is evident. The man who labours with thew and sinew at horse labour – crane labour – not for himself, but for others, is not the man who saves. If he worked for his own hand possibly he might, no matter how rough his labour and fare; not while working for another. Roger reached his distant home among the meadows at last, with one golden half-sovereign in his pocket. That and his new pair of boots, not yet finished, represented the golden harvest to him. He lodged with his parents when at home; he was so far fortunate that he had a bed to go to; therefore in the estimation of his class he was not badly off. But if we consider his position as regards his own life we must recognise that he was very badly off indeed, so much precious time and the strength of his youth having been wasted.

Often it is stated that the harvest wages recoup the labourer for the low weekly receipts of the year, and if the money be put down in figures with pen and ink it is so. But in actual fact the pen-and-ink figures do not represent the true case; these extra figures have been paid for, and gold may be bought too dear. Roger had paid heavily for his half-sovereign and his boots; his pinched face did not look as if he had benefited greatly. His cautious old father, rendered frugal by forty years of labour, had done fairly well; the young man not at all. The old man, having a cottage, in a measure worked for his own hand. The young man, with none but himself to think of, scattered his money to the winds. Is money earned with such expenditure of force worth the having? Look at the arm of a woman labouring in the harvest-field – thin, muscular, sinewy, black almost, it tells of continual strain. After much of this she becomes pulled out of shape, the neck loses its roundness and shows the sinews, the chest flattens. In time the women find the strain of it tell severely. I am not trying to make out a case of special hardship, being aware that both men, women, and children work as hard and perhaps suffer more in cities; I am simply describing the realities of rural life behind the scenes. The golden harvest is the first scene: the golden wheat, glorious under the summer sun. Bright poppies flower in its depths, and convolvulus climbs the stalks. Butterflies float slowly over the yellow surface as they might over a lake of colour. To linger by it, to visit it day by day, at even to watch the sunset by it, and see it pale under the changing light, is a delight to the thoughtful mind. There is so much in the wheat, there are books of meditation in it, it is dear to the heart. Behind these beautiful aspects comes the reality of human labour – hours upon hours of heat and strain; there comes the reality of a rude life, and in the end little enough of gain. The wheat is beautiful, but human life is labour.

Appendices

Evidence in Support of New Articles Attributed to Jefferies[1]

'Drought and Water', *Pall Mall Gazette*, 28 June 1870

This article has connections with 'Water' (*FF*), which first appeared in the *Livestock Journal* on 6 April 1877. 'Water' was confirmed by a payment slip in Jefferies' papers. 'Drought and Water' has further connections with *Wild Life in a Southern County*, first serialised in the *Pall Mall Gazette* in 1878.

In 'Drought and Water' Jefferies observes: 'Above all, and except in our **chalk ranges**, we have **springs** bubbling up in **every** hill and stream, **bursting down every** valley.' In 'Water' he writes of the western counties, 'where the low-lying plains and valleys are fed with clear streams from the **chalk hills**, and where in the winter half of the year **springs burst out** in almost **every** meadow'. In 'Drought and Water' the description of the water drying up – 'what little was suffered to accumulate in the small duck pond by the farmyard or the little hollows by the field corners has long given out' – echoes a similar line in 'Water', where the ponds 'become mere hollows of black mud'.

In 'Drought and Water' Jefferies writes:

> **there is no sap in the shrivelled grass**; the **cattle** and the very sheep have to be driven twice a day to the distant stream. His horses, men, and wagons are **hauling the precious fluid**, and the expenditure of labour on water carriage is something heart-breaking.

Very similar observations appear in the description of the drought on the Downs in *WLSC*: 'the grass becomes dull in tint and touches like wire - **all the sap dried from it**, and nothing but fibre left'. Again, in *WLSC* he writes:

> The cattle of course suffer too; all day long files of watercarts go down into the hollows where the springs burst forth, and at such times half the work of the farm consists in **fetching the precious liquid** perhaps a mile or more.

1. More can be read about my research methods, along with evidence in support of works I have attributed to Jefferies, on the website: <www.richardjefferiesarticles.com>.

A similar observation is made in 'Water': 'he must fetch it from a great distance in iron tanks and water-carts, at the cost of much expensive labour', and 'precious liquid' also features in 'Water': 'the precious liquid which in a few months' time may be worth gold slips away'. A reference to 'gold' also appears in 'Drought and Water': 'in a blazing spring, with plenty of water, he might coin gold'.

The article ends with allusions to the Huerta Valencia and growing practices near the Nile: 'the water regularly let over it steadily manicures it, and everything grows in **tropical** rapidity and **luxuriance**'. The 'tropical luxuriance' of plant growth features in 'The Story of Swindon' (May 1875, *HV*): 'on this sewage farm some most extraordinary results have been obtained, such as mangolds with leaves four feet in length – a **tropical luxuriance** of growth'. It also occurs in 'Village Hunting' (1877) (*LL*): 'Go and sit by the mill sluice, where the ferns grow among the damp stones in **tropical luxuriance**' (p. 44). In 'Drought and Water' Jefferies writes of the overly elaborate banks flanking the quiet streams that 'the **tradition lingers** of some mediaeval flood', and in *WLSC*, of the Downs, he writes that 'There is a **tradition lingering** still that they were in the olden times almost covered with wood.'

'Farmers at Bay', *Pall Mall Gazette*, 8 February 1871

The mention of disputes between the farmers and the Archdeacon in Wiltshire is a strong clue to Jefferies' authorship of this piece. At the time he was living at his birthplace, Coate Farm, in Swindon, and he would have been one of the few journalists able to make such observations concerning the condition and education of the farmer. Furthermore, he mentions copies of the *Marlborough Times* – a paper that he is presumed to have had a connection with.[2] In February 1871 Jefferies wrote to his aunt, explaining that he was finding it difficult to earn a living through his writing, and that he had briefly worked for a Marlborough paper as their correspondent.

The piece has significant connections with 'The Farmer at Home' (*TF*), published in *Fraser's Magazine* in August 1874. Both articles address the education of the farmer and his children, and 'Farmers at Bay' can be seen as a form of prequel to the longer, more in-depth article. 'The Farmer at Home' argues that farmers are 'peculiarly well-informed', which is 'contrary to the **popular** belief, which represents the farmer as rude and ignorant, a pot-bellied beer drinker . . . but the **popular** belief is a delusion'. In 'Farmers at Bay' Jefferies writes: 'The picture of a fat man in a broad-skirted coat, leather gaiters, a low-crowned hat, and a thick stick, in a state of profound bewilderment over some very

2. See Matthews and Trietel, p. 44.

simple question of politics or economy, is the **conventional type** of the British farmer.' 'Conventional type' also occurs in *AF*: 'The **conventional type** is so easy – so accepted – so **popular**; it would pay better, perhaps, to make him out a victim in some way.'

The phrase 'the unfortunate farmer' features in 'The Farmer at Home' as 'the unfortunate agriculturalist'. 'Unfortunate farmer' also appears in 'The Labourer's Daily Life' (*TF*), which followed 'The Farmer at Home' in *Fraser's* (November 1874): 'So our typical unfortunate farmer folds his hands, and in point of fact slumbers away the rest of his existence.' In 'Farmers at Bay' Jefferies observes that the farmer 'is awkward in the evolution of ideas, chews the cud of a generalization a long while before he can digest it, and is liable consequently to be thrown into utter confusion'. The phrase 'utter confusion' appears in 'Choosing a Gun' (*HV*): 'I found that the effect of carefully studying the subject had been to plunge me into utter confusion.' The phrase also features in *WM* ('the barbarian host turned and fled in utter confusion') and in *FF* ('there must have been **utter confusion** of refraction').

The phrase 'Practical wisdom' features in *HHM*, specifically in relation to the vicar, who did things slowly: 'After the first revolt of the old folk there was little opposition, because the vicar, being a man who had studied human nature and full of practical wisdom as well as learning, did all things gradually.' The phrase 'practical wisdom' can be traced to Aristotle's *Nicomachean Ethics*, in the line:

> Virtue, then, is a state of character concerned with choice, lying in a mean, i.e. the mean relative to us, this being determined by a rational principle, and by that principle by which the man of practical wisdom would determine it.[3]

Jefferies very likely read Aristotle. W. J. Keith suggests that a passage from *WE* concerning the reading habits of hero Aymer Malet can be read as an autobiographical allusion, and has resonance with Jefferies' 'conscious desire to explore the classic works of ancient wisdom':

> he bought many of Bohn's fine series - the finest and most useful, perhaps, ever issued - he read Plato and Aristotle, Livy, Xenophon - the poets, the philosophers, the dramatists of ancient Rome and Greece; and although it was not in their original tongue, the vivid imagination of the man carried him back to their day.

---

3. Qtd in Howard J. Curzer, 'Aristotle and Moral Virtue', in *The Oxford Handbook of Virtue*, ed. Nancy Snow (Oxford: Oxford University Press, 2018), pp. 104-29 (p. 120).

Keith continues,

> we have in any case a special reason for trusting the autobio-
> graphical nature of Aymer's education. A few pages later, he
> makes Aymer carry around in his pocket, a 'tiny edition of Shake-
> speare's Poems and Sonnets' which, as we know from another
> context, was Jefferies' own habit.[4]

The article mentions the farmer's 'power' twice, which anticipates
Jefferies' article of June 1874 in the *Fortnightly Review*, 'The Power of the
Farmers'. The phrase 'utterly sterile' is echoed in a sentence in *WE*: 'It
was utterly dry and sterile – not a tree nor a shrub to shelter a cow or a
horse.' The phrase 'the modern farmer' appears in *HHM*: 'Here, again,
he was in direct conflict with the modern farmer. The modern man, if he
has a good harvest or makes a profit, at once buys a "turnout",' and 'First,
of course, the modern farmer paid his landlord.'

The quotation from John Keats's *Hyperion* is not uncharacteristic. As
W. J. Keith has noted, Jefferies tended to quote in his earlier writings.
His quotations come from a range of texts, including Shakespeare,
Longfellow and Drayton.[5] A notable similarity can be found in 'High
Pressure Agriculture' (1876), where Jefferies quotes from Faust in a
similarly dry tone:

> The earth is so idle; like Nature in Faust,
>
>> And what to yield she does not freely choose,
>> You cannot wrest from her with wheels and screws'
>
> Not only with wheels and screws, but with drugs and chemicals,
> superphosphates and what not. (*LL*, pp. 119-20)

In 'Farmers at Bay' he writes:

> They will, however, when hard pressed occasionally turn to bay,
> and then, like Enceladus:
>
>> *Once tame and wild,*
>> *As ox unworried in the grazing meads*
>
> they become really dangerous.

---

4. W. J. Keith, 'Jefferies' Reading', *Richard Jefferies Society Journal*, 2 (1993), pp. 17–22 (pp.
17-18).
5. Ibid.

'The Old Sporting Man', *Pall Mall Gazette*, 1 February 1872

This article is a portrait of an old-school squire of a large estate – a subject of a number of Jefferies' other studies, including 'A King of Acres' and the papers for 'The Squire and the Land', some of which were published in *FF*. The article is based on an estate in Kent. Jefferies lived in Sydenham with his aunt for most of his childhood and often returned to visit. At that time, prior to the formation of the County of London in 1889, Sydenham was a small town, part of Kent, and it would have been just a short journey into the countryside. The squire owns an estate of 'fifteen hundred acres', the same size as the estate in *DM* ('the tenant of fifteen hundred acres').

The description of the powerful build of the squire, which remains visible despite his age, is echoed in Jefferies' descriptions of men elsewhere. Jefferies describes the old sporting man as having a 'lithe, powerful frame': 'Hard and hale, he still resembles what he was when fifty years ago he succeeded to the paternal acres. At two-and-seventy he retains the same square shoulders, the same **broad, open chest**.' 'Paternal acres' echoes 'ancestral acres' in *HHM*. In *HHM* Harry Hodson, 'like so many countrymen', is 'built proportionately broad across the shoulders and chest', which seems to have been a certain type of build that Jefferies noticed and admired. In *GFF* we again see the 'powerful frame': 'Now that his labour was over and the excitement had subsided, even his powerful frame felt the effect of unusual exertion.' In *HHM* a similar observation is made, but about an older man: '"You be got into a good upstanding piece, John," replied the old man sharply in his thin jerky voice, which curiously contrasted with his still powerful frame.' The 'broad chest' and 'powerful frame' both feature in *AL*, in reference to the older Baron, who remains strong:

> The Baron's arm was bare, his sleeve rolled up; and as he pointed to the tree above, the muscles, as the limb moved, **displayed themselves** in knots. . . . Those mighty arms, had they clasped him about the waist, could have crushed his bending ribs. The heaviest blow that he could have struck upon that **broad chest** would have produced no more effect than a hollow sound; it would not even have shaken that **powerful frame**.

As we see in the *AL* quotation above, the muscles 'displayed themselves'. In 'The Old Sporting Man' Jefferies writes: '**Still on the backs of his powerful hands you can see the muscles coiling themselves like whipcord, although they are lost somewhat**

in gathering flesh.' A further significant similarity can be found in *GH*, where Jefferies specifically refers to the elderly gamekeeper's hands, the sinews of which are corded and surrounded by wasted tissue: '**his trembling hand, upon the back of which the corded sinews are so strongly marked now the tissue has wasted**, and over which the blue veins wander, can set a trap'.

The phrase '**It must be remembered, in common fairness**, that he spared himself no more than the brute creation' is echoed in 'The County Franchise' (May 1872, *PMG*): '**Still we have further to consider in common fairness** how far it is equitable to pour this alien element into the county constituencies.'

The article is similar in style and tone to 'The Gentleman Farmer' (1877, *LL*). The squire's feeling that 'Times are not what they were. England is **going to the dogs**' is echoed in 'The Gentleman-Farmer' (1877), specifically in relation to the changes taking place in rural life:

> You would hardly think, if you sat at that well-appointed table and glanced at the furniture and the pictures on the walls and the silver prize-cups yonder, sipping your champagne and trifling with fish or game, that agriculture was **going to the dogs**.

Another connection between the two pieces is the mention of how the squire (or farmer) is regarded by the locals. In 'The Gentleman-Farmer' the farmer leaves the bar 'and gallantly lifted his hat to the buxom landlady (who pronounces him "*such*" a gentleman!)'. In 'The Old Sporting Man' 'Buxom landladies beamed on him from bar-parlours.'

Jefferies writes of Squire Badger that society 'regards him as a type of the English gentleman-yeoman of the old school' and the sporting paraphernalia denotes 'the hall of a sportsman of the old school'. 'Of the old school' is a phrase that Jefferies often uses elsewhere, in 'Christmas: Then and Now' (1877, *FF*): 'For the rising generation somehow never can be got to feel that absorbed interest in corn and cattle characteristic of the old school'; in 'The Size of Farms' (1874, *LL*, p. 133): 'Take say a hundred acres of marshy pasture land under a wood overrun with rabbits and choked with coarse furrow-grass; put a sturdy, half-educated, rude man of the old school in charge of it'; and in *RGE* (1880, p. 111), in relation to the drinking farmer: 'Not many years since it was not unusual for some well-to-do farmer of the old school to ride off.'

In *HHM* the description of the squire who attends church – 'he went to church on Sundays with unfailing regularity' – is similar to that of the squire of 'The Old Sporting Man', who 'holds himself a staunch pillar of the parish church. He would as soon think of missing a meet as morning service.' In *HHM* the professor gives a lecture to the farmers, instructing them on how they ought to drain their meadow-land and crop fields. In 'The Old Sporting Man' the reference to 'snipes in the undrained meadow-land' infers that the Squire manages his land by traditional methods. It also implies specialist knowledge of where to find snipe, which Jefferies refers to elsewhere (*GH*, *AP*, 'Snipe-Shooting at Home' (SFW)). The reference to finding 'ducks occasionally in the sedgy ponds in the gloomy wood' is echoed in *Bevis* (1881), when shooting wildfowl in the 'sedgy covers'. The word is again used in *Bevis*, when the boys, in pursuit of a heron, row across the lake to 'the sedgy banks at the southern extremity of New Formosa'.

A further connection occurs in *WLSC* concerning the crumbling mortar of the farmhouse, which is made worse by the activities of birds. In 'The Old Sporting Man' Jefferies writes of the Grange, 'The keeping up those roods of red-tile roof is as good as an annuity to the bricklayer, thanks to the flights of pigeons perpetually pecking at the mortar,' and in *WLSC* he describes a 'flight' of martins continually pecking the orchard wall: 'working their very hardest at the mortar between the stones'.

Further significant similarities with 'The Old Sporting Man' appear in *GFF*. The ninety-year-old Andrew Fisher recalls the days of his youth:

> So, too, the old boon companions dropped away. Squire Thorpe –
> not the present, but the ancient one of evil days, wild and head-
> strong – was still enough at last in the vault under the chancel. He
> could swear and drink no more, nor fight a main of cocks every
> Sunday afternoon on his dining-room table. . . . The big black
> horse that carried him in the mad steeplechase at Millbourne –
> still talked of by the country-side – and in many a run with the
> Hunt in the vale, lay eight feet deep in the garden, and a damson-
> tree had grown over him.

In 'The Old Sporting Man' Jefferies twice refers to 'boon companions'. The squire 'often sits solitary, with the memories of the jolly old times for his sole boon companions'. The swearing and drinking Squire Thorpe echoes Squire Badger, who is considered 'a most discreditable example' to the parish. Squire Thorpe who used to watch cocks fighting on his dining-room table, also reflects Squire Badger, who 'was permitted to see his pet cocks peck each other to death' and 'improvises on occasion a cockpit in his parlour'. Squire Thorpe's legendary equine pursuits echo Squire Badger's coach-driving ability, for which 'he was celebrated far and wide'.

'The County Franchise', *Pall Mall Gazette*, 1 May 1872

The phrase 'the enfranchisement of the agricultural labourer' occurs in *DM* (1884): 'You can now understand how an enormous power was taken from the hands of Robert Godwin when the new Magna Carta was passed, and why Letitia, clever woman as she was, dreaded **the enfranchisement of the agricultural labourer**.' *DM* was probably a rework of *In Summertime*, written in the 1870s.

Regarding 'the farmer can bring to bear upon his labourer a kind of pressure', I can find only two other instances of the phrase 'bring to bear' in Jefferies' published works, and both are used in relation to a landowner: they are in 'A King of Acres' (*HV*): 'with all the skill, science, and expenditure Thardover could **bring to bear** upon it, all his personal effort was in vain'; and 'An English Deer Park' (*FH*): 'in the gun-room there is a field-glass, said to have been used at the siege of Seringapatam, which the squire can **bring to bear** upon the road in an instant'.

The allusion to the farmer being wary of dismissing labourers because he will probably need the labour at any given time in order to secure his crops is echoed in 'The Farmer at Home'. In 'The County Franchise' Jefferies writes:

> if a farmer cannot get his land ploughed, his corn sown, and his crops carried at the right season of the year and when the weather gives him his chance, the consequences are tenfold more serious. He knows pretty well the whole stock of labour on which he has to depend.

In 'The Farmer at Home' he writes:

> just as the scythes begin to lay the tall grass prostrate again, there is a growl in the sky, and down comes the rain. A thunderstorm unsettles the weather, and here is perhaps another week lost. The farmer dare not discharge his haymakers, because he knows not but that he may require them any day.

Regarding 'the ballot would be **a dead letter**', the phrase 'a dead letter' appears in 'Village Organisation' (1875, *HV*):

> the age at which children may be employed in agriculture was also an extension of an original Act, passed to protect the interest of children in cities and manufacturing districts. There is no objection to the Act except that it is **a dead-letter**.

Jefferies writes of plovers' eggs in *GH* (1878): 'they are protected now by law, but it is to be feared that the enactment is to a great extent **a dead letter**', and in 'The Farmer at Home' (1874, *TF*) he says of the farmers: 'They are eagerly fond of foxhunting, coursing, and shooting, but fishing is **a dead letter**.'

Other phrases that feature in 'The County Franchise' and elsewhere in his work include 'practical utility'. This appears in *Beauty is Immortal* (1948): 'Instead of there being any cause of wonder in the science of the present day, and in the inventions of **practical utility** now in use, the marvel is that more has not been done.' 'Not likely to be surpassed' is echoed in *WE*: 'could not be surpassed'. 'Power to the farmers' obviously connects with 'The Power of the Farmers' (1874).

The suggestion that the farmers are in a greater position of power than the manufacturers is made in 'The Farmer from his own Point of View' and again in 'The Future of Country Society' (1877, *LL*, p. 97): 'The town and manufacturing district rule us now. When the agricultural labourer obtains the franchise, there will be a re-distribution of power.' 'The hands of the farmers' features in 'The Farmer at Home' (*TF*, p. 44): 'the cottages were chiefly in the hands of the farmers'.

'The Poetry of Steam Ploughs', *Graphic*, 5 October 1872

We know that Jefferies wrote in different styles for different publications, and it would be remiss to assume that we yet fully understand the nuances of his early style. Jefferies' earliest known publication in the *Graphic* is 'Women in the Field' (11 September 1875), which is about female agricultural workers. 'The Poetry of Steam Ploughs' predates this by three years. 'The Poetry of' had already been used by Jefferies in the title of his series for the *Broad Churchman*, 'The Poetry of the Bible' (1871). The quotations from literary texts are a stylistic clue because Jefferies uses them in several of his early contributions to the *Graphic* (for example, 'In a Pine Wood', 'The Commonest Thing in the World' and 'The Old Mill'). A specific reference to the blackness of the ash buds in the hedges – 'the few ash trees which alone are suffered to grow in them at sparse distances are black in bough, and, still blacker in bud' – matches an allusion in 'The Haunt of the Hare' (*OA*): 'the black bud-sheaths of the ash may furnish a comparison for his ear-tips', and in *RGE*: 'Ash-stoles, the buds on whose boughs in spring are hidden under black sheaths'.

The descriptions of the steam plough closely resemble those elsewhere in Jefferies' works. In 'Notes on Landscape Painting' (*LF*) (included in this collection as 'The Beauty of the Fields') Jefferies observes that agricultural machinery soon grows old:

> Such memories read strange to the present generation, proving thereby that the threshing-machine has already grown old. It is so accepted that the fields would seem to lack something if it were absent. It is as natural as the ricks: things grow old so soon in the fields.

In 'The Poetry of Steam Ploughs' he writes:

> the village lads soon grow familiar with the steam-plough after all their original amazement; and here, too, a practical mind sees the result upon man of the mightiest physical discoveries. Familiarity speedily breeds, if not contempt, at least indifference.

A notable similarity occurs between the line 'At once the earliest instrument of civilisation and the latest, the history of mankind's progress from the savage is contained in the grimy boiler which works the plough' and the observation in 'Patchwork Agriculture':

> By how much does this patriarchal implement differ from the wooden ploughs depicted upon the monuments of Egypt which were in use upon the teeming soil of that land thirty centuries since? How closely it resembles the true primitive and prehistoric original of the plough which was a forked branch. . . . This is our boasted civilisation and improvement indeed!

'The Poetry of Steam Ploughs' describes the plough as an 'iron monster': 'A fanciful mind might almost recognise instinct in this ungainly iron monster, while the store of coal and water which it bears proclaims loudly enough, that it has an appetite, like any sentient creature.' Jefferies again calls the steam plough an 'iron monster' in *HHM* ('The Village Factory', p. 75), and imagines that it has a 'thirst':

> in the ploughing seasons the engines are forever on the road, and with their tackle dragging behind them take up the highway like a train. One day you may hear the hum and noise from a distant field. . . . The visitor, driving about the neighbourhood, cannot but notice the huge and cumbrous-looking plough. . . . He will meet the **iron monster** which draws this plough **by**

the bridge over the brook, pausing while its insatiable thirst is stayed from the stream. He will see it patiently waiting, with a slight curl of steam over the boiler.

In 'The Beauty of the Fields' he describes the plough as a prehistoric monster: 'Like the claws of some prehistoric monster, the shares rout up the ground; the solid ground is helpless before them'. In 'The Beauty of the Fields' the engine pants, hums and clanks:

> by the trembling of the **monster** as it strains and tugs . . . you know how **mighty** is the power that thus in narrow space works its will upon the earth. Planted broadside, its four limbs – the massive wheels – hold the ground like a wrestler drawing to him the unwilling opponent. Humming, panting, trembling, with stretched but **irresistible** muscles, the **iron creature** conquers. . . . This is force – Thor in another form. If you are near you cannot take your eyes off the sentient iron.

In 'The Poetry of Steam Ploughs' the monster is also pictured crossing a brook, but the analogy is elaborated to include reference to an elephant:

> the creature is completely under the control of human will, as those two sooty stokers evince, who calmly smoke their pipes while they regulate the monster's steps from their seats behind. It has a very complicated arrangement of taps and tubes; yet the internal arrangements of an elephant are probably far from simple until you have learnt to look at them with the eye of an anatomist; and, indeed, this creature as it slowly feels its way over a dubious brick **bridge**, spanning a country **brook**, is **not unlike the elephant**, who cautiously explores with foot and trunk the plank bridge which crosses a jungle torrent, before he will trust his vast weight upon it.

The analogy to a prehistoric monster and its force features in 'Unequal Agriculture', where Jefferies specifically refers to the steam plough as a mastodon – an extinct prehistoric relation of the elephant: 'these ploughing engines stand out solitary and apart from other machinery, and their shape itself suggests **crude force**, such **force** as may have existed in the **mastodon** or other unwieldy **monster of the prehistoric ages**'. In this passage Jefferies refers to the 'ease' with which the machine does its work: 'The huge engines . . . work with

a graceful ease which deceives the eye; the ponderous cranks revolve so smoothly, and shine so brightly with oil and polish, that the mind is apt to underrate the work performed.' The same observation is made in 'The Poetry of Steam Ploughs': 'Resistless and almost superhuman in its might does the machine seem; and the difficult work on which three horses would scarcely make any impression, is accomplished with **an appearance of ease which much adds to the beauty of the sight**.' The references to the 'force' of the creature made in 'Unequal Agriculture' are also echoed in 'The Poetry of Steam Ploughs': 'resistless natural force'; 'the mighty forces which lurk within'; and 'Like all, beneficent forces, it yet contains a mighty terror latent in its womb'. In 'The Poetry of Steam Ploughs' the comment 'It is not unpleasing to behold the terror of partridges and hares, as they flee from the monster's approach' is echoed in 'Unequal Agriculture' in the line about the smoke from the funnel of the 'beast' 'smothering and driving away the partridges and hares'.

Both essays suggest that the size and noise of the machine draw the eye and produce a strong impression. In 'The Poetry of Steam Ploughs' Jefferies writes:

> And when the ungainly fabric, puffing out clouds of smoke, and snorting jets of steam from its enormous interior, draws near with slow yet imposing motion, its immensely broad iron wheels crunching the gravel into dust, with a loud murmurous rattle, such as might proceed from some fabulous creature of the nether world, **it is impossible to escape a sensation of awe**.

In 'Unequal Agriculture' he says: 'When the furrows run up and down a slope, the savage force, the fierce, remorseless energy of the engine pulling the plough upwards, **gives an idea of power which cannot but impress the mind**.' The 'resistless natural force' of the plough in the earlier essay becomes 'remorseless energy' in the later one.

Elsewhere, 'resistless' is used in relation to force. In *TF*, in relation to the wind, Jefferies writes: 'His house is lonely, perched on the side of a hill, and exposed to the bitter blasts of winter which sweep over the downs with **resistless** fury'; in *SMH*: 'I felt the presence of the sun as I felt it in the solitary valley, the presence of the **resistless** forces of the universe'; in *AL*: 'the midday raging in waves dashing **resistlessly** upon the beach, and the evening still again'; and in *HV*: 'These pieces are carried to the furnace, heated to an intense heat, and then placed under the **resistless** blows of a steamhammer, which welds them into one solid bar of iron, longer than the separate pieces were.'

The idea of a machine being a 'black . . . monster' that threatens to grind anyone who gets too close to powder – 'Make way, make way, my masters! else some resistless natural force it will speedily grind you to powder!' ('The Poetry of Steam Ploughs') – appears in *GFF* ('The Nether Millstone, serialised in June 1879), in the description of a water wheel in the mill: 'Looking through into the semi-darkness, a heaving monster, black and direful, rolled continually past, threatening, as it seemed, to crush the life out of those who ventured within reach . . . the individual grain ground into the general powder'.

'The Farmer from his own Point of View', *Pall Mall Gazette*, 23 April 1874

The subject, style and title of this article would fit into the 'Summary of the Farmer's Case' section of the book Jefferies proposed to Longman in 1874. The article was published on 23 April, and Jefferies sent 200 completed folios for the project on 8 June. In the ways that it considers the political power of the farmer, the article anticipates the themes of 'The Power of the Farmers' (1 June 1874). In 'The Farmer from his own Point of View' Jefferies writes that 'It is to the farmers accordingly that political aspirants and their friends chiefly pay their court, and for whom they promise either to uphold existing advantages or to obtain the concession of new ones,' and that 'The farmer is the man to whom candidates address themselves.' In 'The Spirit of Modern Agriculture' he suggests that 'Perhaps nothing is more remarkable in recent political history than the rapid rise to power of the party representing modern **agricultural interests**.' The phrase 'agricultural interest' features six times in 'The Farmer from his own Point of View' and I cannot find it anywhere else in Jefferies' works.

'The Farmer from his own Point of View' refers to the farmer being in a unique position compared to merchants or manufacturers. In 'The Power of the Farmers' he also makes a comparison with other industries, arguing that the farmers 'have shown an amount of patience and forbearance which no other business men in the kingdom would have shown. Neither the colliery-owners, nor the ironmasters, nor the cotton-mill men – none of the great trades would have waited so long.'

His argument that the farmer is not so pivotal as he thinks in the agricultural interest – and indeed is more of a middle man – is also echoed in 'The Power of the Farmers'. In 'The Farmer from his own point of View' Jefferies writes that the farmer is in reality the member of that interest who is the least essential to its existence. . . . in the nature of things the middle man is only a convenience. . . . You must have ownership in some shape or another, and you must have either tillage or pasturage. Proprietors, then, on the one hand, and ploughmen, shepherds, or herdsmen on the other are inseparable from the existence of land in any civilized community.

In 'The Power of the Farmers' he says: 'there is indeed no trade or occupation in the country which seems to depend so much upon the labouring man as farming'.

'The Farmer from his own Point of View' includes the phrase 'we may depend upon it', specifically in relation to land tenure. I am yet to find the phrase anywhere else in Jefferies' works except in 'The State of Farming' (Part II): 'We may depend upon it, the greater the liberty the landlord gives, and the more he as the seller can encourage confidence in the farmer as the buyer, the more profit there will be got out of the land.'

With regard to 'the farmer has for many years past occupied rather an exceptional position among the English industrial classes, and the mental peculiarities which it has produced in him . . . will perhaps repay investigation', the reference to the 'peculiarities' of the British farmer echoes Jefferies' use of the word elsewhere. In *RHH* (1875) he writes: 'this is the **peculiarity** of these women: they hate each other to the death'; in *WE* (1877): 'This is the **peculiarity** of the law in such cases'; in *RD* (1884): 'The men of Red Deer Land are ethnographically separate from those to the east of them, and they cannot be taught out of their racial **peculiarities**'; in *OA*: 'It is a **peculiarity** of the swallow that you cannot make it afraid of you'; in *CH*: 'It is a **peculiarity** of flowing water to work itself a deeper groove under a bridge'; in *HHM*: 'to know all the **peculiarities** of the covers is only given to those who have ridden over the country these forty years'; in *WLSC*: 'It is a **peculiarity** of our usually changeable climate'; in *JL*: 'in recording little **peculiarities**, like that of the "cow-shorne"; and in 'The Spirit of Modern Agriculture': **'local peculiarities'**.

He also uses the phrase 'comparatively few' ('the squires are comparatively few; and the freeholders who are neither squires nor farmers are, or were, comparatively few too'). Elsewhere, the word 'comparatively' is quite often used in his articles on practical subjects: 'The numerical loss from these inflictions was comparatively small' ('The Future of Farming',

1873); in 'Patchwork Agriculture': 'comparatively high cultivation is resorted to'; and in his second letter to *The Times*: 'He rents a large piece of arable land, and ought to be comparatively well off.'

'The Cost of Agricultural Labour in 1875', *Standard*, 1 October 1875

This article was attributed to Jefferies by Walter Besant in *The Eulogy of Richard Jefferies*. Besant had access to letters and notebooks of Jefferies that are no longer in circulation or known. On this basis, Matthews and Trietel include Besant's attributions in *The Forward Life of Richard Jefferies*. Notably, Besant's reference to this article is quite specific. He states that Jefferies wrote 'Village Organisation' (October 1875), and 'for the *Standard* on "The Cost of Agricultural Labour"' and 'The Power of the Farmers' (1874, p. 124). Besant's other attributions have not been doubted and there is no reason to challenge this one. The article is compatible with the subject of Jefferies' other works from the early to mid-1870s. The sentences 'As a natural consequence, the arable farmer, like the occupier of grass lands, has felt the **burden** of high-priced labour more this season than he has ever done before' and 'The price of unskilled labour is so high that, added to other **burdens**, it absorbs that percentage upon capital invested which is called profit' are similar to observations made in 'The Prospects of Farming' (1877). In the latter he refers to '**a new burden**' for the farmer in relation to the pressures of foreign imports, the need for additional labour, and the increase in the cost of labour:

> in addition to these old sources of apprehension, the farmer has now to encounter a totally new burden. The cost necessary for production has immensely increased. More labour is needed under the new system of farming than under the old, and the **wages of labour** have, as a consequence of the movement of which the strikes were only a symptom, risen on an average at least 30 per cent.

'The Power of the Farmers' (1874) also comments that 'the very **price of labour** has taught the tenant to do his utmost to reduce the expenditure in that direction'. The 'cost of labour' is also referred to in 'The Spirit of Modern Agriculture' (1876):

> Yet it is questionable, even now, as the pressure of competition is made heavier by the **rise in the cost of labour**, whether a

sufficient return or percentage can be got out of the land with the limited capital invested in it.

'The Agricultural Labourer's Vote', *Pall Mall Gazette*, 24 May 1877

As with the majority of his articles for the *Livestock Journal*, Jefferies takes the example of Swindon and applies it in general to other districts. The phrase 'hedgers and ditchers' is significant as it appears only three times in *PMG* in the 1870s – the other two instances are in *GH* and *AP* – and there are only two occurrences of the phrase in the *Standard*, one of which is in 'Hodge at His Work' by Jefferies. The reference to 'the establishment at Swindon station of a depot of the Aylesbury Dairy Company' recalls his description of Swindon and surrounds in his letter to the *Standard* about local taxation.

In 'The Power of the Farmers' Jefferies writes: 'the hour approaches when the ploughman will vote and his voice will sway the State. Though postponed, there is no doubt the franchise must at last be extended to the agricultural labourer.' An observation about the agricultural labourer's vote is made in 'The Country Franchise':

> it is clear that farmers would have to think twice before dismissing any number of workmen because of an obnoxious vote; and that if they dismissed them one day they might have to take them on again the next. But, secondly, we must remember what some people do not know, and what many are apt to forget, that the population who would be enfranchised by household suffrage in the counties is far from exclusively agricultural.

The comment 'the name of Mr. Arch was well known, and he had himself addressed an audience of at least 2,000 people in the Corn Hall at Swindon' alludes to Arch's attendance at the Swindon Corn Exchange in January 1874, and the statement that 'any undue influence of the farmers and landowners was in 1874 of necessity prevented' also relates to 'The Power of the Farmers' (1874). The mention of Sir Daniel Gooch, the chairman of the Great Western Railway Company, and Mr Goddard, both of whom belonged to the Conservative Party, is significant as Jefferies was personally known to them. Jefferies wrote a memoir of the Goddard family, and he was known to have socialised with Sir Daniel Gooch.[6]

6. See Matthews and Trietel, p. 70.

'Joint-Stock Agriculture', *Pall Mall Gazette*, 16 March 1877

'Joint-Stock Agriculture' was identified by Samuel Looker in an unpublished list of works.[7] The article would fit in well with the section 'Agriculture as a Business' in the book that he proposed to Longman in 1874. In 'The Spirit of Modern Agriculture' Jefferies refers to joint-stock agriculture three times: 'As I suggested three years ago, the direction of events seems to point irresistibly to the conclusion that at no distant date joint-stock farming will have to be resorted to'; 'We will henceforth form ourselves into one vast firm, a joint-stock company'; and see below. In 'Joint-Stock Agriculture' he refers to 'the various cheese factories scattered over the country'. In 'The Spirit of Modern Agriculture' he writes:

> Factories for the manufacture of cheese are rapidly spreading, and here again the joint-stock principle, the true commercial spirit, appears in all its vigour. The cheese-factory is usually situated near a railway, in the midst of a dairy district, and the farmers send their milk to the factory, and receive in return a proportioned share of the profits.

This last reference specifically connects with the mention of the Aylesbury Dairy Company in Swindon in 'Joint-Stock Agriculture' and is a strong clue to Jefferies' authorship.

The article is very similar in style to 'The Landowner's Difficulties', written in the same month, for the same paper. Instead of repeating 'American meat' he rephrases it as 'dead meat from America': 'It is true that the importation of American meat has not sensibly affected the general cost of living to the consumer, but it is equally certain that it has materially depreciated the value of cattle in the market' ('The Landowners' Difficulties', 29 March 1877).

'The Prospects of Farming', *Pall Mall Gazette*, 19, 23 July 1877

This article is similar in style to *HHM* and pieces written for the *LSJ*. Jefferies' observations about milk, butter, cheese and foreign imports repeat those made in the *LSJ* articles and elsewhere. A linguistic clue that Jefferies is the author both of this piece and of 'The State of

---

7. See Miller and Matthews, p. 41.

Farming' (1881) may be found in the concluding paragraph of 'A Dairy District' (1877) (*FF*): 'these remarks arise out of a review of the **state of** things in a particular dairy district . . . the circumstances of one locality may assist in throwing light upon the progress and **future prospects of** many'. The three pieces – 'The Future of Farming' (1873), 'The Prospects of Farming' (1877) and 'The State of Farming' (1881) – fit together, and were written with four years between each. 'The State of Farming' makes reference to the sheepwalks of Australia, which connects with a line in *HHM*: 'When the young ploughman resolves to quit the hamlet for the backwoods of America or the sheepwalks of Australia, he comes here to engage his berth.'

The sentence 'this disturbance in the **established order of things** is not due to any temporary or accidental cause' is echoed in *HHM* concerning the changing condition of the labourer in country districts: 'the labourer brings a pressure to bear upon almost every aspect of country life. That pressure is not sufficient to break in pieces the **existing order of things**; but it is sufficient to cause an unpleasant tension.' 'The order of things' is again used in *HHM*:

> The old men, working so many years on a single farm, and whose minds were formed in days when a change of tenancy happened once in half a century, have so identified themselves with the **order of things** in the parish that it seems to personally affect them when a farmer leaves his place.

'The Prospects of Farming', II

Regarding 'the straw of a crop is often worth almost as much as the grain, and therefore it is a cruel injustice to the farmer to prohibit him from selling', the phrase 'cruel injustice' features in *AP*: 'The sense of the **cruel injustice** of that act will never quite depart. But they could not burn the barrel, and we almost succeeded in fitting it to a stock of elder.' The sentence concerning the farmer who 'watches not merely the rise and fall of markets, but studies what crops give the best profits, and **seizes every advantage** offered by locality or season' is echoed in Jefferies' references to shrewdness elsewhere. In 'Footpaths' (*NNL*) (3 November 1880) he writes: 'Unless the rook, therefore, be ever in his castle his labour is torn down, and, as with men in the fierce struggle for wealth, the meanest **advantages** are **seized** on.' In 'The Spirit of Modern Agriculture' Jefferies says:

> The typical agriculturist of the day is a man who knows books as well as bullocks, science as well as sheep; a man **quick to**

discern possible advantages, eager to seize them, and willing to lay out his money rather than to hoard it.

In 'Fictitious Manure' (April 1878) he argues that, rather than relying on artificial manure, it is better to rely on 'farm-yard manure' and 'if they made the "common **farm-yard manure" in their own stalls** they might at least feel certain it was genuine' (*FW*, p. 194). In 'Prospects' he states that 'to raise both these profitable crops he adds to his **farm-yard manure (itself made in boxes or stalls**) heavy dressings of artificial manure'.

In 'Prospects' he observes that 'the landlord who is the most **liberal** in bargaining and most **large-minded** in intercourse will secure the best tenants'. A similar observation about being liberal and large-minded is made in Jefferies' second letter to *The Times* on the Wiltshire labourer (*TF*):

> The farmer's books show that this labourer, his wife, and two children received 28s. 6d. per week, his cottage rent free, and a very large garden at a low rent. Yet he could not afford the 3d. a week which would enable his children ultimately to take a better position in the world! The same farmer, who is a **liberal** and **large-minded man**, has endeavoured, without success, to introduce the practice of paying in cash instead of beer, and also the system of payment for overtime.

The observation of the need for a Squire to be 'large-minded' or broad-minded' is also made in 'A King of Acres': '**Broad-minded** himself, he understood the immense value of education, looked at generally; and he thought, too, that by its aid the farmer and the landowner might be enabled to compete with the foreigner.' Again, in 'The Spirit of Modern Agriculture' a similar observation is made: 'With broader views, higher education, and that species of knowledge which is acquired by travelling occasionally, old local prejudices are no longer believed in; a more liberal spirit arises.'

Further,

> there seems, then, no reason to despair of **the future of farming**. But they unquestionably imply a change, which may be very gradual, but is inevitable, in the character of the English farmer and the relation between him and his landlord; for at the basis of any chance of progress there lies the **indispensable** element that the farmer of the future must be a better educated man and a richer man.

'The future of farming' was the title of his letter to *The Times* in 1873, and the title of his major article in *Fraser's*. The comments made in 'Prospects' are also compatible with his observations about the farmer and his education in 'The Farmer at Home' (1874). 'Indispensable' appears elsewhere in the context of agricultural matters: in 'The Wiltshire Labourer' (1883, *HV*): 'A supply of labour on an estate is like water-power in America – **indispensable**'; and in *TF*: 'It was the end of the harvest, and Absalom had plenty of money in his pocket: a week's holiday was therefore **indispensable**' ('A True Tale of the Wiltshire Labourer' – Dartnell dates this work to 1867.[8] 'Indispensable' also features in 'The Farmer from his own Point of View': 'We do not mean to deny that he is **indispensable** to the English system', and in 'The Spirit of Modern Agriculture': 'The engineer indeed is **indispensable** to the modern agriculturist.'

The points about farming becoming a commercial enterprise, and being supplemented by education, are made in *HHM*. In 'Prospects' Jefferies writes:

the farmer of the future must be a better educated man and a richer man. His education must go beyond the study of the clouds and the soil as they appear to the eye; he must have book-learning and be an acute man of business, as wide in survey and as prompt in action as a manufacturer or trader; and both he and the landlord must be prepared to put more capital into the business.

In *HHM* he says:

Cecil had gone into farming, in fact, as a 'commercial speculation,' with the view of realising cent. per cent. He began at the time when it was daily announced that old-fashioned farming was a thing of the past. Business maxims and business practice were to be the rule of the future. Farming was not to be farming; it was to be emphatically 'business,' the same as iron, coal, or cotton. Thus managed, with steam as the motive power, a fortune might be made out of the land, in the same way as out of a colliery or a mine. But it must be done in a commercial manner; there must be no restrictions upon the employment of capital. . . . Cecil was a man of capital. He really had a large

8. George E. Dartnell, 'Richard Jefferies', *Wiltshire Archaeological and Natural History Magazine*, 27, June (1893), pp. 69-99, qtd in Miller and Matthews, pp. 742, 751.

sum of money, and this short-sighted policy (as he termed it) of the landlords only made him the more eager to convince them how mistaken they were to refuse anything to a man who could put capital into the soil.

'Milk Supply', *Pall Mall Gazette*, 26 December 1877

This article focuses on the changes that have been happening in the dairy industry, and reflects Jefferies' thoughts in 'The Spirit of Modern Agriculture' and his articles for the *Livestock Journal*. In 'A Dairy District' (*FW*, p. 105) he writes,

> looking back only a short period of time the change that has come over the dairying industry is really extraordinary; and there is perhaps no department of agriculture which has developed so rapidly, or which shows equal signs of future prosperity.

In 'Milk Supply' he comments:

> the milk trade . . . was for the most part in the hands of small trades-men, and prior to the year of the cattle-plague, when London was studded with small cowsheds, the arrangements of the small dairies at London retained something of old-world simplicity, and were accepted with little questioning as belonging to a traditional type.

By comparison, in the modern day, 'milk from **fifty farms** is brought to London twice a day in cans'. This change is also discussed at length in 'The Spirit of Modern Agriculture', where Jefferies observes the change from farms producing their own dairy products to farms that now send their products to London:

> The cheese-factory is usually situated near a railway, in the midst of a dairy district, and the farmers send their milk to the factory, and receive in return a proportioned share of the profits. It is as if **fifty dairies** all cast their milk into one common cheese-tub. Now nothing could be more opposed to the feelings of the old farmer than such a course as this. He always had the most perfect confidence, the most implicit belief in the milk, and butter, and cheese made from that milk, of his own dairy.

'Fifty dairies' echoes the 'fifty farms' mentioned in 'Milk Supply'.

A similarity in the use of the term 'sweep away' can be found in
'The Spirit of Modern Agriculture'. In 'Milk Supply' Jefferies writes:
'When, however, cows were swept away by the rinderpest and cowsheds abolished, London had to supply itself from the surrounding
counties.' In 'The Spirit of Modern Agriculture' he says: 'The entire
drift of modern circumstance, the pressure of events domestic and foreign, has been to sweep away the system, and to substitute for it its very
antithesis.'

'Milk Supply' begins with a note concerning 'the formal opening of
a cluster of model dwellings attached to the premises of the Aylesbury
Dairy Company at Bayswater'. 'The Future of Farming' also alludes
to Bayswater – 'the crowded dairies of Islington or Bayswater'. The
new depot of the Aylesbury Dairy Company that opened at Swindon is
mentioned in 'The Agricultural Labourer's Vote':

> The exports of the district are cattle, butter, cheese, and milk,
> of which latter article immense quantities are daily forwarded to
> London, and the fact of the establishment at Swindon station of
> a depot of the Aylesbury Dairy Company is a clear proof of the
> general character of the country.

The same company is also mentioned in 'Joint-Stock Agriculture':
'That the joint-stock principle is not entirely inapplicable to agriculture
may reasonably be concluded from the success of such concerns as the
Aylesbury Milk Company, of the various cheese factories scattered over
the country.'

'The Preservation of Game in England', St. James's Gazette, 25 October 1881

As we know, by this time Jefferies had already showed his thorough
knowledge of gamekeeping in *The Gamekeeper at Home*. This article,
identified by Looker in an unpublished list, is in keeping with Jefferies'
contributions on subjects concerning the land from the *LSJ* and those
in the *PMG*. The opening sentence – 'Preservers of game **have for
some time past been labouring under many difficulties**' –
echoes the first line of the second paragraph of 'The Landowner's
Difficulties': 'the residents in "the stately homes of England" **have for
some time past been labouring under a constantly increas-
ing pressure**'.

The reference to the game-preservers' 'intimacy with the fields and copses through which they loved to **stroll gun in hand**' is echoed in *WLSC* in relation the squire at Wick:

> He is seldom seen **without a gun on his shoulder** from November till towards the end of January. No matter whether he **strolls** to the arable field, or down the meadows, or across the footpath to a neighbour's house, the inevitable double-barrel accompanies him.

The phrase 'fields and copses' appears in Jefferies' other works as 'fields and woods' – see *RHH*: 'She could have lingered about the **fields and woods**, wandering with him in a dream of pleasure for ever and ever, had he not asked her to fly with him'; *AP*: 'it was an overpowering instinct for **woods and fields**'; *CH*: 'A Defence of Sport': 'Our **fields and woods**, moors and rivers, are our playgrounds, from which we emerge, strong and ready, to fight the battles of the world.'

The line 'game-preserving in a really effectual way is no longer practicable for a **man of moderate means**' is echoed in 'The Game Question' (1878) regarding a 'desire on the part of **moderate men** to see some rational . . . solution of the game question'. The reference to the new system of agriculture – 'Of the new difficulties which confront the preserver of game several may be traced to an altered and improved system of agriculture' – is repeated elsewhere. For example, the loss of cover for game due to new farming methods is discussed in 'Thoughts in the Stubbles' (1877, *LSJ*).